JOSEPH NAVEH

EARLY HISTORY OF THE ALPHABET

EARLY HISTORY OF THE ALPHABET

AN INTRODUCTION TO
WEST SEMITIC EPIGRAPHY AND PALAEOGRAPHY

By

JOSEPH NAVEH

1982

THE MAGNES PRESS, THE HEBREW UNIVERSITY, JERUSALEM

LEIDEN E.J.BRILL

Distributed by
N.V. Boekhandel en Drukkerij V/H E.J. Brill
Oude Rijn 33a, Leiden
Holland

ISBN 965-223-436-2
Printed in Israel
at Astronel Press, Jerusalem

CONTENTS

Preface   VII

I.   Introduction   1
      1. Inscriptions and Manuscripts   2
      2. Epigraphy and Palaeography   5
      3. The Development of Scripts and Script Styles   6
      4. Semitic Languages and Scripts   8

II.   The Rise of the Semitic Script   13
      1. Background   13
         a. Sumerian cuneiform writing   13
         b. Egyptian hieroglyphic script   14
         c. The Hittite "hieroglyphic" script   18
         d. The Cretan script   19
         e. Undeciphered scripts in Syria-Palestine   21
      2. The Beginnings of the Alphabet   23

III. The South Semitic Scripts   43

IV.   The West Semitic Scripts   53
      1. The Phoenician Script   53
      2. The Hebrew Script   65
      3. The Aramaic Script   78
      4. Comparative Aspects of the Phoenician, Hebrew and
         Aramaic Scripts   89
      5. The Scripts of Israel's Neighbours   100
      6. The Change from Hebrew to Jewish Script   112

Contents

V.   The Development of the Later Aramaic Offshoots   125
        1. Aramaic Writing in the Iranian World   127
        2. The Aramaic Script in the East   132
            a. The South Mesopotamian branch   133
            b. The North Mesopotamian branch   138
            c. The Palmyrene-Syriac branch   143
        3. The Nabataean Script and the Rise of the Arabic
           Script   153
        4. The Jewish Script   162

VI. The Antiquity of the Greek Alphabet   175

Abbreviations   187

Illustrations   189
    Figures   189
    Plates   198

Index   203

PREFACE

Alphabetic writing is one of the principal features of Western culture. The adoption of the alphabet by the Greeks and the Romans, successively, contributed to the development of classical civilization; it should be remembered, however, that the origins of the Greek script go back to the alphabetic writing used by the Canaanites since about 1700 B.C. The respective cultures of the West and of the Near East were thus interwoven from early on.

Our knowledge of the early history, development and spread of the alphabet is constantly changing. Collating the new data that keep coming to light is like working on a puzzle with an irregular supply of pieces. These have to be fitted together carefully and a constant re-examination of the data must be accompanied by the re-evaluation of accepted views. This introduction to West Semitic epigraphy and palaeography is my personal way of introducing this field of study on the basis of the evidence available to date.

This book is intended for readers with no previous knowledge of Semitic epigraphy and palaeography. This does not mean that scientific problems have been avoided, however, nor that the discussion is not on a scholarly level. On the contrary, in addition to describing the story of the alphabet in antiquity, the book deals with a series of questions which are the subject of scholarly controversy. Some sections (mostly in chapters IV-VI) are the result of my own study, while others are more in the nature of a summary of the research of other scholars, mainly W. F. Albright and F. M. Cross. Although in general my work follows the same lines as theirs, I quite often find myself differing with their views, or at least reviewing their conclusions with a degree of criticism or reservation.

While I have tried to express my thoughts clearly and concisely, I have not refrained from illustrating the various scripts as thoroughly and fully as possible. Since only a limited number of plates could be used, most of the illustrations are line-drawings. However, it always has to be borne in mind that a drawing does not portray the written text with the same precision as a phogographic reproduction, and that the drawing is an interpretation of the inscription, representing the reading of the scholar who executed the drawing (or who instructed the draughtsman). About forty figures were drawn by Mrs. Ada Yardeni and a few by the author; most, however, were taken from previously published works (although I do not necessarily agree with the interpretation conveyed in the drawing).

No attempt has been made to produce here a history of research. I have sought to concentrate on the most important arguments without going into excessive detail. More extensive argumentation, as well as a detailed bibliography, can be found in the studies mentioned in the footnotes. If a problem has already been dealt with in one of my previous papers, the reader is referred to the relevant paper. However, if new evidence has since come to light, this book may offer a revised interpretation.

I wish to express my gratitude to everybody who has come to my aid in the preparation of this book and first of all to my teachers, colleagues and friends with whom I discussed through the years many of the subjects dealt with here. Since the list is quite long, I would like only to mention Prof. N. Avigad and Prof. F. M. Cross, who introduced me to epigraphy and palaeography. I am indebted to Mrs. Inna Pommerantz and Miss Jennifer Goldman who read the manuscript and improved its style. I owe much to Mrs. Ada Yardeni, who invested all her talents in the design of this book, and to my wife, Tamar, who so patiently typed the manuscript, read the proofs and prepared the index. The proofs were also read by Miss Adèle Zarmati. The printing was carried out by Astronel Press and the offset printing — by Art Plus. I wish to thank the Management of Brill, Leiden and Mr. Ben-Zion Yehoshua, Director of the Magnes Press, for their efforts to publish this book in such a handsome form.

The following persons and institutions were kind enough to grant me permission to reproduce illustrations: Prof. N. Avigad, Prof. F. M. Cross,

Dr. G. Gerster, Dr. A. R. Millard, Dr. B. Porten, Dr. Chr. Robin, Prof. J. B. Segal, Mrs. G. E. Wright and Prof. Y. Yadin; the editors of Bible et Terre Sainte, Discoveries in the Judaean Desert, Enṣiqlopedia Miqra'it, Iraq and Revue Biblique; the authorities of Accademia Nazionale dei Lincei, American Schools of Oriental Research, Andrews University Press in Berrien Springs (Michigan), British Academy, British Museum, Egyptian Museum in Cairo, Harvard University Press, Israel Academy of Sciences and Humanities, Israel Department of Antiquities, Israel Exploration Society, Israel Museum and its Shrine of the Book, Istituto Italiano per il Medio ed Estremo Oriente, Libraire Orientaliste of M. Paul Geuthner, Museum of Fine Arts in Boston, Oxford University Press, University of Chicago Press and Yale University Art Gallery — Dura Europos Collection.

Jerusalem, January 1982   J.N.

I. INTRODUCTION

Writing, that is, the use of graphic signs for the systematic description of spoken language, is a major achievement in the history of mankind. The earliest inscribed objects have been found at various archaeological sites in Mesopotamia and Egypt among the remains of settlements dated to the end of the fourth millennium B.C. The appearance of such inscriptions marks the beginning of the historic age, succeeding the pre- and proto-historic ages when men had no knowledge of writing. Pre-historic man did give expression to his aspirations and desires in drawings on rock faces and cave walls, but only in the historic era did man begin to depict single words. Early scripts consisted of a large number of pictographs, representing words or syllables. The reduction of the number of symbols to a minimum — that is, the invention of the alphabet — took place about one and a half millennia after the invention of writing and marked a further step in its development.

The present study attempts to trace the evolution of alphabetic writing from its inception around 1700 B.C. up to the crystallization of modern scripts. Since the alphabet was used primarily by the West Semites, we shall deal mainly with the history of West Semitic writing, but also with its adoption by other peoples, South Semites and non-Semites (Greeks and Iranians), and we shall trace the first phase in the evolution of the alphabet among these peoples. The East Semites (Akkadians, Babylonians and Assyrians) used the cuneiform script which was in fact a Sumerian system, and as such does not come within the scope of our study.

The development of each script is deeply rooted in the characteristics of its users. The historical and geopolitical factors and the cultural features of different peoples come into play in their respective scripts.

1

Language and writing, the prime means of cultural expression, reflect individual and collective cultures. Ancient inscriptions and manuscripts are historical documents, and both epigraphy and palaeography are auxiliaries to history. Historians look to epigraphers and palaeographers not only for a rendition of these texts, but also, for the dating of written historical records. Epigraphy and palaeography could contribute to history more extensively than they do at present, and the close scrutiny of documents and their scripts could yield additional data on the cultural backgrounds of peoples which used and developed individual scripts (see below, pp. 5 f.)

1. *Inscriptions and Manuscripts*

Systematic archaeological excavations have been carried out in the lands of the Fertile Crescent for over a hundred years. During the last century, many inscriptions of great importance for the study of Ancient Near Eastern history have been deciphered. Archives of forgotten cities and civilizations have come to light, contributing significantly to our existing knowledge of the history of certain peoples. In earlier times, biblical scholars had had to base their historical research only on the Bible and on ancient historical works, like those of Josephus Flavius, which had been copied and preserved across the ages. Although ancient inscriptions are much shorter than these historical texts, they are generally more reliable. Historians' accounts, which have come down to us through the centuries and through many hands, contain copyists' mistakes and even deliberate emendations, whereas inscriptions found in the debris of ancient towns reach us directly in their original form. If the epigraphic material has been well preserved and the written text has survived undamaged, they constitute historical documents of primary importance. Even short inscriptions are of value: a proper name may add to our knowledge of the ethnic composition of a certain people; a phrase or even a word may shed light on the language of a certain society; even single letters may contribute to our knowledge of a specific script.

The number of known Semitic inscriptions has increased so greatly that there now exists a substantial corpus, written in various languages and dialects. Excluding the Ugaritic texts, which are written in alphabetic cuneiform script on clay tablets, the material can be divided into two main groups: inscriptions made with a pointed instrument, mainly on stone or metal, and manuscripts written in ink on papyrus, parchment and even on potsherds. As we shall see, it is sometimes difficult to determine the correct group for certain types of text.

The first group comprises the following types of inscriptions:

Graffiiti — these are short inscriptions which consist generally of a proper name incised on various objects as a sign of ownership, for example, on pottery or metal vessels. Sometimes inscriptions were incised on potsherds (ostraca; see below). In ancient times, many graffiti were inscribed on the walls of places of pilgrimage. For instance, scores of Phoenician and Aramaic graffiti have been discovered on the walls of the temple of Osiris at Abydos in Egypt,[1] and thousands of Nabataean graffiti are still visible on the rock faces in many wadis in Sinai.[2] Short texts of this kind were written in ancient times in almost every language and script. Sometimes the names are accompanied by blessings similar to those of dedicatory or votive inscriptions.[3]

Votive inscriptions are written on objects that are dedicated to deities, such as silver bowls, figurines, stelae, etc. The custom of writing votive inscriptions was widespread among all ancient peoples. In Carthage, for instance, thousands of votive stelae were found which bear the following formula: "To (divine name and title); which (proper name) vowed, because he heard his voice. May he bless him!"[4]

Burial inscriptions or *epitaphs* sometimes mention only the name of the deceased. In such a case, and particularly when the inscription was made by an unskilled hand, it may be considered as a graffito. Other burial inscriptions give additional details on the deceased, or warnings accom-

---

1. M. Lidzbarski, *Ephemeris für semitische Epigraphik*, III, Giessen 1915, pp. 93-116; W. Kornfeld, Neues über die phönikischen und aramäischen Graffiti in den Tempeln von Abydos, *Anzeiger d. phil.-hist. Klasse d. Österreichischen Akad. d. Wiss.* 115 (1978), pp. 193-204.
2. *CIS*, II, Nos. 490-3233.
3. J. Naveh, Graffiti and Dedications, *BASOR* 235 (1979), pp. 27-30.
4. *CIS*, I, Nos. 180-5940.

panied by curses against persons who would try to open the tomb or damage it.

Memorial stelae were erected by kings and rulers to glorify their deeds which are sometimes described as the fulfilment of divine will. Despite their subjective nature, these inscriptions contain important historical data. Here, too, we find curses against whosoever would damage the monument or deface the inscriptions (see below, note 7).

In this category, the four types listed above are the most significant, but other kinds of texts written on hard surfaces, such as boundary inscriptions, could also be included. In addition, three types of shorter texts, inscribed on weights, seals and coins should be mentioned here:

Weights were made of stone or metal. Some are uninscribed; where inscriptions do exist, they are generally short, indicating the name of the weight and the number of units.

Seals — The earlier seals were uninscribed and ownership was indicated by engraved designs. Later, names were added. Next, there appear seals bearing letters only, so that the owner of the seal could be identified only by reading its impression (the letters on the seal were engraved in the negative). The seals were generally made of hard, semiprecious stone, or of softer stone or metal. They were impressed on pieces of wet clay which held the strings binding the papyrus rolls (such an impression is called a *bulla*), or on the handles of jars before they were fired. The latter indicate ownership or certify the jar's capacity.

Coins are a relatively late invention. The Lydians began to mint coins in the seventh century B.C.; in the sixth and fifth centuries they were introduced into Greece and made their appearance in the East. Previously pieces of gold and silver were used, their value being determined by their weight. Coin legends may give the name of the king (or ruler), the location of the mint, the date of minting and the value of the coin. Although, strictly speaking, the study of coins belongs to the realm of numismatics, the epigrapher's experience can make a substantial contribution to the correct reading of a coin legend.

Turning to inscriptions written in ink, we shall begin by mentioning the simplest text, the *dipinto*, which resembles the graffito except that the letters are painted instead of incised. As a rule, ink was used for writing on papyrus or parchment, but less important texts were also written on potsherds, called ostraca.

Ostraca were used for short notes, name lists, dockets, messages, and private letters. *Papyrus* was the usual writing material for private and official letters, legal documents and literary compositions. However, the use of papyrus was not common in Mesopotamia, where sometimes even private letters were written on parchment.

Private and official letters and deeds, as well as stelae, votive inscriptions and epitaphs, followed fixed structural patterns. Letters began with the name of the addressee, generally followed by the name of the sender; then came the greeting formulae; after the main section, the letter sometimes closed with a further phrase of greeting.[5] Deeds generally open with the exact date and place of writing; then follow the names of the parties, the details of the deed, and the names of the scribe and the witnesses.[6] Similarities and differences in the formulae may be indicative of cultural links between various ancient societies.[7]

2. *Epigraphy and Palaeography*

These terms were first used in classical studies. There is a clear distinction between them: while epigraphy denotes the study of inscriptions inscribed on hard surfaces, palaeography deals with manuscripts written in ink. (Given the very large number of Greek papyri, most of them from Egypt, there is a separate discipline, called papyrology, for the study of manuscripts written on papyrus). This sharp division is less acknowledged in Semitic studies. While adopting the classical system in

5. J. A. Fitzmyer, Some Notes on Aramaic Epistolography, *JBL* 93 (1974), pp. 201-225; P. S. Alexander, Remarks on Aramaic Epistolography in the Persian Period, *JSS* 23 (1978), pp. 155-170.
6. R. Yaron, *Introduction to the Law of the Aramaic Papyri*, Oxford 1961.
7. For examples of the various types of inscriptions and documents, see the following textbooks: G. A. Cooke, *A Textbook of North-Semitic Inscriptions*, Oxford 1903; *KAI* and Gibson.

part, scholars in West Semitic studies tend to distinguish between these terms not on the basis of the writing materials, but according to the field of interest. Palaeography is considered to be the study of ancient scripts which traces the development of letter forms so that documents (both inscriptions and manuscripts) may be read correctly and, if necessary, dated. Epigraphy, on the other hand, is defined as the study of the written sources which archaeology has revealed. If we adopt the latter differentiation, it is often difficult to draw a clear line between epigraphy and palaeography. Since any treatment of the texts must be based on exact readings, a thorough knowledge of the scripts' evolution is a prerequisite. We believe, therefore, that both terms, epigraphy and palaeography, comprise one field of study, an auxiliary to history which specializes in every aspect of ancient written documents.

Scholars who specialize in this field must have a thorough knowledge of history and thus be acquainted with the non-epigraphic written sources, on the one hand, and with the non-epigraphic archaeological finds, on the other. Above all, epigraphers have to know the languages in which the texts are written. Epigraphy-paleography has very close links with linguistics and philology.

For the study of ancient languages, the principal source material consists of inscriptions and manuscripts. In addition to their usefulness in any attempt to reconstruct the spoken language, which is the task of the linguist, ancient records contain information on many aspects of human civilization which can be studied by the epigrapher-palaeographer. Whereas the dating of an undated inscription is based on typologic-diachronic factors, the synchronization of contemporaneous, related scripts may reflect the respective cultures of peoples and societies which developed in different geopolitical circumstances. The latter aspect, that is, comparative palaeography, will accompany our approach to several problems that are discussed in the following chapters of this book.

3. *The Development of Scripts and Script Styles*

Systematic palaeographical research should be based on a methodical study of the development of the script. The process of development was evolutionary. A new letter form would first appear sporadically in the writing of a few individuals, usually alongside the older form. Even after the new form had become entirely accepted, the older one remained in use for several decades. Often the new form continued to develop, though sometimes it would disappear and the older form would prevail.

The script as a whole develops as a result of modifications in the individual letters, such as the omission of elements, the positional shift of strokes, alterations in stance, the joining of elements formerly written separately and, occasionally, the introduction of new elements.

The gradual development of a script takes place on several parallel planes, and depends on the distribution of writing activity. When confined to a royal court or to the priesthood, the script was used mainly for stelae and thus remained conservative, preserving the older forms. At that stage there existed only one style, known as lapidary. Since this was confined to script inscribed on stone, it did not lend itself to rapid development. In time, however, writing was required on a wider scope for administrative purposes, and royal, temple and court scribes developed a faster script which demanded a certain streamlining. This furthered the evolutionary process. Such trends influenced the lapidary script, although the latter remained intact alongside the cursive, a style developed by writers in ink.

Writing became more widespread as people other than professional scribes learned to use it. These non-professionals adopted the scribes' cursive script, but unlike them, were not obliged to write in a calligraphic and conservative hand. Some individuals who could not master the pen wrote in a clumsy fashion; others became quite adept and could write freely.

The spread of writing activity beyond professional scribal circles to laymen who use it either systematically or intermittently is typical of every literate society excepting this generation. Nowadays the typewriter replaces the calligraphic writing of official scribes. In the Latin script of the nineteenth century, for example, there is a clear distinction between cursive and printed scripts. The cursive itself, however, is further divisible. A professional clerk would calligraphically emphasize the thicker descending strokes, and his script would be conservative and formal. As an official, he was required to maintain certain standards and could not invent new forms. But many others who knew how to write, for the most part people from the educated class who had completed their schooling, were not restricted by the rules of penmanship and unwittingly developed individual means of writing faster. Some of these innovations were adopted by others and thus the script gradually changed and evolved. Those who learned to read and write in the course of only a few years' schooling had but a limited use for this knowledge. A carpenter or shoemaker in the nineteenth century knew how to set down the measurements of a table or a shoe, and possibly also to read a newspaper, but writing a letter was a far more complicated matter. Although the clerk, the cultured person and the craftsman all used basically the same cursive script, there were distinctive stylistic differences. These may be classified as sub-styles of the cursive: (a) free (or extreme) cursive — that of the cultured person; (b) formal (or conservative) cursive — that of the professional scribe; and (c) vulgar cursive — that of persons of limited schooling.

This terminology serves to emphasize the unrestricted development of the first sub-style, in contrast to the others, which were influenced by it but did not develop at the same rate. Lapidary script, which may be compared with modern print although it is far more stable, was also influenced by the cursive. Thus, although lapidary script gave birth to cursive script, the offspring grew up to influence its parent; similarly, the free cursive influenced the formal. In other words, older, more conservative, forms were continuously influenced by newer, freer forms.

It should be remembered that not every cursive script can be conveniently classified as one of these sub-styles; moreover, an inscription cannot always be characterized as lapidary or cursive. Occasionally, a professional scribe would take liberties with the formal cursive, and thus introduce "free" forms at random; we may call this style semi-formal. Varying levels of competence in writing also make it difficult to distinguish between free and vulgar cursives. Indeed, many more subdivisions could be discerned, but the usefulness of such distinctions is questionable. At any rate, to regard a script as a homogenous entity or as comprised of only two styles, lapidary and cursive, would undoubtedly obscure analysis and impede valid conclusions.

4. *Semitic Languages and Scripts*

In antiquity Semitic languages were spoken in three areas in the Ancient Near East: in Mesopotamia in the north-east, in Syria-Palestine in the north-west and in the Arabian Peninsula in the south-west. These zones can be defined also as East, West and South. Accordingly, the Semitic languages have a threefold classification:

Eastern: Akkadian, Babylonian, Assyrian.
Western: Canaanite (including Hebrew, Phoenician, Moabite, Ammonite and, probably, Ugaritic), Aramaic.
Southern: South Arabian, Ethiopian, Arabic.

Some languages can be further classified into dialects, but this will be dealt with in the forthcoming chapters. Our aim here is not to discuss details, but merely to show that the division of Semitic scripts does not parallel that of Semitic languages. The East Semitic languages were rendered not in Semitic writing, but in the Sumerian cuneiform script. In other words, Semitic writing can only be either Western or Southern.

The ramification of the Semitic and other alphabetic scripts can be illustrated by a family tree, the trunk of which is the Proto-Canaanite script (see Fig. 1). From this there grew, *c.* 1300 B.C., the Proto-Arabic script (ancestor of the South Arabian and the Ethiopian scripts), and, *c.* 1100 B.C., the archaic Greek script. The Proto-Canaanite script, however, continued to flourish, and its direct offshoot, the Phoenician script, existed until the first centuries A.D. The Hebrew and the Aramaic scripts branched off from the Proto-Canaanite or Phoenician. Aramaic script was widespread throughout the ancient East; it was adopted by the Jews, who developed the Jewish (= square Hebrew) script for Aramaic and Hebrew texts, even though the latter is a Canaanite tongue. Classical Arabic, although a South Semitic language, is written in a script that was another offshoot of the Aramaic. The Arabic script developed from that Aramaic branch which was crystallized by the Nabataeans.

All the letters of the Semitic script stand for consonants. This system has been improved in Aramaic and Hebrew by the use of some consonant letters, called *matres lectionis*, to indicate vowels. In the first stage, these were used mainly at the end of words (*he* served for -a, -e and -o, *waw* for -u and *yod* for -i), but later also in medial positions. It was the Greeks who changed some letters into vowel signs: *alef* became A, *he* — E, *'ayin* — O, etc. This has led Gelb to postulate that only Greek and Latin scripts are alphabetic, while the Semitic script is a syllabary system. Gelb rightly claimed that each Semitic letter represents a consonant plus any

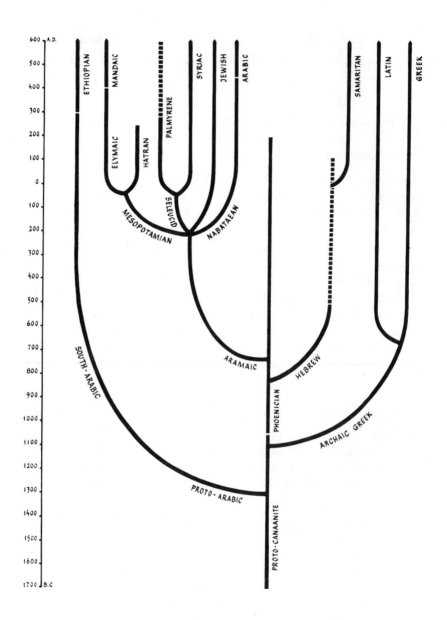

Fig. 1. Family tree of the early alphabetic scripts

one of the vowels (or zero vowel). Only in Greek and in its offshoots does each letter stand for either a consonant or a vowel.[8]

It is true that the Greek system is more evolved than the Semitic one. Acknowledging this handicap, medieval writers in Semitic scripts introduced vowel punctuation in order to facilitate the learning of reading and writing, but this auxiliary practice never became an integral part of the writing system. Nevertheless, we cannot accept Gelb's suggestion that Semitic writing be regarded as a syllabary system and that the term "alphabet" be confined to Greek, Latin and Cyrillic scripts. The definition of "alphabet" is not predicated on the values of the letters; the word denotes a system of writing with a limited number of signs (20-30) which have a fixed, "alphabetic" order. The order of the letters in the Greek and Latin alphabets is essentially the same as in the West Semitic scripts. This order was presumably established at the very beginning of the Proto-Canaanite writing. The earliest abecedary — that is, letters written in the fixed alphabetic order — comes from Ugarit and dates back to the fourteenth century B.C. (see below, p. 30).

In order to avoid potentially confusing terminology such as "ancient Hebrew" or "Phoenician-Hebrew", on the one hand, and "square Hebrew" on the other, we shall use "Hebrew" to denote the script which was commonly used by the Hebrews in both Israel and Judah in the First Temple period, and which was later confined to limited Jewish circles (although accepted by the Samaritans, who still use it today). This is what is meant by "Hebrew script" in Talmudic sources. The other Talmudic term, "Assyrian script", known today as "square Hebrew", is that which the Jews developed from Aramaic writing. Following Cross' usage, this script is here termed "Jewish". The Jewish script is a national script which developed from the Aramaic, as did Nabataean, Palmyrene, etc.[9]

---

8. I. J. Gelb, *A Study of Writing*², Chicago 1963, pp. 72-80; 122-153; idem, New Evidence in Favour of the Syllabic Character of West Semitic Writing, *BO* 15 (1958), pp. 2-7.

9. F. M. Cross, The Oldest Manuscripts from Qumran, *JBL* 74 (1955), pp. 147-172; idem, The Development of the Jewish Scripts, *BANE*, pp. 170-264.

Fig. 2. Sumerian pictographic inscription

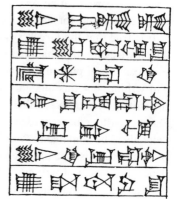

Fig. 3. Babylonian cuneiform text

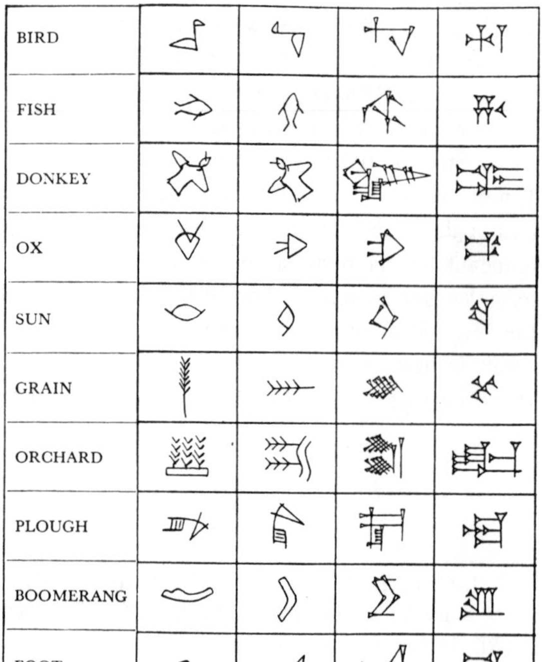

BIRD				
FISH				
DONKEY				
OX				
SUN				
GRAIN				
ORCHARD				
PLOUGH				
BOOMERANG				
FOOT				

Fig. 4. Pictographic origin of ten cuneiform signs

II. THE RISE OF THE SEMITIC SCRIPT

1. *Background*

When alphabetic writing came into existence in Syria-Palestine in the eighteenth or seventeenth century B.C., other scripts were already flourishing in the ancient world. In the East, various peoples, including Babylonians and Assyrians, used cuneiform writing, which they had adopted from the Sumerians; in the South, the Egyptians wrote in hieroglyphs; in the North, the Hittites developed their own pictographic script; and in the West, on the Mediterranean islands and the Greek mainland, there evolved another script. Before discussing the Semitic alphabet, let us take a short look at these non-alphabetic writings.

a. *Sumerian cuneiform writing*

In the late fourth and the third millennium B.C., the Sumerians had a well-developed civilization in southern Mesopotamia. Sumerian does not resemble any of the other ancient or modern languages known to date, as regards either grammar or vocabulary. Initially, pictures were scratched on tablets to designate various words (Fig. 2). In time they improved their writing: the pictographs gave way to wedge-shaped linear signs which were impressed by a stylus on the wet clay, and many signs came to indicate syllables (Fig. 4). The Akkadians, who settled in this area in the third millennium, took over this script and used it for their Semitic tongue (Fig. 3). They adopted the signs representing Sumerian words and terms, but read them as the Akkadian equivalents; these are named ideograms. For instance, the cuneiform symbol which originally designated the Sumerian word LÚ (= man) was read by the Akkadians as "awilum"; GAL (= great, big) — "rabum"; LUGAL (= king, originally:

LU+Gal=great man) — "šarrum". But the symbol for GAL could also represent the syllable -gal- as part of an Akkadian word. Another example: the Sumerian sign KA meaning "mouth" could be read by the Akkadians both as "pum" (the Akkadian word for mouth) or as the syllable -ka-. In cuneiform writing, there evolved a series of symbols which, when placed before a certain name or word, served as determinative indicators. Thus, when the Sumerian sign KUR (= land), in Akkadian "matum", preceded the word Aššur, it meant Aššur (the land) and was read *mat-Aššur*, whereas URU Aššur indicated Aššur (the city) and was read *al-Aššur*. These auxiliary symbols were in widespread use in syllabary scripts. Sumerian cuneiform writing was also adopted by non-Semites, among them the Elamites, the Hurrians and the Hittites.

The Akkadian language developed in two areas of Mesopotamia, and thus two East Semitic dialects came into being: Babylonian in the South, and Assyrian in the North. The history of these dialects can be traced for more than three thousand years. During this long period the Babylonians and the Assyrians preserved the tradition of cuneiform writing. In the eighth century B.C., the Neo-Assyrians introduced the alphabetic Aramaic script in order to facilitate communication between the newly-conquered provinces. Nevertheless, the Assyrians did not abandon their own script and both the Assyrian and Babylonian languages were always written in the complex cuneiform script. The latest cuneiform tablets were written in the first century A.D.

b. *Egyptian hieroglyphic script*

"Hieroglyph" is a Greek word meaning "sacred carving". When the Greeks occupied Egypt they were impressed by the monumental inscriptions engraved on the walls of the Egyptian temples. However, hieroglyphic writing was used not only for engraving texts, but also — and primarily — as a pictographic script consisting of drawn pictures. As in Sumerian writing, each pictograph initially designated a word, and later there evolved a series of syllabic symbols. However, unlike the cuneiform script in which the signs also represented the vowels within each syllable or word, the Egyptian hieroglyphic script did not indicate the vowels between consonants, and the vocalization of the Egyptian language is not known. The symbol drawn as a house represented *pr*, but we do not know with what vowels this sign was pronounced; it could stand for par, per,

SIGN	TRANS-LITERATION	OBJECT DEPICTED
 𓄿	ꜣ	Egyptian vulture
𓇋	i	flowering reed
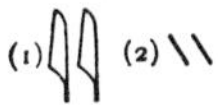 (1) 𓇋𓇋 (2) \\	y	{ (1) two reed-flowers (2) oblique strokes
𓂝	ꜥ	forearm
 𓅱	w	quail chick
 𓃀	b	foot
𓊪	p	stool
 𓆑	f	horned viper
 𓅓	m	owl
𓈖	n	water
 𓂋	r	mouth
𓉐	h	reed shelter in fields
 𓎛	ḥ	wick of twisted flax
𓐍	ḫ	placenta (?)
 𓄡	ẖ	animal's belly with teats
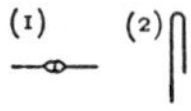 (1) 𓋴 (2) 𓊪	s	{ (1) bolt (2) folded cloth
𓈙	š	pool
𓈎	ḳ	hill-slope
 𓎡	k	basket with handle
𓎼	g	stand for jar
𓏏	t	loaf
 𓍿	ṯ	tethering rope
𓂧	d	hand
 𓆓	ḏ	snake

Fig. 5. The uniconsonantal signs in the Egyptian hieroglyphic script

15

pura, peru, etc.; the pictograph for "mouth" could be read ra, re, ri, ru or r.

In Egyptian writing there were symbols of one, two or three consonants. Had the Egyptians used only the uniconsonantal signs, their writing would have been alphabetic like that of the Semites (Fig. 5). Since they also preserved bi- and triconsonantal pictographs, the number of signs remained large (Fig. 6).

Egyptian belongs to the Hamitic family of languages, which has some affinity to the Semitic family. Although the Egyptians continued to use pictographs in their formal writing until the late first millennium B.C., they also developed a cursive style of writing. The earlier scripts of this style are called hieratic, and the later ones demotic (Fig. 7).

Fig. 6. Egyptian hieroglyphs engraved on a stele

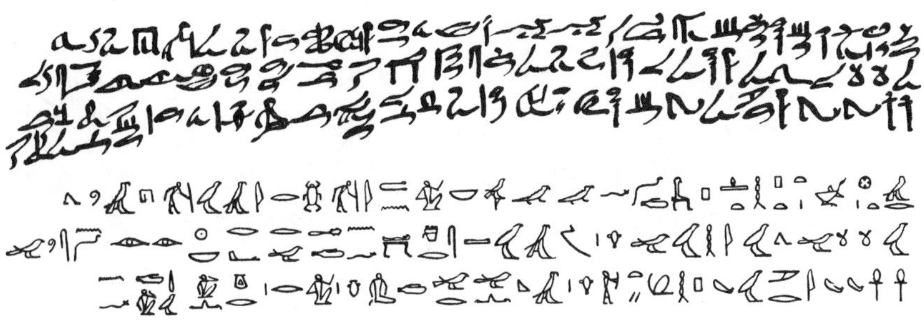

LITERARY HIERATIC OF THE TWELFTH DYNASTY (*Pr.* 4, 2-4),
WITH TRANSCRIPTION

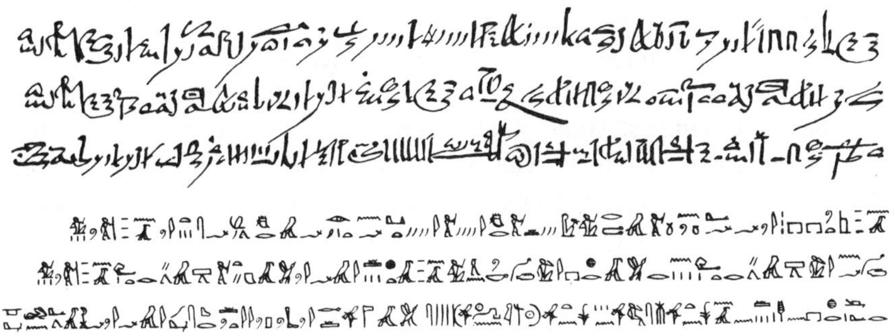

OFFICIAL HIERATIC OF THE TWENTIETH DYNASTY (*Abbott* 5, 1-3),
WITH TRANSCRIPTION

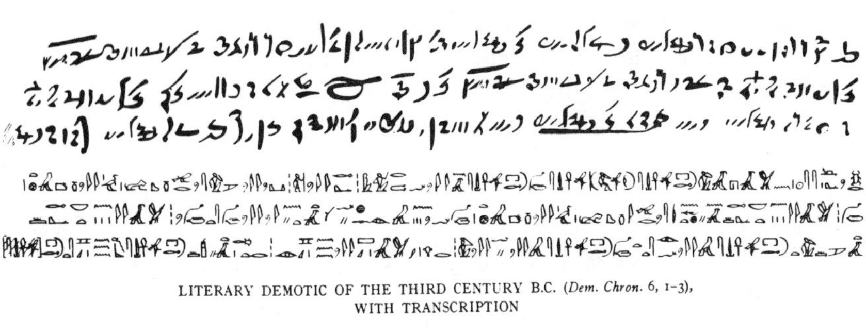

LITERARY DEMOTIC OF THE THIRD CENTURY B.C. (*Dem. Chron.* 6, 1-3),
WITH TRANSCRIPTION

Fig. 7. Hieratic and demotic scripts with hieroglyphic transcriptions in a modern
Egyptological hand

Fig. 8. Hittite pictographic script

c. *The Hittite "hieroglyphic" script*

Hittite is an Indo-European language akin to Greek, Latin and the German and Slavic tongues. The term "Hittite hieroglyphs" does not indicate any relation to Egyptian writing, except for the fact that both were pictographic writings. Hittite studies simply adopted the inexact term for Egyptian writing (Fig. 8). The Hittites also used the Sumerian cuneiform writing, but some monumental inscriptions were written in their native script. This pictographic writing was generally carved in relief in the Hittite empire during the second half of the second millennium, and in the Neo-Hittite kingdoms during a 300-year period from the start of the first millennium B.C. A very important key to the decipherment of the Hittite pictographic script was the relatively long bilingual (Phoenician-Hittite) inscription found at the city gate of Karatepe in Cilicia, which in the eighth century B.C. was the fortress of a ruler named Azitawadda (Fig. 9). However, most information on the Hittite language is drawn from their cuneiform inscriptions.

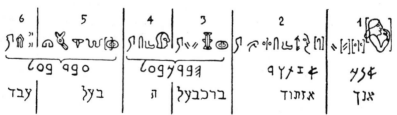

Fig. 9. The opening phrase of the Karatepe bilingual (Hittite and Phoenician) inscription; the text in square Hebrew letters is a word-by-word translation of the Hittite into Phoenician

Fig. 10. Cretan pictographic script

d. *The Cretan script*

Another pictographic writing evolved on the island of Crete (Fig. 10).
It is probably from these pictographs that there developed the scripts
known as Linear A and Linear B, which were used in Greece in the
second millennium B.C., and the Cypriote syllabary. Modern scholars
can read the Cypriote syllabic script (Fig. 11), which the Cypriote Greeks
employed along with the Greek alphabet as late as the Hellenistic period.
Linear B was deciphered in the last generation by a British architect
named Ventris (Fig. 12), while Linear A, and the Cretan pictographic

	α, αι	ε, η	ι	ο, ω	u
Vowels					
k					
t					
p					
l					
r					
m					
n					
j					
f, v					
s					
z		(?)			
x	(?)				

Fig. 11. Cypriote syllabary

script, are still enigmatic. Linear B was a syllabic and ideographic writing practised by the Mycenaean Greeks until *c.* 1100 B.C., when the Mycenaean civilization was destroyed by the Doric invasion. The Cypriote Greek community was probably an offshoot of the Mycenaean.

Fig. 12. Linear B script

Fig. 13. Enigmatic inscription from Byblos

e. *Undeciphered scripts in Syria-Palestine*

The excavation of Byblos on the Phoenician coast brought to light some inscribed stelae, presumably from the second millennium (Fig. 13).

Their partly pictographic and partly linear script has not yet been deciphered. Another illegible stele was found at Balu'ah in Moab (Fig. 14), and some inscribed tablets at Deir 'Alla in the Jordan valley (Fig. 15). Some scholars believe that the script of the Deir 'Alla tablets can be related to the Cypro-Minoan type of writing thought to have been used there by the Philistines:[1] the Byblos and Balu'ah scripts may perhaps be regarded as West Semitic attempts to invent some system of syllabic writing. At any rate, these attempts were abandoned with the introduction of the alphabet.[2]

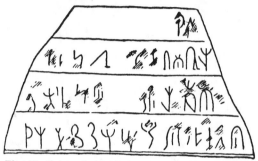

Fig. 14. Enigmatic inscription on a stele from Balu'ah

Fig. 15. A tablet from Deir 'Alla

1. G. E. Wright, Fresh Evidence for the Philistine Story, *BA* 29 (1966), p. 73.
2. For a more detailed description of the cuneiform, hieroglyphic and other non-alphabetic scripts, see the respective chapters in the following: D. Diringer, *The Alphabet*, New York 1948; G. R. Driver, *Semitic Writing from Pictograph to Alphabet*[3], London 1976; Gelb, *A Study of Writing*[2], Chicago 1963.

2. *The Beginnings of the Alphabet*

The origins of the alphabet have intrigued human curiosity since ancient times. Herodotus, the "Father of History" who lived in the fifth century B.C., informs us that the knowledge of writing was brought to Greece by the Phoenicians and a certain legendary person named Kadmos. There was a consensus among ancient historians that the Greeks had learned the alphabet from the Phoenicians, but opinions differed as to the origin of the Phoenicians' knowledge of writing. Diodorus Siculus and Pliny believed that the Assyrians had introduced writing, whereas Plato and Tacitus claimed that it was an Egyptian invention. Nineteenth-century scholars revived this debate: the majority adhered to the theory of Egyptian and Assyrian origin, but some suggested that the alphabet had evolved from the Cypro-Minoan or even the Hittite hieroglyphic writing.[3]

The turning point that marks the beginning of modern research on the origin of the alphabet was Petrie's discovery in 1905 of the temple at Serabit el-Khadem on the Sinai peninsula.[4] In this temple, dedicated to the Egyptian goddess Hathor, and in the turquoise mines nearby, there came to light about a score of relatively short inscriptions in a formerly unknown script. The script consisted of pictures, but these pictographs numbered fewer than thirty. It was soon realized that this was an alphabetic — albeit pictographic — script. The first step towards its decipherment was made in 1916 by Gardiner, who pointed out that in these so-called Proto-Sinaitic inscriptions a certain series of pictures recurs several times: ox goad — house — eye — ox goad — cross. He suggested that these pictographs have acrophonic values of the equivalent Canaanite words *lamd-bet-ʿayin-lamd-taw*, i.e. each picture symbolizes not the depicted word, but only its initial sound. Gardiner thus discerned the Canaanite word *lbʿlt* "to the lady" (Fig. 16, Pl. 1:A).[5] The word *bʿlt*

3. For more detailed discussions, see bibliography in n. 2.
4. W. M. Flinders Petrie, *Researches in Sinai*, London 1906, pp. 129-132.
5. A. Gardiner, The Egyptian Origin of the Semitic Alphabet, *JEA* 3 (1961), pp. 1-16.

Fig. 16. The word *(l)b'lt* in the Proto-Sinaitic inscriptions

is an epithet of a Canaanite goddess, probably to be identified with Egyptian Hathor. Since then, there have been further attempts at deciphering on the basis of different axioms concerning the language in which these inscriptions were assumed to have been written. Thus, for example, Van den Branden tried to read the Proto-Sinaitic inscriptions as a South Semitic dialect akin to the language that appears on South Arabian monuments.[6] However, it is generally thought that these texts were written in Canaanite, and efforts to decipher them are for the most part based on our knowledge of Canaanite in the second millennium B.C., in which Ugaritic is of key importance.

Albright, whose decipherment is based mainly on the Ugaritic vocabulary and grammar, believed that he could identify twenty-three of the probable twenty-seven letters of this script (Fig. 17).[7] His decipherment is based on other axioms too: that these texts are votive inscriptions dedicated to a certain goddess called here Ba῾alat, and that the people who wrote them were Canaanite or West Semitic miners employed by the Egyptians in the turquoise mines at Serabit el-Khadem. Despite some readings which are indisputably correct, it would be premature to state that the Proto-Sinaitic inscriptions have been satisfactorily deciphered. However, these texts include quite a large number of pictographs which were definitively identified as the original forms of the Phoenician letters. Thus the main importance of this discovery is the contribution which these inscriptions make to the origin and the early history of the alphabet.

6. A. van den Branden. Les inscriptions protosinaïtiques, *Oriens Antiquus* 1 (1962), pp. 197-214.
7. W. F. Albright, *The Proto-Sinaitic Inscriptions and their Decipherment*, (Harvard Theological Studies, XXII), Cambridge (Mass.) 1966.

Now, the question arises: Did these West Semitic workers or slaves in Sinai invent the first alphabetic writing? For some decades after the discovery, the answer was positive. Scholars believed that these Semites, who were in daily contact with Egyptian writing, improved it and restricted it to uniconsonantal signs, thereby inventing the alphabetic system of

Phon. Value	Schematic Forms	Early North-west Semitic	Early South Semitic	Early Letter Names	Meaning of Names
ʾ	𝖄 𝖄	𝄐 (14th) 𝄐 (13th)	𝖄 𝄐 (Jamme)	ʾalp-	ox-head
b	◻ 𝄐	◻ (17th) 𝄐 (13th)	Π	bêt-	house
g	∟	∧ (15th) ⟩ (12th)	⊓ Γ	gaml-	throw-stick
d	↦ 𝄐	◁ △ (10th)	𝄐 (Jamme)	digg-	fish
ḏ	= ⊂	?	H N (Jamme)	?	?
h	𝄐 𝄐	⌐ (10th)	𝄐	hô(?)	man calling
w	—○ 𝄐	Y (10th)	⊕ (? used for y)	wô(waw)	mace
z	?	⅀(16th) I (10th)	𝄐	zê(n-)	?
ḥ	Ⅲ 𝄐	Ⅲ (12th) 𝄐 (10th)	𝄐⟩	ḥê(t-)	fence (?)
ḫ	𝄐 𝄐	?	𝄐 (Jamme)	ḫa( )	hank of yarn
ṭ	?	‖○ (16th) ⊕ (10th)	⊞	ṭê(t-)	spindle?
y	𝄐 𝄐	𝄐 (13th) 𝄐 (10th)	𝖯 (orig w)	yad-	arm
k	Ⱳ Ⱳ	Ⱳ (17th) Ⱳ (13th)	𝄐 𝄐	kapp-	palm
l	𝄐 𝖯 𝖢 𝄐	𝄐 (14th) 𝄐 (13th)	𝄐 L (Jamme)	lamd-	ox-goad
m	𝄐 𝄐	𝄐 (15th) 𝄐 (13th)	𝄐 (9th) 𝄐 (8th)	mêm-	water
n	𝄐 𝄐 ⌐	𝄐 (14th) 𝄐 (12th)	𝄐 𝄐 𝄐	noḥš-	snake
ś	?	𝄐 (10th)	𝄐 𝄐	(śamk-?)	?
ʿ	⟋ ⟍	○ (12th) ○ (10th)	○	ʿên-	eye
ḡ	𝄐	⊏ (15th)	⊓ 𝄐 (Jamme)	ḡa( )	?
p	𝄐 𝄐	⟩ (10th)	◊ ◊	puʾt-(?)	corner?
ṣ/ẓ	𝄐 𝄐	𝄐 (10th)	𝄐 𝄐	ṣa(d-)	plant
ḍ	?	?	⊟	?	?
q	⊂◯ 𝄐	⊂◯ (14th) 𝄐 (10th)	◊ φ (Jamme)	qu(p-)	?
r	𝄐 𝄐	𝄐 (16th-14th)	) (	na'š-	head of man
ś/ṯ	𝄐	𝄐 (13th) 𝄐 (10th)	⟩ ⟨	ṯann-	composite bow
š	𝄐 𝄐	?	𝄐 𝄐 (Jamme)	?	?
t	+	+ ✕ (13th)	✕ + (Jamme)	tô(taw)	owner's mark

Fig. 17. Albright's chart of letters in the Proto-Sinaitic inscriptions

25

writing. In addition, there were scholars who tried to relate this script to the Israelites, who after the Exodus lived for a generation in the Sinai peninsula.[8] Nowadays these romantic views are no longer accepted. There are at least three short pictographic inscriptions of the same type which were found in Palestinian sites — Shechem (Fig. 18), Gezer (Fig. 19, Pl. 1:B), and Lachish (Fig. 20) — and which antedate the corpus of the Proto-Sinaitic texts. The latter are dated to *c.* 1500 B.C., whereas the above-mentioned three Palestinian inscriptions seem to belong to the

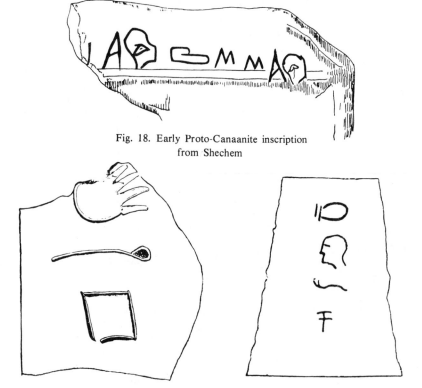

Fig. 18. Early Proto-Canaanite inscription
from Shechem

Fig. 19. Early Proto-Canaanite letters
(*klb*) on a potsherd from Gezer

Fig. 20. Early Proto-Canaanite letters
on a dagger from Lachish

8. H. Grimme, *Althebräische Inschriften vom Sinai*, Hannover 1923.

seventeenth and sixteenth centuries.[9] The pictographs on the Palestinian inscriptions are drawn realistically, whereas the same symbols in the Serabit el-Khadem texts are more schematized. Further schematization can be traced in other Palestinian pictographic inscriptions from the thirteenth and twelfth centuries B.C. Thus we are inclined to conclude that although the Proto-Sinaitic inscriptions form a relatively large group, they are an integral part of the corpus of the early alphabetic inscriptions called Proto-Canaanite.

Apart from the pictures representing the consonantal signs b, l, ‘ (fricative pharyngal) and t, the following pictographs can be identified with certainty: ’ (plosive laryngal, the first consonant of the word ’*alp* — "ox"), w (*waw* — "peg"), y (*yod* — "hand"), k (*kaf* — "palm"), m (*mem* — "water"), n (*naḥaš* — "snake") and r (*roš* — "head"). It seems likely that not all the pictographs represented acrophonic values. However, bearing in mind that from these pictographs there evolved the Phoenician letters, on the one hand, and the South Arabian script, on the other, we can often identify the original form of additional letters as they appear in the middle of the second millennium (Fig. 17). In fact, the development of the Proto-Canaanite pictographs into linear letters can be traced in the later Proto-Canaanite and early Phoenician inscriptions.

The chief importance of the Proto-Canaanite and Proto-Sinaitic inscriptions is their contribution to the history of writing. However, since their decipherment, particularly that of the earlier texts, cannot be considered conclusive, they cannot be taken as data for the Canaanite language spoken in the second millennium. The sources for such information should be sought in records written in other scripts. In this period, Akkadian was a *lingua franca* which various peoples used for the purposes of communication. At Tell el-Amarna in Egypt, letters sent from Canaanite rulers to Pharaohs Amenhotep and Akhenaton were found. These letters were written in Akkadian, but Canaanite words in cuneiform script were frequently included. Thus these syllabic transcriptions of Canaanite words are of prime importance for the vocalization of the Canaanite language as early as the fourteenth century B.C. From the

---

9. Cf. Albright (above, n. 7), p. 10; F. M. Cross, The Origin and Early Evolution of the Alphabet, *EI* 8 (1967), p. 10*; *IR*, No. 1.

hundreds of Akkadian documents found at Mari, scholars concluded that the inhabitants of the city were West Semites ("Amorites" or "East Canaanites"). The Canaanite proper names and certain other words that occur in these texts throw some light on the West Semitic language spoken in the eighteenth century B.C. Even Egyptian documents mentioning Canaanite towns and rulers add to our knowledge. However, the main source is the corpus of texts found at Ugarit.[10]

Fig. 21. Cuneiform alphabetic script from Ugarit

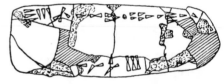

Fig. 22. Cuneiform alphabetic script from Beth-Shemesh

10. See W. L. Moran, The Hebrew Language in its Northwest Semitic Background, *BANE*, pp. 59-84; H. B. Huffmon, *Amorite Personal Names in the Mari Texts*, Baltimore 1965; J. C. Greenfield, Amurrite, Ugaritic and Canaanite, *Proceedings of the International Conference of Semitic Studies*, Jerusalem 1969, pp. 92-101. Since 1975 thousands of clay tablets from the third millennium B.C. have been discovered in Ebla (Tell Mardikh in North Syria). About 80% are in Sumerian, the others are in a Semitic language. While Pettinato and Dahood believe that the latter is West Semitic (Old Canaanite), Gelb and others maintain that it is an East Semitic dialect, i.e. closer to Akkadian. See I. J. Gelb, Thoughts about Ibla: A Preliminary Evaluation, *Monographic Journals of the Near East, Syro-Mesopotamia Studies* 1/1 (May 1977), pp. 3-30.

Since 1928 systematic archaeological excavations have been carried out at Ras-Shamra on the Mediterranean coast of North Syria. The archives found at that site indicate that in the fourteenth and thirteenth centuries a city named Ugarit flourished here. In addition to the Akkadian syllabic cuneiform tablets, many tablets were inscribed with a cuneiform script comprising a limited number of signs. This is an alphabetic cuneiform script, which adapted the techniques of cuneiform writing — i.e. clay tablets and stylus — to the alphabetic principle (Fig. 21). In Ugarit, thirty cuneiform characters were used to write letters, administrative documents and literary works: the last are a most important source for Canaanite mythology and poetry.[11] It seems likely that the use of the alphabetic cuneiform script was not restricted to Ugarit. Such texts were also found in some sites in Palestine, such as Beth Shemesh (Fig. 22), Ta'anach (Fig. 23) and Nahal Tavor (Fig. 24); however, these belong

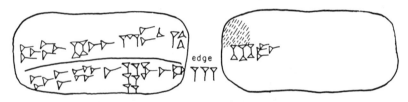

Fig. 23. Cuneiform alphabetic text from Ta'anach

Fig. 24. Cuneiform alphabetic text from Nahal Tavor

11. C. H. Gordon, *Ugaritic Textbook*, Rome 1965.

to the thirteenth and twelfth centuries B.C.[12] Cross suggests the following schema for the general ordering of the early alphabetic texts:[13]

  I. The Proto-Canaanite Texts
      (a) Old Palestinian, 17th-12th centuries B.C.
      (b) Proto-Sinaitic, 15th century B.C.
  II. Canaanite Cuneiform Texts
      (a) Ugaritic, 14th-13th centuries B.C.
      (b) Palestinian, 13th-12th centuries B.C.

As mentioned above (p. 11), the earliest evidence for the present-day alphabetic sequence was found at Ugarit, where the thirty cuneiform alphabetic letters were inscribed on clay tablets. The transcription of one of these tablets is as follows (Fig. 25):

$$'a \; b \; g \; \underline{h} \; d \; h \; w \; z \; \underline{h} \; \underline{t} \; y \; k \; \check{s} \; l$$
$$m \; \underline{d} \; n \; \underline{z} \; s \; {}^{\backprime} \; p \; \d{s} \; q \; r \; \underline{t}$$
$$\dot{g} \; t \; {}^{\backprime}i \; {}^{\backprime}u \; s_2$$

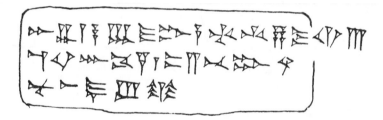

Fig. 25. An abecedary from Ugarit

The number of letters from '(a) to t is twenty-seven; these are the original letters. (According to Albright's reconstruction, the original Proto-

12. See *IR*, No. 3; D. R. Hillers, An Alphabetic Cuneiform Tablet from Taanach, *BASOR* 173 (1964), pp. 45-50; F. M. Cross, The Canaanite Cuneiform Tablet from Taanach, *BASOR* 190 (1968), pp. 41-46. See also J. Teixidor in J. B. Pritchard, *Sarepta*, Philadelphia 1975, pp. 102-104.
13. Cross (above, n. 9), p. 12*.

Canaanite alphabet consisted of the same consonantal system.) The last three letters were presumably added at a later stage: ʾ*alef*+i and ʾ*alef*+u were introduced in order to distinguish in writing between the three possibilities of vocalization (whereas the original ʾ*alef* became ʾ*alef*+a); the last letter was used only in foreign words, e.g. s_2s_2w (= Phoenician *ss*; Hebrew *sws*; Aramaic *swsy*ʾ — "horse"). The Phoenician alphabet omits five letters: ḫ, š, ḍ, ẓ and ġ and thus consists of twenty-two letters, which were also adopted by the Hebrew and Aramaic scripts. As early as the thirteenth century B.C., the South Canaanite dialect, which was written in the Proto-Canaanite script, dropped these consonants from its phonemic system: ḍ became z; ḫ > ḥ; ẓ > ṣ and ġ > ʿ; the consonant ṯ became š, but the letter designating ṯ was preserved and thus the later letter for š (formerly ṯ) came between r and t in the alphabetic sequence.

In order to understand these phonetic changes we shall discuss briefly the Semitic phonemic system (Fig. 26). The ancient South Arabian dialects have twenty-nine consonants. This is the richest Semitic consonantal system. The reconstructed Proto-Semitic language, which may have been the ancestor of all Semitic languages, is considered to have the same twenty-nine consonants. Classical Arabic has twenty-eight consonants. Thus six Arabic letters have no equivalents in the Phoenician, Hebrew and Aramaic alphabets; these are ث (ṯ), خ (ḫ), ذ (ḍ), ظ (ẓ), ض (ḍ) and غ (ġ). However, classical Arabic lacks one letter which does exist in South Arabian. The latter has three sibilants ħ, ℨ and 𐩥, whereas in classical Arabic there are only two: س (s) and ش (š).

As languages evolve, there is a tendency for phonemes to become assimilated. In the South Canaanite dialect and in Phoenician, five consonants assimilated with another five. For instance, the Proto-Semitic word for "land" ʾ*rḍ* (=Arabic ارض) became ʾ*rṣ* (ארץ) in Phoenician and Hebrew, while in Aramaic it was written as ʾ*rq*ʾ (ארקא) and later ʾ*r*ʿ (ארעא); ẓl "shadow": Arabic ẓl (ظل), Hebrew ṣl (צל), Aramaic ṭll*ʾ (טללא). The Proto-Semitic root of certain words can be reconstructed on the basis of Arabic, but if the root does not occur in Arabic, the reconstruction can be based on Hebrew and Aramaic. Words written in Hebrew with z and in Aramaic with d stem from the original ḍ, e.g. Hebrew *zrw*ʿ (זרוע) and Aramaic ʾ*dr*ʿ (אדרע), both indicating "arm"; or the original ṯ became š in Hebrew and t in Aramaic, e.g. "three" in Hebrew is *šlš* (שלש) and in

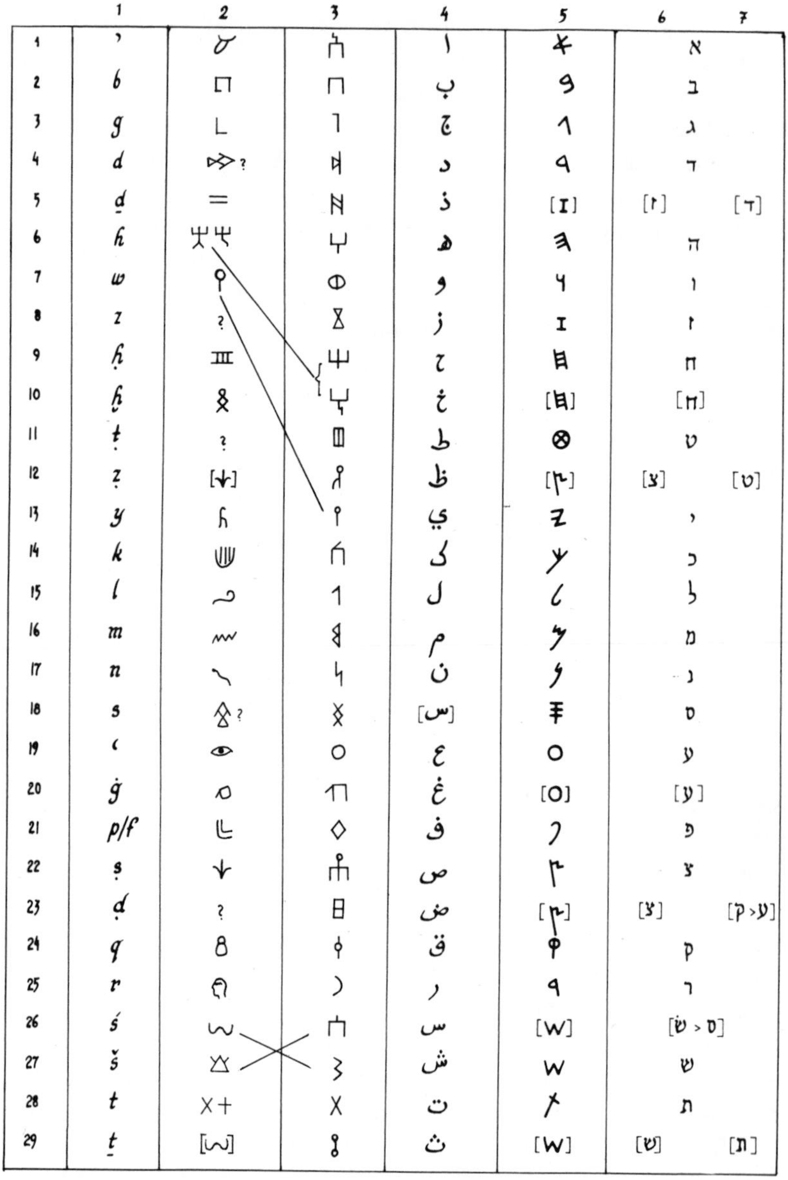

	1	2	3	4	5	6	7
1	ʾ			ا		א	
2	b			ب		ב	
3	g			ج		ג	
4	d			د		ד	
5	ḏ			ذ	[ ]	[ ]	[ז]
6	ḥ			ه		ה	
7	w			و		ו	
8	z			ز		ז	
9	ḥ			ح		ח	
10	ḫ			خ	[ ]	[ח]	
11	ṭ			ط		ט	
12	ẓ			ظ	[ ]	[ ]	[ט]
13	y			ي		י	
14	k			ك		כ	
15	l			ل		ל	
16	m			م		מ	
17	n			ن		נ	
18	s			[س]		ס	
19	ʿ			ع		ע	
20	ġ			غ	[O]	[ע]	
21	p/f			ف		פ	
22	ṣ			ص		צ	
23	ḍ			ض	[ ]	[צ]	[ק>ע]
24	q			ق		ק	
25	r			ر		ר	
26	ś			س	[W]	[שׂ>ס]	
27	š			ش	W	ש	
28	t			ت		ת	
29	ṯ			ث	[W]	[ת]	[ת]

Fig. 26. Phonemic systems in West and South Semitic: 1. Proto-Semitic; 2. Proto-Canaanite; 3. South Arabic; 4. Arabic; 5. Phoenician; 6. Hebrew; 7. Aramaic

Aramaic *tlt* (תלת), while Arabic preserved the form *ṯlṯ* (ثلث).[14] (See below, chapter IV, pp. 54 ff.).

Albright suggested the following readings and translations for two of the Serabit el-Khadem inscriptions (Fig. 27):

No. 349

1. *ʾnt ḏ ṯ*ᶜ	Thou, O offerer,
2. *rb nqbnm ṯ[ᶜ]*	(or) chief miner, an offering
3. *ᶜrkm lbᶜlt*	prepare for Baᶜalat
4. *ᶜl ʾḥn ḏ ṯ[ᶜ ṯ]*	on behalf of ʾAḥena — O offerer — an offering
5. *ᶜ ṯᶜt lbn[h ʾ]*	of a wild ewe. On behalf of [his] son
6. *[ly]ṯᶜ ṯ[n ḏ ṯ]*	[Eli]sha(?) gi[ve, O offer]er,
7. *ᶜ ṯᶜt l[bᶜlt]*	a wild ewe for [Baᶜalat].[15]

No. 357

Vertical line: *ʾnt ṯpn dkm lʾbb mn 8*

Horizontal line: *šm[ʾ] mrʾ rb ᶜ[prm]*

Thou, O Shaphan, collect from ʾAbaba eight minas (of turquoise) Shimea, groom of the chief of car[avaneers(?)].[16]

Whereas in the early Proto-Canaanite (including Proto-Sinaitic) inscriptions, the readings and interpretations of texts are very conjectural, we stand on rather more solid ground when dealing with the later inscriptions. Thus the inscription painted on the shoulder of a decorated ewer found at Lachish was read and interpreted by Cross as follows (Fig. 28):

mtn. šy [lrb]ty ʾlt

Mattan. An offering to my Lady ʾElat.[17]

The offering or tribute was no doubt the decorated ewer itself, and perhaps its contents, presented to the temple of the goddess ʾElat in Lachish by a certain Mattan. The word *šy* (etymological *ṯy*; in the Proto-

14. S. Moscati et alii, *An Introduction to the Comparative Grammar of the Semitic Languages*, Wiesbaden 1964, pp. 22-45.
15. Albright (above, n. 7), p. 18.
16. *Ibid.*, p. 23.
17. F. M. Cross, The Evolution of the Proto-Canaanite Alphabet, *BASOR* 134 (1954), pp. 20-21; idem (above, n. 9), p. 16*; *IR*, No. 4.

Fig. 27. Two inscriptions from Serabit el-Khadem

Sinaitic inscriptions *t‘* [?] and in Ugaritic *t‘y*) "tribute, offering" occurs also in the Old Testament. In the fifteenth century the sign in question (composite bow) was used — according to Albright and Cross — for *t* and *ś*; by the thirteenth century, the shift *t/ś>š* had taken place in South Canaanite.

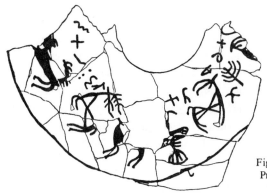

Fig. 28. A 13th-century B.C. Proto-Canaanite text on the Lachish Ewer

In the Beth Shemesh ostracon, probably from the very beginning of the twelfth century B.C., Cross read (in vertical columns) the following name list (Fig. 29):

(obv. 1) *l'z'ḥ* (2) *'bśkr* (rev. 3) *gm'n* (4) *ḥnn*

Belonging to 'Uzzi'aḥ, Abiśakr, Gum'an (and) Ḥannun.[18]

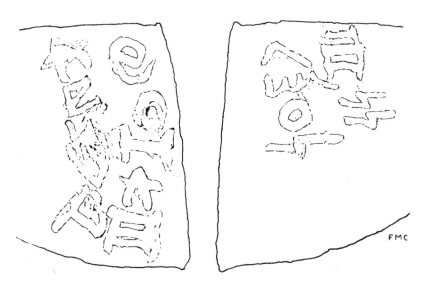

Fig. 29. Proto-Canaanite text on an ostracon from Beth-Shemesh

18. Cross (above, n. 9), pp. 17*-18*.

The first name ʿUzziʾaḥ contains the word ʾaḥ "brother" (used here as a theophoric element). ʾaḥ — etymological ʾaḫ (cf. Arabic) — occurs here with the sign for ḥ, as in Phoenician and Hebrew, whereas, according to Albright, the same element in the proper name ʾḫn — ʾAḫena in the Serabit el-Khadem inscription No. 349 — is written with ḫ.

On an inscribed bowl fragment recently found at Qubur el-Walaydah in the north-western Negev (near Tell el-Farʿah), the preserved letters were dated by Cross to *c.* 1200 B.C. and read as follows (Fig. 30, Pl. 1:C):

šmpʿl. ʾyʾl.š. 10 (?)

Šimi-paʿal (son of) ʾIyya-ʾEl 10 (?) sheep (or sheqels).[19]

Fig. 30. A fragmentary Proto-Canaanite inscription on a bowl from Qubur el-Walaydah

The text is written from left to right, with vertical strokes dividing between the words. Note that in the inscription on the Lachish ewer (Fig. 28) the first word *mtn* is separated from the rest of the text by three vertically placed dots, and that both word-dividers are common in the archaic Greek writing.[20]

The ostracon found at Izbet Sartah, 3 km. east of Tel Aphek, is the largest inscribed item in the scant corpus of late Proto-Canaanite inscrip-

19. F. M. Cross, Newly Found Inscriptions in Old Canaanite and Early Phoenician Script, *BASOR* 238 (1980), pp. 2-4.
20. J. Naveh, Word Division in West Semitic Writing, *IEJ* 23 (1973), p. 206, and n. 8.

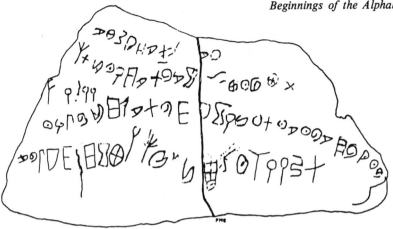

Fig. 31. The ostracon from Izbet Sartah

tions (Fig. 31). It contains more than eighty letters in five lines written by an unskilled hand. This inscription seems to have been scratched by a semi-literate person who, after a rather unsuccessful attempt at writing an abecedary, merely etched an agglomeration of random letters which do not comprise a text in any Semitic language. This ostracon is to be dated to the twelfth century B.C.[21]

In the four above-mentioned inscriptions from Lachish, Beth Shemesh, Qubur el-Walaydah and Izbet Sartah, as well as in the other thirteenth- and twelfth-century inscriptions, the evolution of the former pictographs into linear letters is clearly discernible. This process can be followed in the later Proto-Canaanite inscriptions. On four arrow-heads found at el-Khader near Bethlehem the following text was written in vertical columns (Fig. 32):

ḥṣ 'bdlb't
The dart of 'Abdlabi'at.[22]

21. J. Naveh, Some Considerations on the Ostracon from Izbet Sartah, *IEJ* 28 (1978), pp. 31-35; Cross (above, n. 19), pp. 8-15.
22. J. T. Milik and F. M. Cross, Inscribed Javelin Heads from the Period of the Judges, *BASOR* 134 (1954), pp. 5-15; Cross (above, n. 9), pp. 13*-16*, *IR*, No. 7.

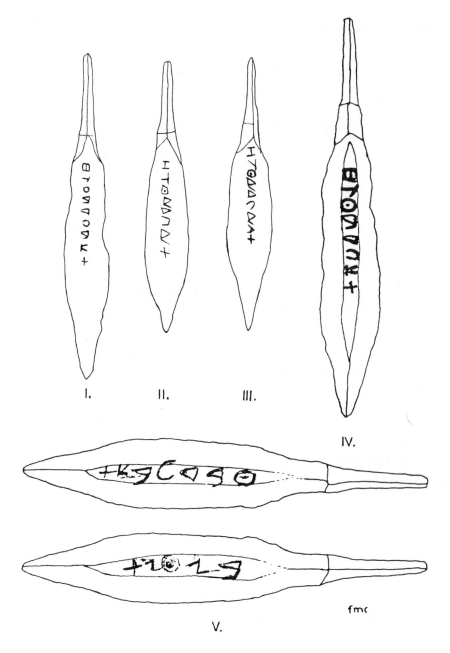

Fig. 32. The inscribed arrow-heads from el-Khader

On the fifth inscribed arrow-head the letters follow each other horizontally from right to left and the text reads as follows:

ʿbdlbʾt / bnʿnt
ʿAbdlabiʾat (son of) Benʿanat.[23]

The name ʿAbd-labiʾat means "servant of the Lion-lady" (i.e. the goddess ʿAnat).

The el-Khader arrow-heads are presumably from the late twelfth century B.C. Four more arrow-heads found at various sites in Lebanon probably date from the eleventh century B.C. Two of these appear to be Proto-Canaanite, while the other two are written in Phoenician script. The two which bear respectively the inscriptions *ḥs grbʿl / ṣdny* and *ḥṣ rpʾ / bn yḥš* can be dated to the early or mid-eleventh century (Fig. 33); the

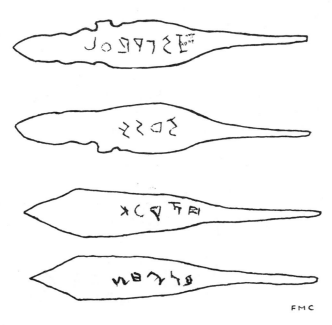

FMC

Fig. 33. Inscribed arrow-heads from the first half of
the 11th century B.C.

23. Cross (above, n. 19), pp. 4-7.

inscribed arrow-heads found at Biqaʿ (*ḥṣ zkrb[ʿl] / bn bnʿn[t]*) and Ruweisah (*ḥṣ ʾdʾ / bn ʿky*) should be dated to the late eleventh century (Fig. 34). In the former, the stances of some letters had not yet been stabilized; this means that the pictographic conception still existed.[24]

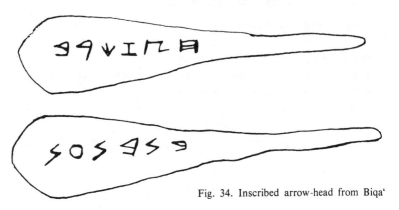

Fig. 34. Inscribed arrow-head from Biqaʿ

Two eleventh-century fragmentary inscriptions come respectively from Nora in Sardinia and Tekke near Knossos in Crete. The stele fragment from Nora was first published in 1890 (*CIS*, I, 145), but only recently did Cross note that the text runs in boustrophedon (Fig. 35). In the first

Fig. 35. The Nora fragment

24. See Cross (above, n. 9), pp. 19*-23* and bibliography there.

sinistrograde line there can be read]'*n. p*ʿ*l*["there is no one to do" or "there is no deed". In addition to the boustrophedal writing, some letters still preserve their pictographic shape; note in particular the ʿ*ayin* with its central dot, indicating the pupil of the eye. The Nora fragment is the oldest West Semitic inscription found in the Western Mediterranean; it should be dated to the first half of the eleventh century and labelled as a Proto-Canaanite inscription.[25]

The other early West Semitic inscription is inscribed on the shoulder of a bronze bowl recently unearthed at Tekke near Knossos. It should be dated to the late eleventh century B.C., i.e. it is an early Phoenician inscription, which can be read with Cross as follows (Fig. 36):

*ks šm*ʿ *bn l*'[

The cup of Šemaʿ son of L[[26]

Fig. 36. Inscribed bronze bowl from Crete

Although the two above-mentioned inscriptions from Sardinia and Crete are fragmentary, their texts are sufficient to indicate that as early as the eleventh century B.C. there were cultural contacts between Canaan and the Western Mediterranean. This new evidence seems to corroborate the theory of the early adoption (i.e. *c.* 1100 B.C.) of the alphabet by the Greeks, which will be discussed below (pp. 175 ff.).

25. F. M. Cross, Leaves from an Epigraphist's Notebook, *CBQ* 36 (1974), pp. 490-493; idem, Early Alphabetic Scripts, *Symposia Celebrating the 75th Anniversary of the Founding of the American Schools of Oriental Research*, I, Cambridge (Mass.) 1979, pp. 103-104.
26. M. Sznycer, L'inscription phénicienne de Tekke, près de Cnossos, *Kadmos* 18 (1979), pp. 89-93; Cross (above, n. 19), pp. 15-17.

For reasons of space we have discussed only the most important texts and have not mentioned all the Proto-Canaanite inscriptions known to date. Certain inscriptions which are usually treated in this context have been intentionally omitted because they do not belong to the Proto-Canaanite series. These are the inscriptions from Tell el-'Ajjul (ancient Gaza), Kamid el-Loz and Tell Jisr.[27]

The characteristics of the Proto-Canaanite script can be summarized in four points:

(1) It was invented *c.* 1700 B.C. by Canaanites who had some knowledge of Egyptian writing.
(2) The number of letters representing the consonantal system was initially twenty-seven. By the thirteenth century it was reduced to twenty-two.
(3) The signs were pictographs and most had acrophonic values. These evolved into linear letters.
(4) The pictographic conception permitted writing in any direction: from right to left, from left to right, in vertical columns and even horizontal or vertical boustrophedon. Vertical writing effectively disappeared *c.* 1100.

When the stances of the twenty-two linear letters became wholly stabilized and were written only horizontally from right to left, the terminology changes: the script is no longer called Proto-Canaanite, but Phoenician. The transition took place in the mid-eleventh century B.C. The Phoenician script is a direct offshoot of the Proto-Canaanite. However, two other scripts evolved from the latter: the Proto-Arabian *c.* 1300, and the Archaic Greek script *c.* 1100 B.C. Both scripts preserved the pictographic conception, being written either left to right or right to left or in boustrophedon (the South Arabic script could even be written in vertical columns). These scripts will be dealt with below.

27. See the discussions of G. Garbini, *Storia e problemi dell'epigrafia semitica*, Napoli 1979, pp. 94-98; Cross, Early Alphabetic Scripts (above, n. 25), pp. 98-101.

III. THE SOUTH SEMITIC SCRIPTS

Thousands of monumental inscriptions were found on the Arabian Peninsula, mainly in its south-western part (Pl. 2:A). These inscriptions, many of which are skilfully carved in relief, come from the area of the ancient kingdoms of Saba, Ma'in, Qataban, Ausan and Hadramauth. Although there were variations between the dialects spoken in these regions in antiquity, notably between the Sabaean and the other dialects,[1] the scripts show hardly any local characteristics.

The latest Old South Arabic monumental inscriptions date from the sixth century A.D. However, scholars have no definitive answer to the problem of the earliest appearance of these inscriptions. There are two main theories: Albright and other scholars believe that the earliest Old South Arabic inscriptions belong to the eighth century B.C.;[2] another school, represented mainly by Jacqueline Pirenne, gives a later date, i.e. the fifth century B.C. The different views are determined by different attitudes and preferences with regard to the available data. Whereas the earlier date is based on a small number of finds which were uncovered in systematic excavations, Jacqueline Pirenne pointed out that the Old South Arabian culture absorbed Graeco-Persian influences which could have penetrated into this region only in the fifth century B.C. and later.[3]

1. K. Conti Rossini, *Chrestomathia arabica meridionalis epigraphica*, Rome 1931; A. F. L. Beeston, *A Descriptive Grammar of Epigraphic South Arabian*, London 1962.
2. W. F. Albright, A Note of Early Sabaean Chronology, *BASOR* 143 (1956), pp. 9-10; G. W. Van Beek, South Arabian History and Archaeology, *BANE*, pp. 300-326.
3. J. Pirenne, *La Grece et Saba*, Paris 1955.

Jacqueline Pirenne also published a detailed study on the palaeography of the Old South Arabic scripts. Her typological and chronological conclusions are based on the relations between the height and width of the letters, on the one hand, and, on the other, the shape of the feet of the letters.[4] However, the claim that such features can provide satisfactory dates is not convincing. The available material does not consist of cursive writing, but only of monumental lapidary inscriptions. Moreover, the Old South Arabic writing hardly underwent any changes during a millennium. It is, therefore, very difficult to substantiate a system of dating.

This type of writing was not limited to South Arabia only. Some inscriptions were discovered in Babylonia, from Ur in the South to Nippur in the North (Fig. 37). These so-called "Chaldaean" inscriptions were

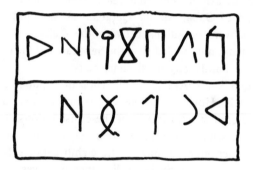

Fig. 37. A South Arabic inscription from Ur

dated to the seventh century B.C. on the basis of the archaeological finds unearthed together with them.[5] At Tell el-Kheleifeh, near Elath, two Old South Arabic letters were discovered on a jar from the eighth or seventh century B.C. (Fig. 38). These letters were considered as Minaean (from Ma'in), but according to Albright they are Proto-Dedanic (Dedan, or modern El-'Ula, was an oasis in North Arabia).[6]

4. J. Pirenne, *Paléographie des inscriptions sud-arabes*, I, Paris 1956.
5. W. F. Albright, The Chaldean Inscriptions in Proto-Arabic Script, *BASOR* 128 (1952), pp. 39-45.
6. N. Glueck, The First Campaign at Tell el-Kheleifeh (Ezion-geber), *BASOR* 71 (1938), pp. 15-16; Albright (above, n. 5), pp. 43-44.

Although some Minaean inscriptions were found in North Arabia, the main inscribed material discovered there consists of other types of South Semitic writing. In the arid areas surrounding Syria and Palestine, i.e. in North Arabia, Transjordan and the Syrian wilderness, thousands of Lihyanic, Thamudic and Safaitic inscriptions were found; these are generally graffiti inscribed on rock faces by nomadic Arab shepherds of the Lihyan, Thamud and Safa tribes. Whereas the Safaitic graffiti were found mainly in the Syrian Desert, the Lihyanic and Thamudic inscriptions are prevalent in North Arabia and Transjordan. Some Thamudic inscriptions were also found in Sinai and in the Negev (Pl. 2:B).

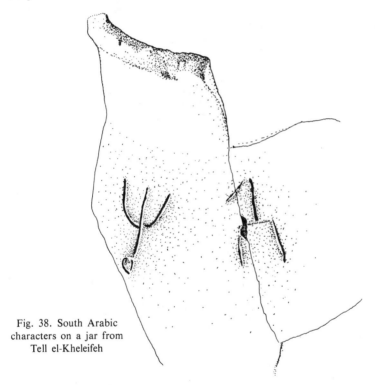

Fig. 38. South Arabic characters on a jar from Tell el-Kheleifeh

The dating of these vast numbers of inscriptions is not easy. Winnett suggested that the Dedanic script should be dated to the period between *c.* 700 and 450 B.C. and the Lihyanic script to the fifth-early fourth centuries B.C. As for the Thamudic scripts, Winnett proposed classifying

45

them in five groups: A) — early fifth century B.C. (followed by Lihyanic); B) — third-first centuries B.C.; C) — first or second century A.D.; D) — third century A.D.; E) — third-fourth centuries A.D. According to Winnett, Safaitic belongs to the fourth century A.D.[7]

Winnett's suggested date for group D is based on a bilingual Nabataean-Thamudic D inscription, found in Ḥejra in North Arabia. This is a burial inscription of a certain Raqaš, the daughter of ʿAbdmanutu. The Nabataean text contains various data, including the date 267 A.D., whereas the Thamudic mentions only the name of the deceased (Fig. 39). At any rate, this dated bilingual inscription indicates that Thamudic D was used in the third century A.D.[8] The dating of the other groups is not as firmly established as that of group D. For example,

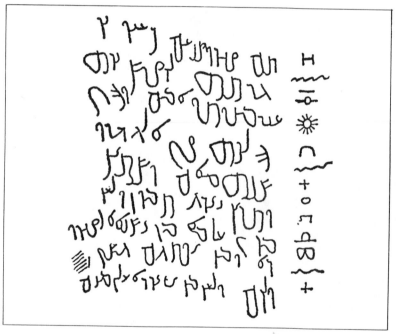

Fig. 39. The bilingual (Nabataean-Thamudic) inscription from Ḥejra

7. F. V. Winnett, *A Study of Lihyanite and Thamudic Inscriptions*, Toronto 1937.
8. *Ibid.*, pp. 38, 52.

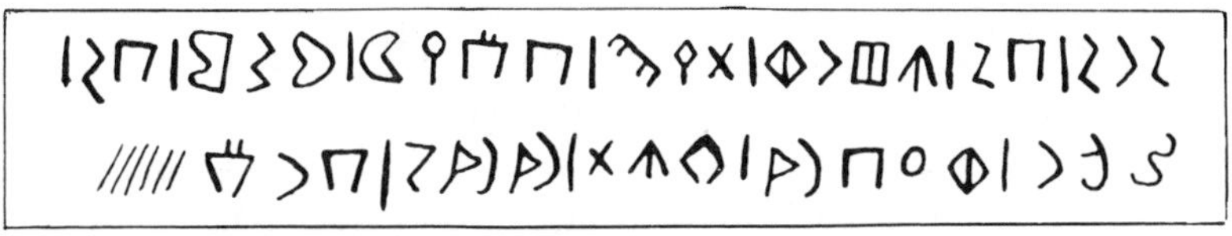

Fig. 40. A Lihyanic text mentioning Gashm

Thamudic B was dated by Winnett on the basis of four letters of this group incised on a seal beneath a figure of a mounted elephant. As the elephant was the emblem of the Seleucid dynasty, Winnett assumed that the Thamudaean artist might have been influenced by the Seleucids in his choice of a design.[9] Recently, however, a slightly longer Thamudic B inscription was found in North Sinai, to the west of El-ʿArish, inscribed on a bowl supported by an archaic Greek winged figure: it can be dated to *c.* 500 B.C. (Pl. 2:C-D).[10] This seems to indicate that people wrote in the Thamudic B script as far back as the early Persian period. Winnett's date for the Lihyanic script is based on the mention, in a Lihyanic inscription, of a certain Gashm, whom he suggests should be identified with Geshem the Arab, a contemporary of Nehemiah (Fig. 40).[11]

Other attempts have been made to date this epigraphic material, but because of the dearth of dated inscriptions (except for the above-mentioned bilingual one), none of these can be accepted without reservation. At any rate, these Old North Arabian scripts were used for more than a millennium. In order to establish more reliable dates for the various groups, we shall have to wait until more evidence is obtained, mainly through systematic archaeological excavations, which are still very limited in Arabia.

Archaeological surveys carried out in Arabia brought to light various graffiti typoligically antedating both above-mentioned types of inscrip-

9. *Ibid.*, p. 52.
10. J. Naveh and E. Stern, A Stone Vessel with a Thamudic Inscription, *IEJ* 24 (1974), pp. 79-83.
11. Winnett (above, n. 7), p. 51; see also F. V. Winnett and W. L. Reed, *Ancient Records from North Arabia*, Toronto 1970, pp. 115-117. In this book Winnett changed the classification of the Thamudic script and introduced (p. 70) the terms Najdi (former Thamudic B), Hijazi (Thamudic C-D) and Tabuki (Thamudic E).

tions.[12] Their script, called Proto-Arabic, seems to provide us with letter forms of the intermediate stage between Proto-Canaanite, on the one hand, and both South and North Arabian, on the other (Fig. 41). It seems likely that the Proto-Arabic script evolved from the Proto-Canaanite *c.* 1300 B.C., and that both South Semitic writing traditions, that of the North and that of the South, branched off from Proto-Arabic.

The South Semitic scripts have twenty-nine letters, whereas Proto-Canaanite, it has been suggested, has only twenty-seven. (See above Fig. 26 on p. 32). Either early Proto-Canaanite also had twenty-nine letters, or, alternatively, it can be assumed that when the ancient Arabs adopted

Fig. 41. An archaic South Arabian inscription in vertical columns

12. A Jamme, Preliminary Report on Epigraphic Research in Northwestern Wadi Ḥaḍramaut and at al-ʿAbar, *BASOR* 172 (1963), pp. 41-54. See also A. Jamme, An Archaic South Arabian Inscription in Vertical Columns, *BASOR* 137 (1955), pp. 32-38; W. F. Albright, The Early South Arabic Inscription in Vertical Columns, *BASOR* 138 (1955), p. 50.

the Proto-Canaanite alphabet, they added two letters to allow for the written representation of all the consonants existing in their language. The available data is not sufficient to determine which of the two alternatives is more feasible.

The South Semitic scripts remained flexible with regard to the direction of writing, a feature which characterized the Proto-Canaanite script. Although most of the inscriptions were written from right to left, the reverse direction also existed in both the North and the South. Some Thamudic inscriptions, mainly Thamudic D, were written in vertical columns.[13] Horizontal boustrophedal writing was very common in the Old South Arabic monumental scripts. Thus any word in the same inscription could be written with leftward and rightward profiles (e.g. the word ʾ*dm* "slave" was written either ᗡ ᗄ ᖾ or ᖾ ᖾ ᗡ) depending on the direction of the line. Given the length of South Arabic monumental inscriptions which covered huge walls, the use of boustrophedon was virtually inevitable; the reader had to walk several yards in order to read a line, but he could read the next line when he retraced his steps and thus he could continue walking and reading.

The modern offshoot of the South Semitic writing is Ethiopic which evolved from the Old South Arabic script. The South Arabians probably introduced this script into nearby Africa, just across the Bab el-Mandeb straits. The consonantal system of Ethiopic is not as rich as that of South Arabic. Five Old South Arabic letters do not exist in the Ethiopic script: ᙭ (s_3), ᙿ (ṭ), ᑎ (ġ) and ᕁ (ẓ); ḍ > z, but instead of ᙭ (the South Arabian sign of z) the letter for ḍ (ᕼ) survived and came to stand for z. Thus of the twenty-nine South Arabic letters only twenty-four survived, but two additional letters were added: p and p^s (South Arabic ◊ designated f).[14]

Initially, the Ethiopic script was as consonantal as any other Semitic writing. However, in the fourth century A.D., a specific Ethiopian system

13. See above (n. 12), Jamme and Albright on a South-Arabian inscription in vertical columns, which according to Albright should be dated to the tenth or ninth century B.C.
14. S. Moscati et al., *An Introduction to the Comparative Grammar of the Semitic Languages*, Wiesbaden 1964.

	I. Ground-form pronounced with *ă*	II. With *ū*	III. With *ī*	IV. With *ā*	V. With *ē*	VI. With *ĕ* or without any Vowel	VII. With *ō*	Minao-Sabaic	Phonetic Value and Transcription	Corresponding Hebrew *or* Arabic Letters
1.	ሀ	ሁ	ሂ	ሃ	ሄ	ህ	ሆ	𐩠	*h*	ה
2.	ለ	ሉ	ሊ	ላ	ሌ	ል	ሎ	𐩡	*l*	ל
3.	ሐ	ሑ	ሒ	ሓ	ሔ	ሕ	ሖ	𐩢	Originally strong *h* (*ḥ*); pronounced later like No. 1	ح
4.	መ	ሙ	ሚ	ማ	ሜ	ም	ሞ	𐩣	*m*	ם
5.	ሠ	ሡ	ሢ	ሣ	ሤ	ሥ	ሦ	𐩦	Originally *sh* (*š*); pronounced later like No. 7	ש
6.	ረ	ሩ	ሪ	ራ	ሬ	ር	ሮ	𐩧	*r*	ר
7.	ሰ	ሱ	ሲ	ሳ	ሴ	ስ	ሶ	𐩪	*s*	ס
8.	ቀ	ቁ	ቂ	ቃ	ቄ	ቅ	ቆ	𐩤	Guttural *k* (*q*)	ק
9.	በ	ቡ	ቢ	ባ	ቤ	ብ	ቦ	𐩨	*b*	ב
10.	ተ	ቱ	ቲ	ታ	ቴ	ት	ቶ	𐩩	*t*	ת
11.	ኀ	ኁ	ኂ	ኃ	ኄ	ኅ	ኆ	𐩭	Originally *ch* hard (*ḫ*); pronounced later like No. 1	خ
12.	ነ	ኑ	ኒ	ና	ኔ	ን	ኖ	𐩬	*n*	ן
13.	አ	ኡ	ኢ	ኣ	ኤ	እ	ኦ	𐩱	*Spiritus Lenis* (ʼ)	א
14.	ከ	ኩ	ኪ	ካ	ኬ	ክ	ኮ	𐩫	*k*	ך
15.	ወ	ዉ	ዊ	ዋ	ዌ	ው	ዎ	𐩥	*w*	ו
16.	ዐ	ዑ	ዒ	ዓ	ዔ	ዕ	ዖ	𐩲	Peculiar Aspirate-Guttural (ʻ); pron. later like No. 13	ע
17.	ዘ	ዙ	ዚ	ዛ	ዜ	ዝ	ዞ	𐩸	Soft *s* (*z*)	ז
18.	የ	ዩ	ዪ	ያ	ዬ	ይ	ዮ	𐩺	*y*	י
19.	ደ	ዱ	ዲ	ዳ	ዴ	ድ	ዶ	𐩵	*d*	ד
20.	ገ	ጉ	ጊ	ጋ	ጌ	ግ	ጎ	𐩴	*g* hard	ג
21.	ጠ	ጡ	ጢ	ጣ	ጤ	ጥ	ጦ	𐩷	Emphatic *t* (*ṭ*)	ט
22.	ጰ	ጱ	ጲ	ጳ	ጴ	ጵ	ጶ	—	Emphatic *p* (*p̣*)	—
23.	ጸ	ጹ	ጺ	ጻ	ጼ	ጽ	ጾ	𐩮	Emphatic, explosive Sibilant, *ts* (*ṣ*)	ץ
24.	ፀ	ፁ	ፂ	ፃ	ፄ	ፅ	ፆ	𐩳	Originally a Mute (*ḍ*); pronounced later like No. 23	ض
25.	ፈ	ፉ	ፊ	ፋ	ፌ	ፍ	ፎ	𐩰	*f*	ف
26.	ፐ	ፑ	ፒ	ፓ	ፔ	ፕ	ፖ	—	Slightly assibilated *p* (*pˢ*)	—

Fig. 42. Characters of the Ethiopic Alphabet

of vocalization was invented. In the kingdom of Aksum at this period, both consonantal and syllabic (vocalized) Old Ethiopian scripts were used. In the syllabic writing the vowel which follows each consonant is represented by a slight modification of the basic character. These minor changes indicated whether a certain consonant was to be vocalized by u, i, a, e, o, or was to remain unvocalized; the original letter forms stand for the consonant+ǎ. Thus the Ethiopic alphabet consists of seven series of twenty-six letters (Fig. 42). Another feature of the Ethiopic script is that it was written from left to right.[15]

The order of the letters in the Ethiopic alphabet differs from that found in the West Semitic alphabet. It seems likely that the Ethiopic order follows an ancient tradition. Excavations carried out in Timnaʿ, the capital of the Qatabanian kingdom, at a level dated to about 300 B.C., revealed a pavement some blocks of which were marked by South Arabic letters. These were mason's marks made to identify stones which had to be placed in a particular position in the pavement. No letter is repeated in the series, and it is clear that they were used as serial numbers to indicate the position of the stones in relation to each other. The successive letters on adjacent stone slabs form an order that is similar, but not identical, to the Ethiopic alphabetic order. This discovery may perhaps indicate that the Ethiopic letter order follows an Old South Arabian tradition. As to the reason for this particular sequence of letters, it might be partly explained by the similarity in the shapes of the letters, but there may well be another reason, unknown to us, which caused the older Proto-Canaanite letter order to fall into disuse.[16]

15. A. Dillmann, *Ethiopic Grammar*, London 1907; E. Ullendorf, Studies in the Ethiopic Syllabary, *Africa* 21 (1951), pp. 207-217.
16. A. M. Honeyman, The Letter-Order of the Semitic Alphabets in Africa and the Near East, *Africa* 22 (1952), pp. 136-147.

Fig. 43. The inscription of Yeḥimilk from Byblos

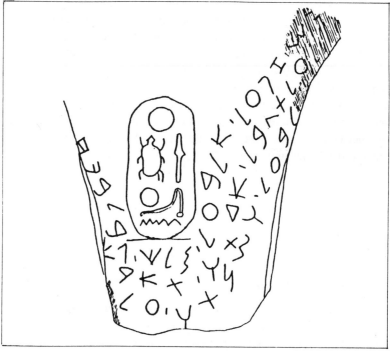

Fig. 44. The inscription of Eliba'al from Byblos

52

IV. THE WEST SEMITIC SCRIPTS

Three alphabetic scripts which had evolved from a common ancestor were used in Syria-Palestine in the first millennium B.C.: Phoenician, Hebrew and Aramaic. Initially, they were national scripts of equal status, but in the course of time, each played a different role in history. Whereas Phoenician had a normal development as a national script, the use of the Hebrew script was restricted and that of the Aramaic was greatly expanded when Aramaic became an international means of communication. In this chapter we shall describe the main phases in the development of each script and its specific characteristics. We shall look at the scripts of the peoples which adopted one of the three writing traditions, and then discuss the changeover of scripts that were used by the Jews. As the history of the Aramaic script is much more complex than that of its two sister-scripts, we shall follow its course only up to the third century B.C. Later Aramaic writing and its various derivatives will be dealt with in the next chapter.

1. *The Phoenician Script*

The script called Phoenician is the direct descendant of Proto-Canaanite. The new term designates that script which took shape from about 1050 B.C., when the twenty-two letters of the later Proto-Canaanite dropped all pictographic features. From the mid-eleventh century onwards, we deal with stabilized, linear letters written in right-to-left, horizontal lines — this is the Phoenician script; its less developed ancestor is termed Proto-Canaanite (see above, pp. 23 ff.). The inscription on the Aḥiram sarcophagus from *c.* 1000 B.C. and the tenth-century inscriptions of Yeḥimilk (Fig. 43), Abibaʿal, Elibaʿal (Fig. 44) and Shiftibaʿal, all from Byblos,[1] are good examples of the early forms of the Phoenician letters.

In the tenth and ninth centuries B.C., the Phoenician language and script enjoyed a certain international status. In the late ninth century, Kilamu bar Ḥaya, king of Yadi-Samʾal (modern Zenjirli on the border of Cilicia and North Syria, today in Turkey), wrote his monumental inscription in this language, although Phoenician was not the local tongue.[2] The name Kilamu is of Anatolian origin. Moreover, although the Aramaic word *bar*, rather than the Canaanite *ben* is used to indicate the word "son", and proper names are written in the Aramaic spelling, the language of the inscription is pure Phoenician (Fig. 45). Even in the eighth century B.C., the Phoenician alphabetic script was used in addition to Hittite pictographic writing in Azitawadda's inscription, erected at the gateway of Karatepe in Cilicia (Fig. 46).[3] In the early first millennium B.C., Phoenician was a language of prestige. The Hebrews and the Aramaeans, who had settled in the area only some two centuries earlier, adopted various cultural features, among them the alphabet, from the Canaanite or Phoenician inhabitants. Both the Hebrews and the Aramaeans began to write in the Phoenician script. At first, their writing did not differ from the Phoenician, but in the mid-ninth century the Hebrew script began to evolve; in Aramaic inscriptions, on the other hand, the earliest, specifically Aramaic features are not discernible before the mid-eighth century B.C.

The Hebrew and the Aramaic alphabets consist only of the twenty-two Phoenician letters, notwithstanding the fact that both languages had more consonants than the Phoenician tongue. In Hebrew there was ś and probably also ġ and ḫ; in Aramaic speech there were ḍ, ẓ, ṭ and a phoneme which evolved from Proto-Semitic ḍ. Except for the latter (which was transliterated in Aramaic by q and later by ʿ), the Hebrews and the Aramaeans followed the Phoenicians in using the letters according to the phonetic shift taking place in Phoenician. So dominant was

1. See *KAI*, Nos. 1-8 and bibliography there.
2. *KAI*, No. 24.
3. *KAI*, No. 26.

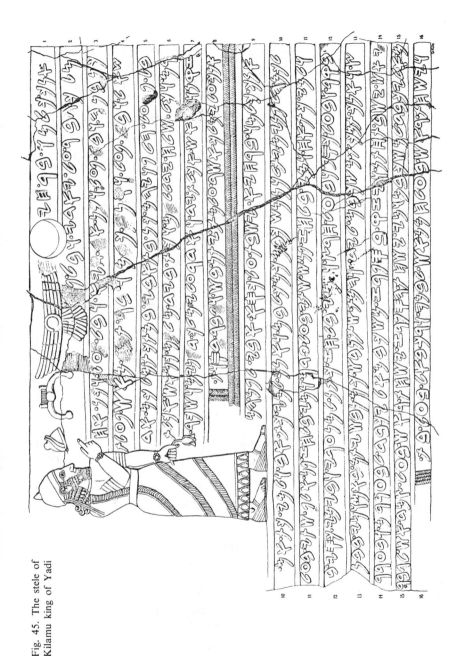

Fig. 45. The stele of
Kilamu king of Yadi

55

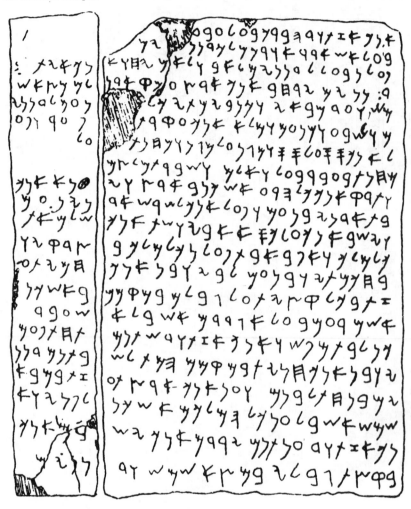

Fig. 46. Part of the Phoenician inscription in Karatepe

the Phoenician influence that neither the Hebrews nor the Aramaeans invented new letters to render those consonants which did not exist in
Phoenician. For the Aramaic words *ḏhb* "gold" and *ṯlṯ* "three" were written in Aramaic, as in Phoenician, *zhb* and *šlš*. Only in the fifth century
B.C. (when the Aramaic phonetic shifts ḏ>d and ṯ>t had taken place)

was Aramaic writing emancipated from the Phoenician legacy and the above-mentioned words began to be written as *dhb* and *tlt* (see above, pp. 31 ff. and Fig. 26).

Peckham's palaeographic study "The Development of the Late Phoenician Scripts" deals with the Phoenician inscribed material from the eighth century B.C. onwards.[4] He assumes that the inscriptions from the tenth century (mainly those from Byblos) and from the ninth century (one from Nora in Sardinia, an archaic inscription from Cyprus [Figs. 47-48] and the above-mentioned stele of Kilamu[5]) were written in the early Phoenician script. This classification may be corroborated by the fact that, in the first two centuries of the first millennium B.C., the Phoenician script was also used for writing Hebrew and Aramaic texts. Only from the eighth century onward did the Phoenician script cease to be international and became a national script like Hebrew and Aramaic.

The Phoenician script is generally divided into three categories: Phoenician proper, Punic and Neo-Punic. Punic denotes the script of the Phoenician colonies in the western Mediterranean, principally Carthage, while Neo-Punic is the script used by the communities in North-west Africa which outlived the destruction of Carthage in 146 B.C. This geographical and chronological division is well suited to the classification of the inscriptions, but it is of little value for the purpose of distinguishing between the scripts. The script used in Phoenician, Punic and Neo-Punic inscriptions was, in fact, standard, with no local variations. Whatever anomalies are discernible in the scripts of the Punic and Neo-Punic inscriptions can easily be explained on stylistic and chronological grounds.[6] There were, however, local peculiarities of language; in addition to Phoenician proper, there were Byblian, Cyprian, Punic and Neo-Punic dialects.[7]

---

4. J. B. Peckham, *The Development of the Late Phoenician Scripts*, Cambridge (Mass.) 1968.
5. *KAI*, Nos. 24, 30, 46.
6. Peckham (above, n. 4), pp. 223-225.
7. Z. S. Harris, *A Grammar of the Phoenician Language*, New-Haven 1936; J. Friedrich – W. Röllig, *Phönizisch-punische Grammatik*, Rome 1951; S. Segert, *A Grammar of Phoenician and Punic*, Munich 1976.

Fig. 47. The 9th-century B.C. Nora inscription

Fig. 48. Archaic Phoenician inscription from Cyprus

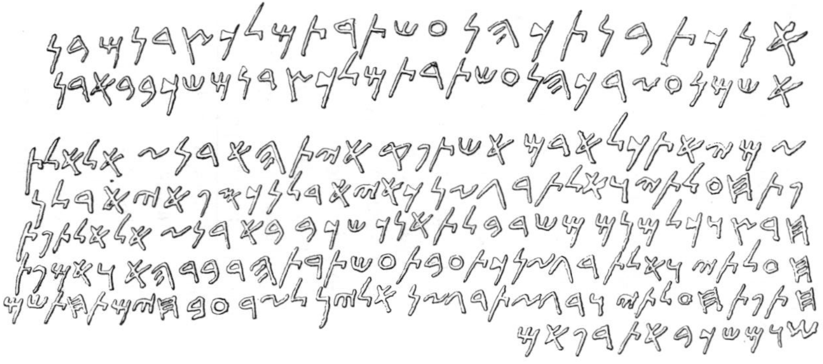

Fig. 49. 5th-century B.C. burial inscription of Tabnit king of Sidon

58

Phoenician inscriptions have been found not only in the Phoenician heartland, but also in Cilicia, Mesopotamia (Pl. 3:A), Palestine, Egypt and other North African lands, in various Mediterranean islands (Cyprus, Crete, Malta, Sicily and Sardinia) and in Southern Europe (Greece, Italy, France and Spain). A fragmentary inscription found at Nora in Sardinia and a dedication on a bowl from Crete belong to the eleventh century B.C. (see above, pp. 40 f.); these indicate, at least, an expansion of Phoenician sea trade. In addition, however, there were Phoenician settlements in most of the territories listed above during the periods that produced the various inscriptions.

The vast majority of the Phoenician, Punic and Neo-Punic inscriptions, which include royal memorial stelae and votive and burial inscriptions, were carved in stone (Fig. 49). Hence we are acquainted mainly with the Phoenician lapidary style. Epigraphic material in ink or paint is relatively sparse: a letter found at Saqqarah in Egypt written on papyrus in the sixth century B.C. (Pl. 4);[8] a *c.* 500 B.C. ink inscription written on both sides of a stone slab found at Kition in Cyprus (Pl. 3:B);[9] some short fifth-century texts inscribed in ink on jars found at Elephantine in Upper Egypt (Pl. 5:A);[10] some inscribed jars and sherds from Egypt (Pl. 3:C),[11] Cyprus[12] and Palestine (Shiqmona and Bat-Yam [Fig. 50]);[13] seven

Fig. 50. The jar-inscription *lb'lṣlḥ* from Bat-Yam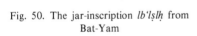

8. *KAI*, No. 50.
9. *KAI*, No. 37.
10. M. Lidzbarski, *Phönizische und aramäische Krugaufschriften aus Elephantine*, Berlin 1912.
11. See mainly, N. Aimé-Giron, Adversaria Semitica, *BIFAO* 38 (1939), Nos. II and III; idem, *Textes araméens d'Égypte*, Cairo 1931, No. I.
12. O. Mason and M. Sznycer, *Recherches sur les phéniciens à Chypre*, Genève-Paris 1972, pp. 92, 112, 119, 121.
13. J. B. Peckham, An Inscribed Jar from Bat-Yam, *IEJ* 16 (1966), pp. 11-17; F. M. Cross, Jar Inscriptions from Shiqmona, *IEJ* 18 (1968), pp. 226-233; *IR*, Nos. 11, 110.

Phoenician ostraca discovered at the temple of Eshmun near Sidon;[14] one ostracon from Tell el-Kheleifeh near Elath (Pl. 5:B);[15] and a *c.* 300 B.C. papyrus found in Egypt (Pl. 5:C):[16] this is the list of the Phoenician cursive material published to date.[17] It is quite obvious, nonetheless, that the same cursive writing tradition was practised both in the East (Phoenicia, Cyprus, Palestine and Egypt) and in the West. It is in the Neo-Punic inscriptions from the last century B.C. and the first two centuries A.D., that we sometimes find the most developed cursive letter forms (Fig. 51), which no doubt derived from the cursive script used in the documents listed above.

The Phoenician lapidary script was preserved chiefly through the practice of dedicating votive inscriptions to the deities, although the script was

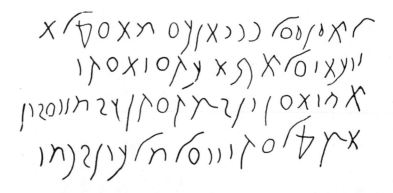

Fig. 51. A Neo Punic votive inscription with cursive letter forms

14. A. Vanel, Six ostraca phéniciens trouvés au temple d'Echmoun, près de Saïda, *BMB* 20 (1967), pp. 45-95; idem, Le septième ostracon phénicien trouvé au temple d'Echmoun, près de Saïda, *Mélanges de l'Université Saint-Joseph* 45 (1969), pp. 345-364.

15. J. Naveh, The Scripts of Two Ostraca from Elath, *BASOR* 183 (1966), pp. 27-28.

16. Aimé-Giron, *BIFAO* 38 (above, n. 11), No. I; *KAI*, No. 51.

17. There are two unpublished cursive texts from Israel: an ostracon found in the excavations of Tel Akko and an inscribed jar purchased in Gaza. The ostracon will be published by M. Dothan and the jar-inscription — by the author.

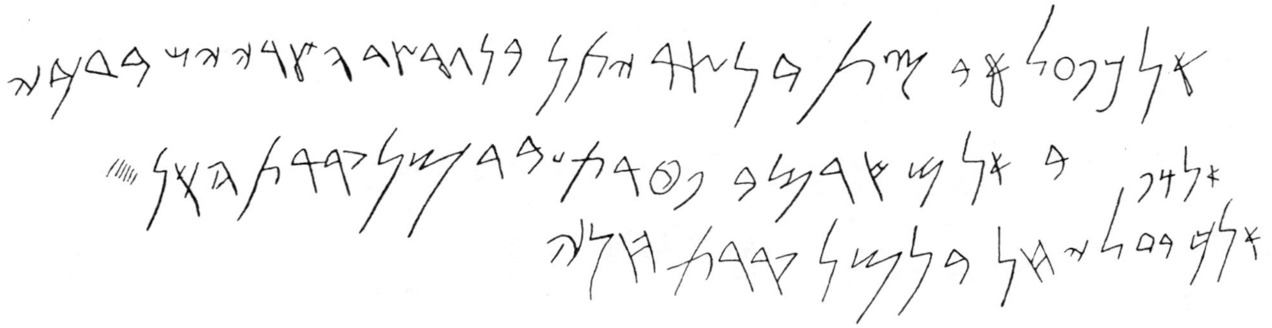

Fig. 52. 5th-century B.C. Phoenician graffiti at Abydos in Egypt

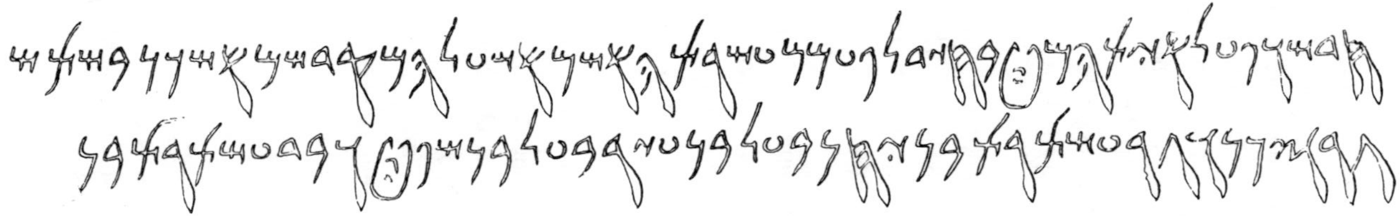

Fig. 53. A Punic inscription from Carthage

61

constantly influenced by the cursive tradition. This influence is clearly visible not only in the Phoenician graffiti inscribed on the walls of the Egyptian temple at Abydos (Fig. 52),[18] but also in Phoenician and Punic votive inscriptions. For instance, in Punic inscriptions we can perceive a thickening of the downstrokes of the letters in imitation of a natural feature of pen-and-ink writing (Fig. 53). It is to be noted that the same writing tradition was accepted both on the Phoenician mainland and in the furthest colonies, a fact which indicates the close bonds that existed between the Phoenician communities, notwithstanding their diverse locations.

In contrast to Aramaic and Hebrew, Phoenician orthography was entirely defective. There were no *matres lectionis* (i.e. letters to indicate vowels) either in the middle or at the end of the words. *Matres lectionis* were introduced into Phoenician writing only in late Punic and — especially — Neo-Punic inscriptions. While the Aramaeans and Hebrews used some letters (mainly *he, waw* and *yod* but sometimes even *alef*) as vowel signs in order to facilitate reading, the Phoenicians adhered strictly to the defective spelling.[19] Moreover, not only did the Phoenician scribes refrain from the use of instructive vowel signs, they even gradually introduced continuous writing, i.e. with no division between words. At the same time, the Hebrew script preserved the ancient practice of separating words by dots, while Aramaic script introduced spaces between words.[20]

The latest Neo-Punic inscriptions belong to the second or early third century A.D. Soon thereafter, the Phoenician script — the direct outgrowth of the original, alphabetic writing — ceased to exist. However, those scripts which branched off from this tree were to flourish and play important roles in the civilizations of mankind.

18. *KAI*, No. 49 and above in chapter I, p. 3, n. 1.
19. F. M. Cross and D. N. Freedman, *Early Hebrew Orthography*, New-Haven 1952.
20. J. Naveh, Word Division in West Semitic Writing, *IEJ* 23 (1973), pp. 206-208.

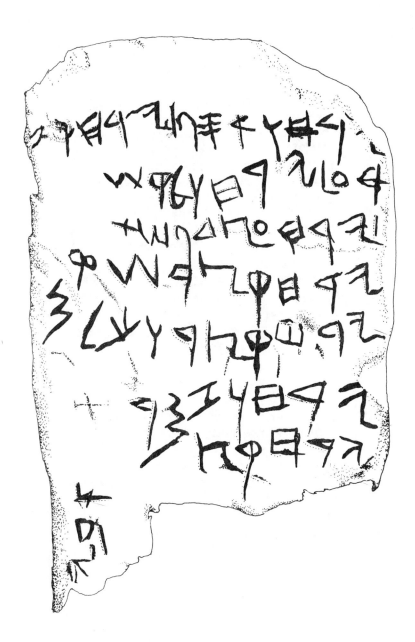

Fig. 54. The Gezer Calendar

63

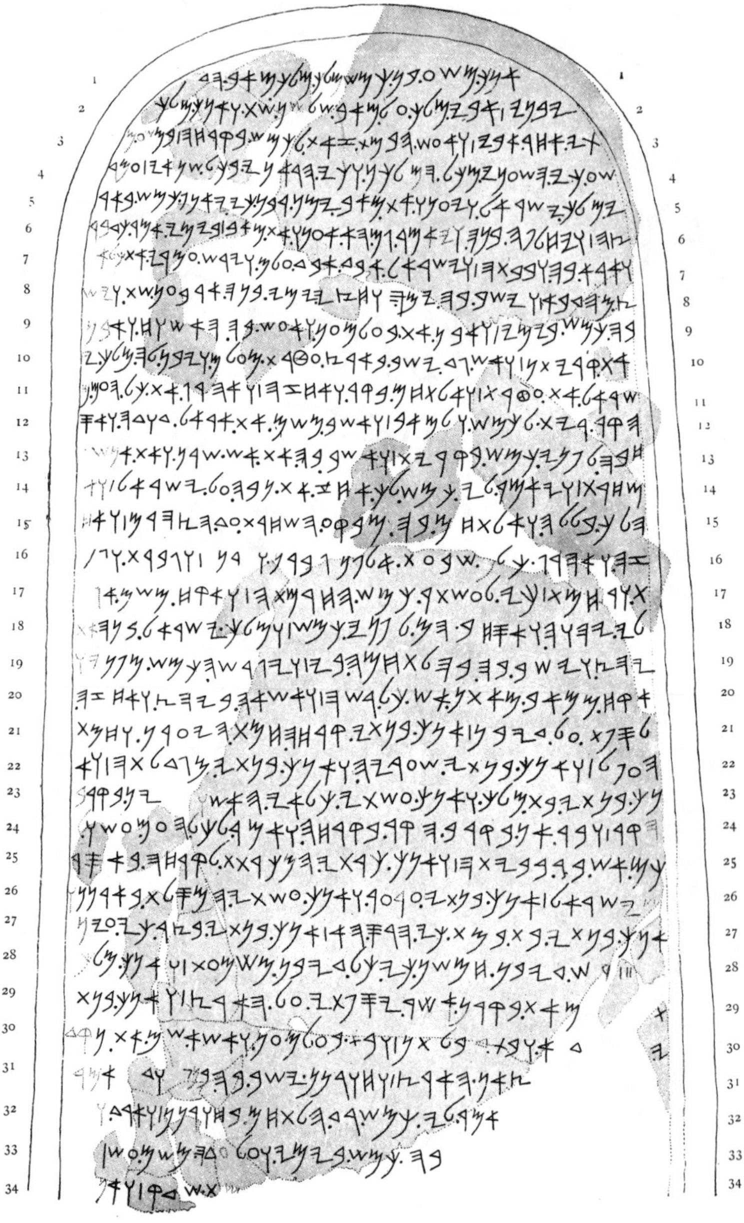

Fig. 55. The Mesha stele

2. *The Hebrew Script*

The cultural values which the Hebrews adopted from the inhabitants of Canaan after their conquest of the land, included the art of writing. This event took place in the twelfth or eleventh centuries B.C.; over a period of about two hundred years, the Hebrews wrote in the script which was used by their Canaanite or Phoenician neighbours. The script of the Gezer Calendar (Fig. 54),[21] thought to be the earliest Hebrew inscription known to date, resembles the writing of the tenth-century B.C. Phoenician inscriptions from Byblos. At this stage no specifically Hebrew characters can be distinguished, and the Hebrew followed the scribal tradition current in Canaan.

Strange as it may seem, the first distinctive features of Hebrew writing can be discerned in the scripts of the ninth-century Moabite inscriptions, namely, the stele of Mesha (Fig. 55) and the fragmentary inscription which mentions Mesha's father Kemošyat (Fig. 56).[22] Although their

Fig. 56. The fragmentary inscription mentioning Mesha's father, Kmošyat

21. *KAI*, No. 182; Gibson, I, pp. 1-4; *IR*, No. 8.
22. *KAI*, No. 181; *IR*, No. 45. W. L. Reed and F. V. Winnett, A Fragment of an Early Moabite Inscription from Kerak, *BASOR* 172 (1963), pp. 1-9; Gibson, I, pp. 71-84.

language is Moabite, a Canaanite dialect akin to Hebrew but not identical to it, their script is Hebrew: the *kaf, mem, nun* and *pe* begin to manifest the curved leftward diagonals; the *waw* is always written with the semi-circular head, and the *taw* is of the X-form. Further developments of these features can be traced in the Hebrew scripts of the eighth century and later. These ninth-century inscriptions of the Moabites, who adopted the contemporary Hebrew script, illustrate the first stage of the Hebrew scribal tradition. Evidence of a Hebrew script in the late ninth century appeared recently in the excavations at Kuntilet 'Ajrud, in the form of Hebrew votive inscriptions inscribed on stone vessels (Fig. 57) and written in ink on pithoi.[23]

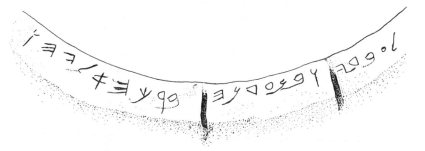

Fig. 57. A short Hebrew votive inscription on a stone vessel from Kuntilet 'Ajrud

The mid-ninth century Moabite inscriptions are carved in stone and are lapidary in style. At first glance, it would be reasonable to assume that contemporaneous ink inscriptions were written in a cursive style that had a more developed script. Indeed, Aharoni suggested that certain fragmentary ostraca found at Arad, which exhibit letter forms similar to those of the Mesha stele (Fig. 58), are earlier than the ninth-century Moabite inscriptions and should be dated to the tenth century B.C.[24] This argument is based on the assumption that the Hebrew script (like the Phoenician

23. Z. Meshel, Kuntillet 'Ajrud, A Religious Centre from the Time of the Judaean Monarchy on the Border of of Sinai, *Israel Museum Catalogue*, No. 175, Jerusalem 1978.
24. Y. Aharoni, *Arad Inscriptions*, Jerusalem 1981, p. 130.

Fig. 58. Relatively early Hebrew letters on an
ostracon from Arad

and Aramaic sister-scripts) developed in two parallel styles — lapidary
and cursive. However, a survey of later Hebrew inscriptions gives no in-
dication of such a parallel development in the Hebrew script. The independent Hebrew script becomes progressively cursive, dropping the
lapidary features as it evolves away from the mother-script. Even in the
Mesha and Kemošyat stelae, the curved diagonal strokes of the *kaf, mem,
nun* and *pe* are cursive developments.

Fig. 59. The Royal Steward inscription

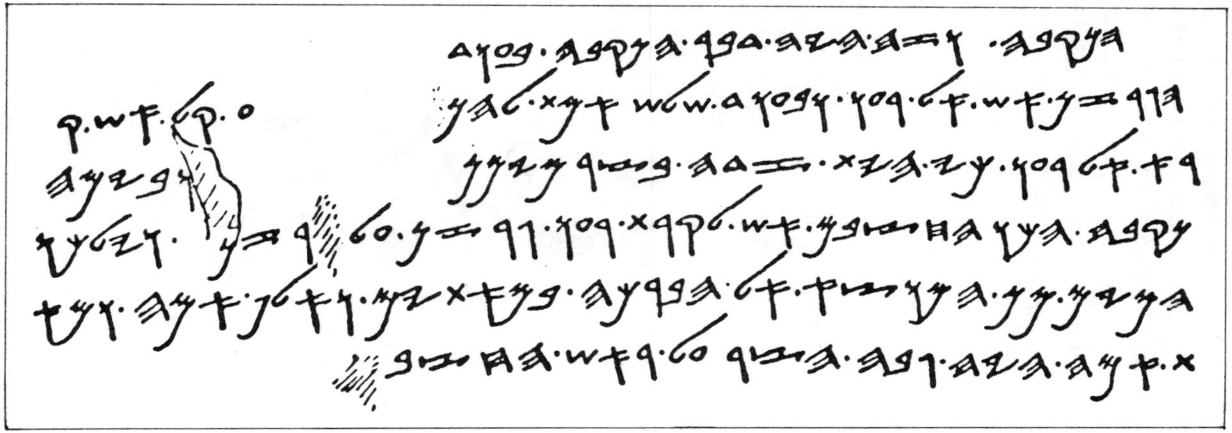

Fig. 60. The Siloam inscription

68

This cursive trend is evident in both the *c.* 800 B.C. Kuntilet 'Ajrud in-scriptions and the eighth-century engraved inscriptions, viz. the Siloam inscription (Fig. 60),[25] the Royal Steward inscription (Fig. 59)[26] and the fragmentary Hebrew inscription on ivory found at Nimrud in Assyria, taken there as booty from Samaria (Pl. 6:A).[27] The use of stone and the monumental content of the engraved inscriptions would have warranted the use of the lapidary style, had such a style existed. But these and other inscriptions, as well as the ivory piece, are written in the cursive style. Moreover, they reproduce the feature of shading which is proper to cur-sive script, being a natural consequence of writing with pen and ink. The shading can be seen also in most seventh- and early sixth-century Hebrew seals, which were carved in hard semi-precious stone (Fig. 61; Pl. 6:B).

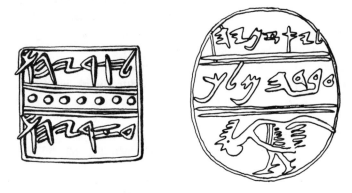

Fig. 61. Two Hebrew seals from the late 7th century B.C.

Hebrew monumental writing emulated the cursive style used by skilful scribes, that is, the formal cursive. This phenomenon may indicate that there was little occasion to develop a lapidary style in Israel and Judah where there was no widespread custom of erecting royal stelae nor of of-fering votive inscriptions to the deity — a fact which might explain why

25. *KAI*, No. 189; Gibson, I, pp. 21-23, *IR*, No. 75.
26. *KAI*, No. 191; Gibson, I, pp. 23-24; *IR*, No. 14.
27. A. R. Millard, Alphabetic Inscriptions on Ivories from Nimrud, *Iraq* 24 (1962), pp. 45-49; Gibson, I, pp. 19-20.

the specific features related to carving in stone disappeared from Hebrew writing.

Up to the present, no Hebrew inscriptions earlier than the late ninth century have been found. This, is, of course, mere coincidence; nonetheless, the quantity of epigraphic material from the eighth century and onwards indicates a gradual increase in the distribution of writing skills among the people of Israel and Judah.

We have some evidence suggesting the common use of papyrus. In addition to a twice-inscribed ("palimpsest") fragment from Wadi Murabbaʿat (Pl. 6:C),[28] which owes its preservation to the dry climate of the Dead Sea area, some scores of seal impressions on clay ("bullae") have been found, seventeen of them in Lachish.[29] Since papyrus did not survive in the humid climate that characterizes most of Palestine, our knowledge of the Hebrew script derives from other, available materials which, in addition to inscriptions on stone (including seals), consist mainly of inscriptions on pottery vessels and potsherds.

Several scores of inscriptions on pottery vessels are known today; some were inscribed after firing or were written in ink, while others were written in the soft clay before the vessels were fired. Many inscriptions indicate the names of the vessels' owners (or of those responsible for determining the vessels' capacity); others indicate the capacity as a measure, e.g. *bt lmlk* — "a royal *bat*" found at Lachish (Fig. 62).[30] Sometimes it

Fig. 62. The *bt lmlk* inscription on the shoulder of a jar from Lachish

28. Gibson, I, pp. 31-32; *IR*, No. 32.
29. Y. Aharoni, Trial Excavation in the Solar Shrine at Lachish, *IEJ* 18 (1968), pp. 164-168; *IR*, Nos. 26-31.
30. S. Moscati, *L'epigrafia ebraica antica*, Rome 1951, p. 121; Gibson, I, p. 70; *IR*, No. 99.

was preferred to impress a seal on the handle of the jar rather than to write in the soft clay. Scores of impressions of "private" seals and hundreds of *lmlk* stamps are known today (Fig. 63); the latter indicate that

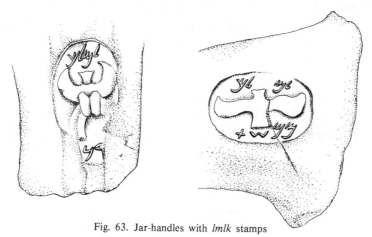

Fig. 63. Jar-handles with *lmlk* stamps

the capacity had the certification "of the king".[31] The distribution of these seal impressions reflects a widespread use of the script. The fact that most of the private stamps and the seals of the late seventh and early sixth centuries do not bear any figures may also, perhaps, indicate that people could identify the ownership of the seal by reading it (see above, Fig. 61 and Pl. 6:B as against the eighth-century seals illustrated in Fig. 64 and Pl. 7:A).

Fig. 64. Two Hebrew seals from the 8th century B.C.

31. See Moscati (above, n. 30) and Gibson, I, pp. 64-66; *IR*, Nos. 80-90.

By far the most important Hebrew epigraphic materials are the ostraca; some of these were incised (Pl. 7:B), but most were written in ink. The latter include sixty-three eighth-century dockets from Samaria (Fig. 65), about a hundred ostraca from Arad (letters, messages, name-lists, etc.) mainly from the seventh and early sixth centuries (Fig. 66; Pl. 7:C), a late seventh-century petition to the local governor found at Meṣad-Ḥashavyahu (Fig. 67), and about a score of early sixth-century letters

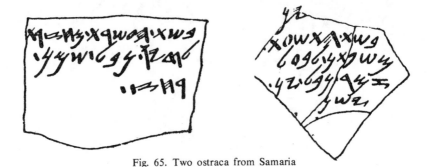

Fig. 65. Two ostraca from Samaria

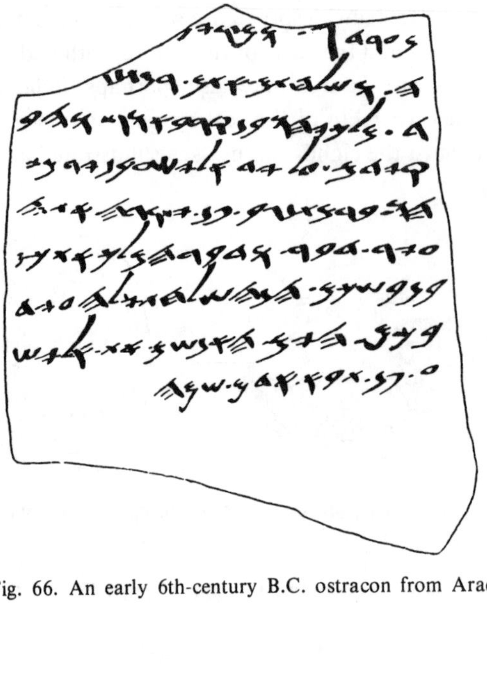

Fig. 66. An early 6th-century B.C. ostracon from Arad

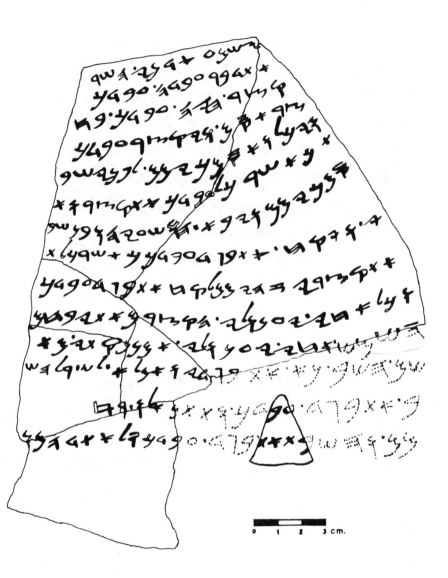

Fig. 67. Late 7th-century petition from Meṣad Ḥashavyahu

73

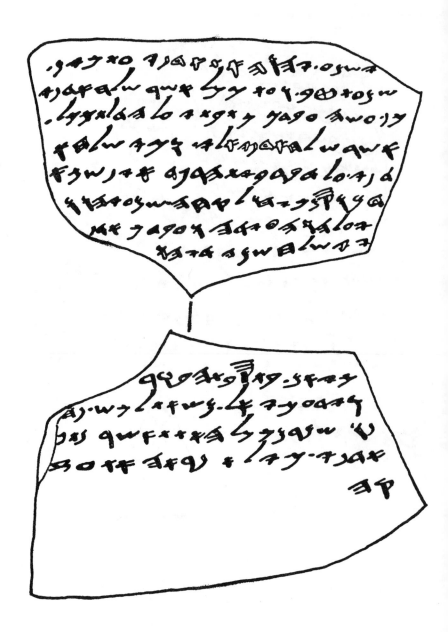

Fig. 68. An early 6th-century letter from Lachish

(most fragmentary) from Lachish (Fig. 68).[32] This material seems to have been written for the most part by professional second-grade scribes. Their writing cannot be regarded as a reliable reflection of the formal script used by first-grade scribes who wrote on papyrus and were employed by the king, the temple and the courts of law. While most ostraca were written in a semi-formal style, some are in the free cursive, which has more developed letter forms and does not emphasize shading.[33]

The vulgar sub-style of the cursive is also represented in the Hebrew epigraphic material, on some seals and stamps, but mainly on sixth-century inscribed jar-handles from Gibeon (Fig. 69).[34] Thus in the late

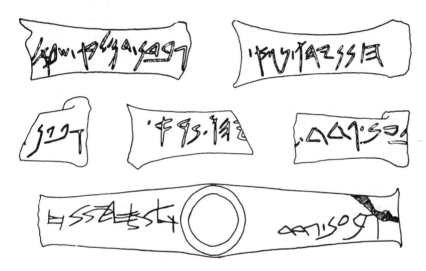

Fig. 69. Some inscribed jar-handles from Gibeon

32. These texts have been dealt with in *KAI*, Nos. 183-188; 192-200; in Gibson, I and mainly in A. Lemaire, *Inscriptions hébraïques*, I: *Les ostraca*, Paris 1977; *IR*, Nos. 33-38, 49-72, 77-78, 166.
33. On the Hebrew cursive scripts in the eighth and seventh centuries see F. M. Cross, Epigraphical Notes on Hebrew Documents of the Eighth-Sixth Centuries B.C.: II. The Murabba‘at Papyrus and the Letter Found Near Yabneh-yam, *BASOR* 165 (1962), pp. 34-42.
34. *Ibid.*: III. The Inscribed Jar Handles from Gibeon, *BASOR* 168 (1962), pp. 18-23; *IR*, No. 106.

seventh and early sixth centuries, when all three sub-styles of the cursive writing were current in Judah, we can consider its people as a literate society. De Vaux arrived at a similar conclusion, stating that "the commandment of Deut. 6:9; 11:20 presumed that every head of family could write".[35] A literate society may well have existed even earlier, but there is no substantial epigraphic material to prove this.[36]

The script of the Gezer Calendar, as mentioned above, is identical with that of the tenth-century Phoenician inscriptions. Moreover, its language does not have any lexical or grammatical features that preclude the possibility of its being Phoenician. Even if we date the Gezer Calendar to the late tenth century and note the fact that Gezer became an Israelite city in the middle of that century, this does not prove that the calendar is a Hebrew inscription. We may conjecture that in the tenth century the Hebrews wrote in the prestigious Phoenician language, as did Kilamu bar Ḥaya, king of Yadi, in the late ninth century, notwithstanding the fact that the tongue spoken in Yadi-Sam'al was a local Aramaic dialect.

The Hebrew spelling is generally defective in the middle of the word, whereas at the end of the word the vowels are rendered by *matres lectionis*: final *he* stands for -a, -e, and -o, final *waw* is -u and final *yod* is -i. There are, however, some instances of medial vowel letters. The spelling *byt* ("house") which occurs in the Judahite inscriptions indicates the pronunciation *bayt*; the same word is written in Phoenician as *bt* which should be read as *bēt*; i.e. the diphthongs *ay* and *au* are contracted in Phoenician. The shifts ay>ē and au>ō are also characteristic of the North Israelite dialect and of Moabite; e.g. "wine" in the Samaria ostraca is *yn* (*yēn*), whereas in the Arad ostraca, *yyn* (*yayn*). In the Gezer Calendar there are two words — *kl* (*kēl* — "measuring") and *qṣ* (*qēṣ* — "summer") — in which the dipthong *ay* is contracted. The language may be considered as reflecting either the North Israelite dialect (Gezer is located on the border of Ephraim) or Phoenician. It seems likely that the spelling of the Gezer Calendar is defective (*yrḥ* probably stands for *yarḥo* — "his

---

35. R. de Vaux, *Ancient Israel*, London 1961, p. 49.
36. These problems are discussed in my paper: A Palaeographic Note on the Distribution of the Hebrew Script, *HTR* 61 (1968), pp. 68-74.

Fig. 70. Development of the Hebrew script: 1. Gezer Calendar; 2. Mesha stele;
3. Siloam inscription; 4. 7th-century B.C. seals; 5. Early 6th-century ostracon from
Arad; 6. 2nd-century B.C. Leviticus fragment; 7. Medieval Samaritan bookhand

month", and *pšt* for *pišta* — "flax"), which does not conform with the Hebrew orthography.[37]

Despite the dialectal differences between Judah and Israel, the same Hebrew script was used in both kingdoms, with no local variations. It was also adopted by both the Moabites and the Edomites, who used it to render their own dialects for as long as they were under the suzerainty of Israel and Judah; afterwards, their scripts absorbed other influences (see below, pp. 100 ff.).

Up to the destruction of the First Temple, the Hebrew script developed as a single, conservative, national tradition of writing. But its course was interrupted by the Temple's destruction and the exile of most of the educated class to Babylonia, followed by the partial return by later generations, born and educated in exile, to Judah — a country which was already a province of the Persian empire. The Jews returning from Babylonian captivity spoke and wrote Aramaic. Aramaic was the official language of the Persian empire and thus also of the province of Judah, called *Yehud*. It seems that Hebrew was still spoken and written, at least by those who had not been exiled, but the prevailing language was Aramaic. From the late third and, especially, the second century B.C. onwards, the Jews wrote in a script which they developed from the Aramaic, that is, the Jewish script. At the same time, the use of the Hebrew script was restricted. In the Second Temple period it appears mainly on coins and in the Pentateuch fragments found at Qumran. The latest known use of this script by the Jews was on the coins of Bar-Kokhba in 132-5 A.D. The Samaritans, however, continued to use it up to the present day (Fig. 70). In the section devoted to the change of scripts by the Jews (see pp. 112 ff.) we shall discuss in more detail the use of the Hebrew — or so-called Palaeo-Hebrew — script in the Second Temple period.

3. *The Aramaic Script*

The Aramaeans adopted the Phoenician script in the eleventh or tenth century B.C. At first, they used the same letters as the Phoenicians. The

---

37. Cross and Freedman (above, n. 19).

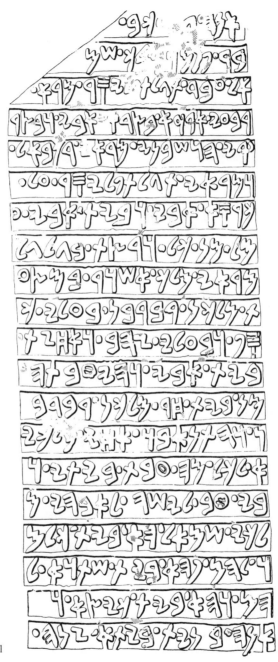

Fig. 71. Inscription of
Bar-Rakib king of Sam'al

79

late ninth-century Kilamu inscription is still Phoenician in language, while the eighth-century Hadad and Panamu inscriptions from Sam'al are written in the local Aramaic dialect, and the later eighth-century Bar-Rakib inscription (Fig. 71) is in standard Aramaic (probably the Damascus dialect).[38] The same standard language is used in the mid-ninth century inscription of Bar-Hadad, king of Damascus, though it is dedicated to the Phoenician deity Melqart and its blessing formula seems to be of Phoenician character (Fig. 72), and in the inscription of Zakur of Hamath from

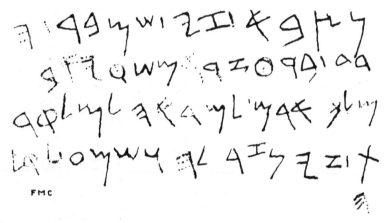

Fig. 72. Inscription of Bar-Hadad, king of Damascus

c. 800 B.C. (Fig. 73).[39] Nevertheless, there are no Aramaic features in the scripts of these inscriptions (except perhaps for the two-bar *ḥet* in Bar-Rakib). The script can be termed Phoenician-Aramaic. The divergence of the Aramaic script from the Phoenician begins roughly in the mid-eighth century B.C.; to this period belong the bricks found at Hamath (Fig. 74) on which short Aramaic texts were inscribed in a cursive script (e.g. *ḥet* with one horizontal bar).[40] From that time onwards the Ara-

38. *KAI*, Nos. 24, 214-216; Gibson, II, pp. 60-93.
39. *KAI*, Nos. 201-202; Gibson, II, pp. 1-4; 6-17.
40. *KAI*, Nos. 203-213; Gibson, II, pp. 17-18.

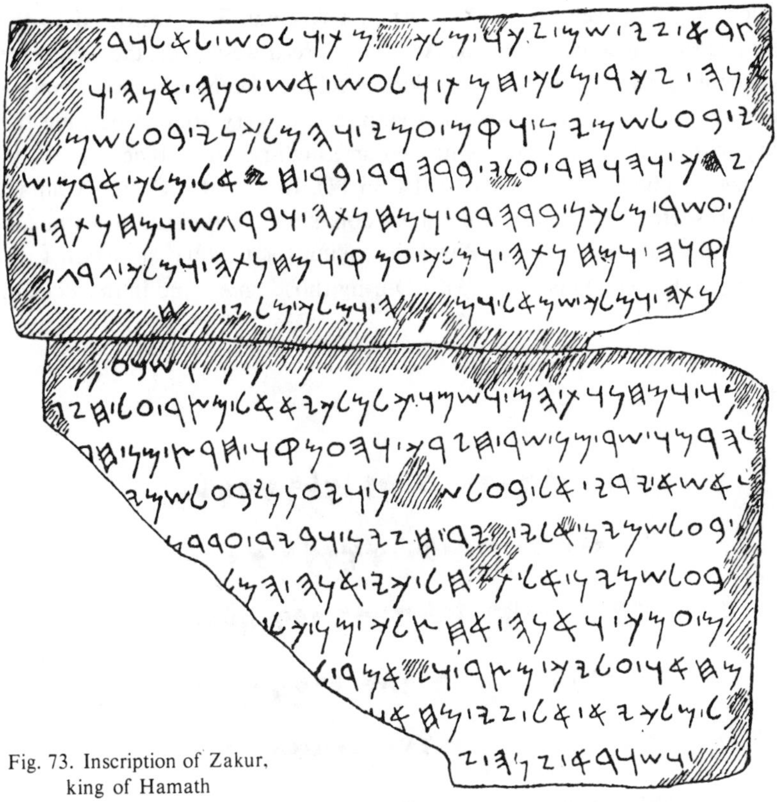

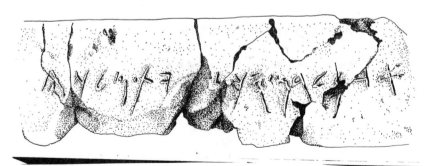

Fig. 73. Inscription of Zakur,
king of Hamath

Fig. 74. An inscribed brick from Hamath

maic cursive developed rapidly. At first Aramaic was restricted to the Aramaean kingdoms, but as the Assyrians spread westwards, they made the Aramaic alphabetic script the official medium of communication among the peoples of the Neo-Assyrian empire, and very soon it became the *lingua franca*. In the late eighth century, high-ranking officers in Judah spoke Aramaic (2 Kings 18:26; Is. 36:11). In *c.* 600 B.C., an Aramaic papyrus letter was sent by a certain Adon, king of a Philistine (or Phoenician) city, to the Egyptian Pharaoh, asking for military aid against the invading Babylonians (Fig. 75).[41] During those times, and in the Persian

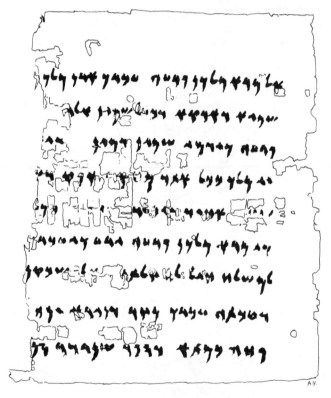

Fig. 75. Letter of Adon found at Saqqarah in Egypt

41. *KAI*, No. 266; Gibson, II, pp. 110-116; B. Porten, The Identity of King Adon, *BA* 44 (1981), pp. 36-52.

Fig. 76. Stele from Nerab

period, especially, Aramaic was widely used throughout an area that extended from Asia Minor as far as Afghanistan, Egypt and North Arabia. Nevertheless, the Aramaic script remained standard and no local traditions of writing emerged even in the remotest provinces,[42] although some dialects are discernable in the Aramaic language. The diversification of the Aramaic script began only a century or two after the fall of the Per-

42. J. Naveh, *The Development of the Aramaic Script*, Jerusalem 1970.

sian empire. At that time, in the Hellenistic period, the official language of the government was no longer Aramaic, but Greek. However, the Aramaic language and script were so deeply entrenched that each nation continued to use them and evolved its own national script from the Aramaic. In the next chapter, we shall discuss the various Aramaic offshoots that developed.

On account of its international status, the Aramaic script developed rapidly. Aramaic was written by persons of various ethnic origins who were not restricted to a national writing tradition; they used the Aramaic script for purely practical purposes, so that unnecessary strokes were dropped from the letters. This happened first in the cursive script, but with time lapidary writing took over many of the cursive elements.

Aramaic lapidary inscriptions are relatively sparse. Two seventh-century funerary stelae were found at Nerab (Fig. 76);[43] an inscription published in 1971 by Caquot is an order issued by the Babylonian (not Assyrian, as Caquot thought) authorities in the early sixth century;[44]

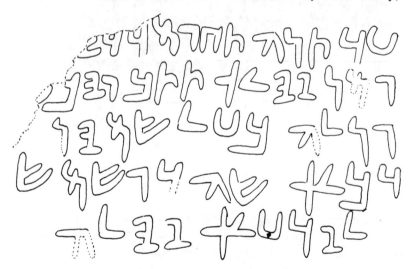

Fig. 77. A lapidary inscription from Gözne in Asia-Minor

43. *KAI*, Nos. 225-226; Gibson, II, pp. 93-98.
44. A Caquot, Une inscription araméenne d'époque assyrienne, *Hommages à A. Dupont-Sommer*, Paris 1971, pp. 9-16.

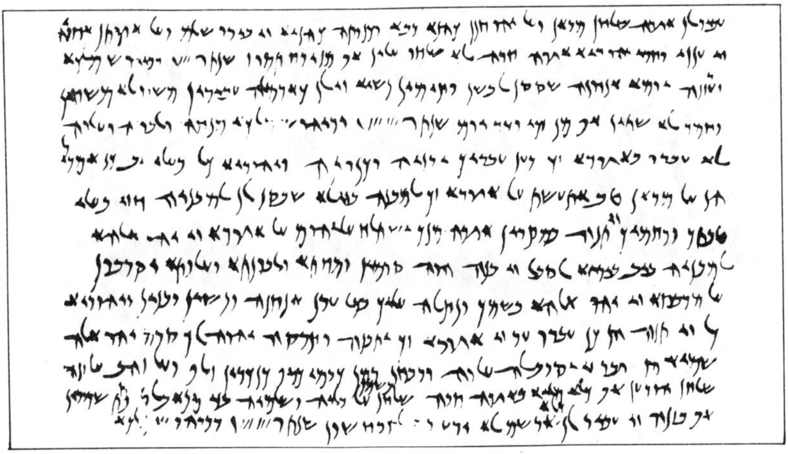

Fig. 78. Petition to the Governor of Judah from Elephantine, 408 B.C.

some Aramaic dockets on clay tablets (or Aramaic endorsements added
to Akkadian texts), written in the lapidary script, date from the seventh
and sixth centuries. But the prevalent style was the cursive (Pl. 8:A).
From the fifth and fourth century we have some stelae, votive and burial
inscriptions, and inscribed boundary stones — originating from North
Arabia, Egypt and Asia Minor (Fig. 77; Pl. 11:A) — as well as some
Judaean seal impressions, Cilician coins, etc. But even for inscriptions on
these materials, the cursive script was frequently used. In the late fourth
century the Aramaic lapidary style ceased to exist.[45]

The rapid development of the Aramaic cursive can be followed in the
documents of the seventh and sixth centuries, which consist of some
papyri, ostraca and dockets on clay tablets. Dating from the late sixth or
early fifth century are eight private letters found in Egypt at Hermopolis
(Pl. 8:B).[46] The most important material from the fifth century consists of
about a hundred papyri found at Elephantine (Fig. 78) and the parchment

45. For the lists of the inscriptions mentioned above and below, see the respec-
    tive chapters in Naveh (above, n. 42).
46. Edda Bresciani and M. Kamil, Le lettere aramaiche di Hermopoli, *Memorie
    Scienze morali, storiche e filologiche, Accademia Nazionale dei Lincei*,
    Series VIII, vol. XII, Fasc. 5 (1966), pp. 361-428.

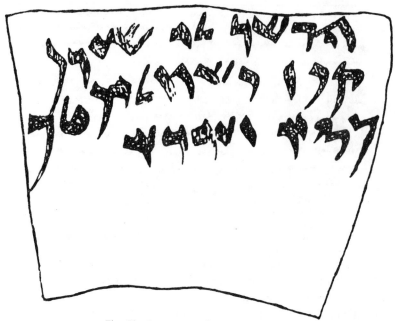

Fig. 79. An ostracon from Elephantine

letters of Arsham, the Persian governor, sent from the East to Egypt (Pl. 9).[47] But the corpus of inscriptions from that century is also rich in ostraca (Fig. 79; Pl. 10:A) and manuscripts and inscriptions of other types. Dating from the fourth century are the papyri found in Wadi Daliyah in the Jordan Valley, east of Samaria (Fig. 80), and the ostraca from Arad and Beer-Sheba (Pl. 10:B) and Egypt. The early third-century papyri and ostraca from Egypt (Pls. 10:C, 11:B) complete the collection of epigraphic material written in the uniform Aramaic cursive.[48]

47. A. H. Sayce and A. E. Cowley, *Aramaic Papyri Discovered at Assuan*, London 1906; E. Sachau, *Aramäische Papyri und Ostraka*, Leipzig 1911; A. Cowley, *Aramaic Papyri of the Fifth Century B.C.*, Oxford 1923; E. G. Kraeling, *The Brooklyn Museum Aramaic Papyri*, New-Haven 1953; G. R. Driver, *Aramaic Documents of the Fifth Century B.C.*, Oxford 1954.

48. See above, n. 45. For the Arad ostraca see Naveh in Aharoni (above, n. 24), pp. 153-176; for those from Beer-Sheba see below, n. 61.

In this brief survey, which covers only the most important items, the Elephantine documents are of primary importance. They consist of name-lists, private and official letters, legal documents and even two literary works (the Aramaic version of the Behistun inscription, and the "Words of Aḥiqar"). The legal documents bear exact dates, the names of the scribes and the signatures of the witnesses, whose handwriting is not always very steady as their writing ability was often limited to composing their own signature. Although formal, the writing of the Elephantine scribes does not fall into the same category as that of the scribes of Arsham, the Persian governor in Egypt. Whether on papyrus in Egypt or on leather in the East, the government scribes employed the most formal version of the script, whereas the Elephantine scribes were less conservative and were influenced by the free cursive style. Thus the script of the Elephantine scribes may be called 'semi-formal'. Some of the legal documents of Elephantine seem to have been written by educated persons serving as occasional scribes. These unprofessional writers wrote in the free cursive style. This style, however, is known to us mainly from private letters, as well as from name-lists and the above-mentioned signatures (although there are many signatures which may be termed vulgar cursive). Thus, just like Judahite society in the late seventh and early sixth

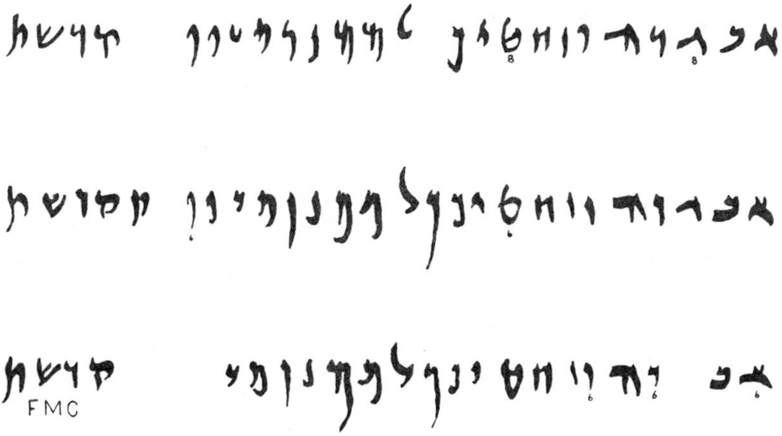

Fig. 80. Script samples of two papyri from Wadi Daliyah: Line 1 from 352/1 B.C.; Lines 2-3 from 335 B.C.

87

centuries (see above, p. 76), the fifth-century Jewish colony in Elephantine can also be considered a literate society. In fact, we can assume that from the eighth century, the knowledge of writing in the ancient East was widespread and that, as a rule, wherever alphabetic writing was practised, there was a literate society. Epigraphic evidence, however, has come to light only in those places where the three cursive sub-styles are discernable.

Formal and semi-formal writing emphasizes shading. In the Phoenician and Hebrew scripts, the descending vertical or rightward diagonal strokes are thicker than the others, but in Aramaic it is the horizontal strokes which are shaded. This phenomenon can be traced from the earliest cursive Aramaic ink-inscription, i.e. the late eighth-century ostracon from Nimrud[49] (which is an Ammonite name-list, see p. 109), through the mid-seventh century Assur ostracon[50] to the *c.* 600 B.C. Saqqarah papyrus.[51] This feature characterizes the Aramaic script throughout the ages and in all its subsequent derivatives. The modern Jewish (= square Hebrew) and Arabic formal scripts, which have thick horizontal and thin vertical strokes, follow the Aramaic tradition from *c.* 750 B.C. The question must be asked: why does the Aramaic shading differ from that of the two sister-scripts? Perhaps the answer should be sought in the origins of the Aramaic cursive, i.e. in the writing practice of the scribes in Assyria and Babylonia. These scribes must have been bilingual, for they inscribed tablets both in Assyrian or Babylonian cuneiform and in Aramaic alphabetic writing. It may well be that the way the stylus was held for cuneiform writing caused the pen to produce thick horizontal strokes, but since we do not know how the cuneiform scribe held his stylus, this explanation remains conjectural.

For those who used it, the Aramaic script was essentially a practical means of communication; hence innovations were made in order to facilitate reading and writing. Soon after the Aramaeans adopted the

---

49. J. B. Segal, An Aramaic Ostracon from Nimrud, *Iraq* 19 (1957), pp. 139-145.
50. M. Lidzbarski, *Altaramäische Urkunden aus Assur*, Leipzig 1921; *KAI*, No. 233; Gibson, II, pp. 98-110.
51. See above, n. 41.

alphabet, they initiated the use of *matres lectionis*,[52] but the simplification of the letter forms and the use of spacing between words began only in the eighth and seventh centuries B.C., when Aramaic became a *lingua franca*. However, the number of letters remained the same twenty-two which had been adopted from the Phoenicians, although Aramaic speech had more than twenty-two consonants.

4. *Comparative Aspects of the Phoenician, Hebrew and Aramaic Scripts*

The independent development of the Hebrew script began, as we have seen, in the ninth century B.C., and that of the Aramaic script a century later. In inscriptions of the tenth century, Phoenician, Hebrew and Aramaic scripts are indistinguishable. In the ninth century, there were differences between certain Hebrew letter forms and the equivalent letters in the Phoenician-Aramaic script, but specifically Aramaic letters appear only in the cursive writing of the mid-eighth century B.C.

Before discussing the comparative aspects of these scripts, we shall trace the development of six letters in the three sister scripts. The letters chosen are *alef, bet, he, waw, zayin* and *het*, but these are also representative of others. The evolution of each letter will be illustrated in three horizontal series, depicting the Phoenician, Aramaic and Hebrew forms, respectively. The development of Phoenician letters will be followed from the tenth century B.C. up to their latest use in the Neo-Punic inscriptions. The Hebrew letter forms will be traced as far as the emergence of the Samaritan characters, and the Aramaic forms, up to the third century B.C. — the later offshoots will be omitted from the following outline.

In the tenth century B.C., the *alef* (Fig. 81) consisted of a downstroke and a V turned on its side (1). In the ninth century the downstroke

---

52. Recently a relatively long bilingual (Akkadian-Aramaic) monumental inscription was found at Tell Fakhariyah in Syria. According to the information gathered so far on this unpublished inscription, it appears to belong to the eleventh century B.C. and the Aramaic text has not only final but also medial *matres lectionis*.

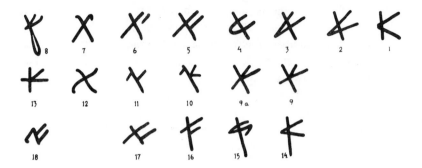

Fig. 81. Development of the *alef*

becomes somewhat slanted and the V, now narrower, shifts slightly to the left (2). In the Phoenician script this development was a continuous process. Later the angle of the V became more acute and was intersected by a diagonal stroke (3); the V was sometimes drawn as a U (4). In the seventh century the V gives way to two parallel bars which do not meet: the upper bar crosses the diagonal downstroke; the lower bar only touches it on the right (5). In about 500 B.C. — in the cursive text from Cyprus — the lower bar is short and does not touch the downstroke (6). The next stage of development can be seen in the Neo-Punic inscriptions, which represent the latest cursive forms: the *alef* is drawn like an X and the former short, lower bar is appended to the top right arm (7). This represents the most developed Phoenician cursive *alef*. In the lapidary script, however, the early forms survived much longer than in the cursive. Under the influence of the cursive, the *alef* in some lapidary Phoenician and Punic inscriptions has a thickened, long downstroke and the V is small (8). The Phoenician *alef* is bigger than most of the other letters in the Phoenician alphabet.

As early as the eighth century, the upper bar of the V in the Aramaic *alef* shifts to the right and meets the junction of the lower bar and the downstroke (9); at the same time, the upper bar sometimes crosses the downstroke while the lower one remains to the right of it (9a). In these forms, the V is on the right of the downstroke, while only a small bar remains on the left. In the seventh century this small left-hand bar moves upwards, nearing the tip of the downstroke (10). By the early fifth century, the right-hand v has become a diagonally drawn bar (11). (This form is basically preserved in the Jewish script.) In the third century, the cursive *alef* is written like an x with two diagonal, wavy lines (12). While lapidary Aramaic script preserves form 9, it generally has a vertical downstroke (13).

In the eighth century, the Hebrew *alef* has a long downstroke (14), and the formal and cursive forms begin to diverge. The latter preserves the v, but sometimes has a tail on the lower bar (15). (A common feature of cursive script is the tendency to draw the pen towards the next letter; cf. Hebrew *zayin, yod, samekh* and *ṣade*; Phoenician *lamed*; Aramaic *lamed, ʿayin*, as well as the later Aramaic development of medial *kaf, mem, nun pe* and *ṣade*.) In the formal *alef* the v becomes two parallel bars, the upper one of which crosses the downstroke, while the lower one remains on the right (16). This form is similar to the Phoenician (5), but these developments occurred independently, without mutual influence. In the seventh century the downstroke becomes much shorter in both the formal and in the cursive forms. In the Second Temple period the cursive *alef* disappears, while the formal *alef* is used in the Pentateuch fragments, on coins, etc. (17). The Samaritan *alef* (18) evolved from this form.

Fig. 82. Development of the *bet*

The classical *bet* (Fig. 82) consists of a triangular head, sometimes rounded on the left, and a downstroke that resembles a leg bent at the knee (1). In the Phoenician and Aramaic inscriptions of the ninth and eighth centuries, the letter is somewhat slanted (2). In cursive writing, however, it was difficult to keep the "knee-bend" in the correct position, and thus the downstroke of the *bet* became a curved line (3). Forms 2 and 3 are both common in the Phoenician lapidary style up to a fairly late period, while the cursive form follows a different path of evolution. The Phoenician papyri and ostraca from the fifth and fourth centuries B.C. give evidence of a tendency to open the closed head at its lower part (4). In the papyrus of *c.* 300 B.C. (see above, n. 16) as well as in Neo-Punic inscriptions, the *bet* is written as a slightly curved, vertical stroke (5). The cursive forms of *dalet* and *resh* developed along the same lines.

The Aramaic *bet* underwent a similar evolution at an earlier date. In the eighth century B.C. the head begins to open at its top (6), and gradually this opening is enlarged to form a cup-shaped curve with a leftward — turning downstroke, all drawn without lifting the pen (7). While the Phoenician lapidary *bet* preserves the closed head, in the Aramaic lapidary script the *bet* is open but the lines are straight and meet at right angles (8).

In the Hebrew script the *bet* has two forms: formal and cursive. Whereas in the formal *bet* the downstroke slants leftward then turns to a horizontal base (9), in the cursive *bet* the downstroke is a single diagonal curve (10). In the Hebrew *bet* the head remains closed; the only open-headed forms of *bet* occur on some Hasmonaean coins (11). During the Second Temple period, the head of the *bet* is generally closed and this form also survives in the Samaritan script (12).

The *he* (Fig. 83) in the tenth century consists of an upright stroke, from which three parallel horizontal bars branch off to the left; the upper bar forms a right angle with the top of the downstroke (1). In the centuries that followed, the *he* acquired a slant (2). In the Phoenician and Aramaic scripts, the two lower bars move away from the downstroke (3, 8). In Phoenician, this development takes place at a later stage, probably in the sixth-century cursive script, and exercises an influence on the lapidary style. In the Aramaic script, the two lower bars were drawn detached from the downstroke right at the inception of the cursive style in the eighth century B. C., and it was in that century that these bars fused into a single diagonal bar (9), which was then appended to the upper line (10). This line was drawn obliquely until the fifth century; from that time, and

Fig. 83. Development of the *he*

mainly in the early fourth century B.C., the *he* had a horizontal upper stroke (11).

In the Phoenician script, the two lower horizontal bars which shifted sideways (3) continued for a while to be drawn separately, but the lowest bar changed its direction (4). The letter came to resemble an inverted R (5), sometimes composed of two separate parts: a downstroke, and a wavy line to the left of it (6). The Phoenician papyrus of *c.* 300 B.C. offers the most developed cursive *he*, consisting of two parallel, slightly curved, vertical downstrokes (7). (Compare with the cursive Phoenician *ḥet*, which has three such strokes.) It should be pointed out that while the lapidary Phoenician script preserves the early types (mainly 2 and 3), the Aramaic lapidary *he* is more developed (10, 11).

The Hebrew script preserves the classical form of the *he*. The main change at the time of the First Temple was the rightward extension of the upper horizontal line (12). (This trait is also exemplified in the Hebrew *dalet*.) From the sixth century onwards, the horizontal bars are not always parallel and their ends tend to meet on the left (13). This leads to the development of a *he* in which the two lower bars converge and are drawn without lifting the writing implement (14). Such forms occur on Hasmonaean coins, in the Pentateuch fragments from Qumran, and in the epitaph from Givʿat ha-Mivtar. At the same time there also existed the *he* with parallel bars, a form which later prevailed. The Samaritan *he* has parallel bars, but the upper bar forms a curved elbow with the downstroke, and the middle bar crosses the downstroke (15).

The *waw* (Fig. 84) has two forms in the tenth century: there is a Y-shaped, but round-headed *waw* (1), and a *waw* shaped like an inverted **h** (2), which was adopted in the Phoenician and Aramaic scripts (3, 7). In the Phoenician script the downstroke becomes longer and somewhat slanted, and the head shallower (4), then forming a right angle with the top of the downstroke (5). Sometimes the upper bar is elongated and extended upwards to the right (6).

Fig. 84. Development of the *waw*

In the Aramaic *waw* the downstroke remains short. The head develops as follows: in the seventh century, the right-hand side of the curve meets the top of the downstroke (8); in the sixth century, it straightens out to form a horizontal bar (9); in the fifth century, the head and the shoulder become rounded (10).

The Hebrew script adopted the Y-shaped *waw* (1; cf. the Mesha stele) and developed it. At first the semicircular head was composed of two rounded bars: the left one was continuous with the downstroke, and the right one joined it (11). Then the right-hand bar forming the head straightened out and the letter was drawn aslant (12). The cursive *waw* was written either without lifting the pen (13), or as a vertical line that was wavy at the top and intersected by a bar just under the wave (14). These forms of the *waw* were current in the period of the First Temple. In the Second Temple period the wavy head straightens (15). The Samaritan *waw* resembles the numeral **7** but is drawn aslant (16).

The tenth-century B.C. *zayin* (Fig. 85) consists of a relatively long vertical stroke with two horizontal bars, one at the top and the other at the base (1). In the ninth century the vertical stroke became shorter (2). In the eighth century B.C. the Aramaic *zayin* was written like a Z (9); later the letter was drawn aslant (10). Then the Aramaic *zayin* became a wavy line (11). As early as the seventh century it dropped its extremities and became a straight line (12). But the Aramaic lapidary preserves the older Z-like form (13). (The Aramaic *yod* had a similar development.)

The Phoenician *zayin* had a more gradual and lengthy evolution. The Z-shaped Phoenician *zayin* (3) appeared only in the sixth century. Later, to the slanted Z-shaped *zayin* (4) a tail was added (5), a trait which originated in the tendency to draw the pen leftward toward the next letter when writing rapidly. A further development is the *zayin* composed of two parallel slanted bars joined at their tops by a concave line (6). Later — mainly in lapidary inscriptions — we find a shape resembling form 2, but slanted (7). There is no direct relation between forms 2 and 7, since the latter evolved from form 6. The rounded *zayin* (8), which is common in Neo-Punic inscriptions, also developed from form 6.

The Hebrew script preserves, in essence, the early form of the letter (2). From the eighth century onward, the horizontal strokes become longer and leftward tails are added to their right-hand tips (14). From the seventh century onward, the parallel horizontal strokes are closer to each other and the vertical stroke is very short (15). In the late seventh-century

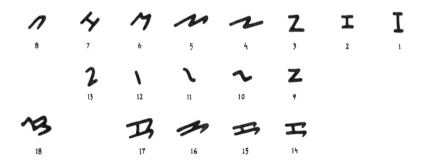

Fig. 85. Development of the *zayin*

and sixth-century cursive script, the upper tail and the small vertical stroke are combined into a single bar (16). The formal *zayin* (15) is the main form used in the Second Temple period, for instance, on the Eleazar coins struck at the time of the Bar-Kokhba Revolt (17). It seems likely that the complicated Samaritan *zayin* (18) evolved from this form.

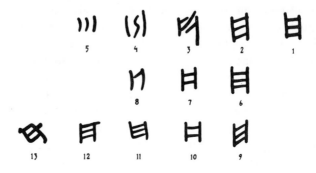

Fig. 86. Development of the *het*

Het (Fig. 86) in the tenth century resembles *he*, but it has also a left downstroke (1). This form, generally somewhat slanted and with elongated downstrokes, occurs in all three scripts (2, 6, 9). The Aramaic and Hebrew scripts tend to drop one of the three horizontal bars (7, 10). However, while in the Hebrew script the two-bar *het* is found along with the more prevalent three-bar *het*, the Aramaic script drops yet another bar, and as early as the eighth century the one-bar *het* becomes common (8).

In the Hebrew *het* of the First Temple period, the upper horizontal stroke is not extended to the right (11; in contrast to the *he*). But a *het* with the upper stroke extended to the right occurs in some Pentateuch fragments from Qumran (12). This seems to be the ancestor of the Samaritan *het* which is drawn like a *he*, but with a slanted stroke on the left side of the letter (13).

The Phoenician *het* initially preserved all three bars, but by the time of the seventh-century cursive, these did not touch the downstrokes (3). Later the three bars were drawn in one S-shaped line (4). Then, from the fifth century B.C., the *het* was written with three curved, sometimes parallel, downstrokes (5). (The two last forms resemble the development of the *he*.)

A comparative study of the development of these six letters — which are representative also of the other letters of the alphabet — clearly shows that the Hebrew script preserved the basic forms of the letters to a greater extent than the two sister scripts. The Aramaic script, at the beginning of its independent development, lost the superfluous lines and became a practical writing system. The Phoenician letters also underwent significant changes, but these were due to a slow and gradual evolution. These processes, which can be traced in almost every letter, are perhaps most pronounced in the comparative descriptions of *zayin, ḥet* and *yod*, as well as in those of *bet, dalet and resh*, which develop open heads in the Aramaic and the Phoenician scripts, whereas in the Hebrew script the heads of these letters remain closed. As for the lapidary script, the Aramaic is much more developed than the Phoenician, while the Hebrew script did not develop a lapidary style.

It can be convincingly argued that the development of the Hebrew script cannot be compared with the evolution of the Aramaic and the Phoenician scripts, given the restricted use of the Hebrew script after the destruction of the First Temple. We shall, therefore, compare these scripts as they appear in the inscriptions and manuscripts of the late seventh and early sixth centuries B.C. (Fig. 87). In this period, which preceded the Babylonian Exile, the inhabitants of Judah still lived a normal national life in their own land. In our comparison we should bear in mind that when the Hebrew script began to diverge from the Phoenician in the mid-ninth century B.C., Aramaic inscriptions continued to be written in Phoenician letters for about a hundred years; only in the middle of the eighth century did an independent Aramaic script begin to evolve. Thus around 600 B.C. the Hebrew script had undergone some 250 years of independent development, while the Aramaic script had a history of only some 150 years. Nevertheless, the Hebrew script perserved the older forms, while the Aramaic script underwent further changes, taking on the aspect of a shorthand. The Phoenician script is more evolved than the Hebrew, but much less than the Aramaic. If we assume that the rate of development of the Phoenician script — the direct descendant of the original Proto-Canaanite alphabet — was normal, then that of the Aramaic script was extremely rapid, while the Hebrew script developed very sluggishly.

Fig. 87. Comparative chart of scripts at the beginning of the 6th century B.C.:
1. Saqqarah papyrus, Aramaic; 2. Lachish ostraca, Hebrew; 3. Ipsambul graffiti (CIS, I, Nos. 111-112), Phoenician

These phenomena can be explained by the different geopolitical and cultural factors that prevailed among the peoples using the various scripts.

At first, the Hebrew script was used by both Israel and Judah; then, from the late eighth century on, it was confined to Judah. Thus the script was written by a nation which dwelt in a mountainous land far from international highways, and which tended to preserve its traditional values. The Hebrew script served a well-defined culture that was steeped in tradition.

As a *lingua franca*, Aramaic was used and developed by scribes and merchants who introduced abbreviated letter forms with a view to making writing more rapid and efficient. People using the Aramaic script were generally not Aramaeans. As a commercial and diplomatic medium of communication for many peoples who had little interest in upholding a conservative tradition of writing, the script was stripped of all national sentiment and became strictly functional.

Given the Phoenicians' trade ties throughout the ancient world, their national script was also a relatively widespread means of communication in the commercial sphere. It is therefore understandable that the Phoenician script should take a middle course, compared to the free development of the Aramaic script, on the one hand, and the conservatism of the Hebrew script, on the other.[53]

From the inception of independent development in each of the three scripts and throughout their history, there was no interaction or reciprocal influence between them. This is also true of the Hebrew script in the Second Temple period, when this script was a relatively weak entity. Purvis, when discussing the development of the Samaritan script, suggests that the Hebrew *yod* in the Second Temple period might have been influenced by the form of the same letter in the Phoenician script.[54] This is difficult to accept. It should be remembered that, since the three

53. J. Naveh (above, n. 42), pp. 64-68; idem, The Scripts in Palestine and Transjordan in the Iron Age, in J. H. Sanders (ed.), *Near Eastern Archaeology in the Twentieth Century, Essays in Honor of Nelson Glueck*, Garden City 1970, pp. 277-279.
54. J. D. Purvis, *The Samaritan Pentateuch and the Origin of the Samaritan Sect*, Cambridge (Mass.) 1968, pp. 44-45.

scripts evolved from a common ancestor, the development of some similar letter forms is almost inevitable. For instance, the contraction of the *shin* from four bars into three came about independently in both the Phoenician and the Aramaic scripts. Moreover, the early sixth-century B.C. Hebrew epigraphic material shows quite clearly that the Hebrew cursive also developed a three-bar *shin*,[55] but the formal script which survived did not adopt it. As the Aramaic script branched off from the Phoenician later than did the Hebrew, the Phoenician and Aramaic scripts have more letter forms in common. However, the identity or similarity of letters appearing in a late stage of evolution cannot be explained by mutual influence. The simplification of a letter often results in similar forms. The following example will serve as an illustration. The X-shaped *mem*, known in the Phoenician cursive, survived in the Neo-Punic inscriptions of the second century A.D.[56] At the same time an X-shaped *mem* appears in the South Mesopotamian branch of the Aramaic script, in the so-called Elymaic script.[57] Now, it is inconceivable that this resemblance was the result of interaction between the two cultures.

The Phoenician, Hebrew and the (uniform) Aramaic scripts reflect three independent cultures. As such, they did not absorb foreign influences. Even when the use of the Aramaic script was greatly expanded and that of the Hebrew restricted, each script preserved its integrity. On the other hand, we shall see below that both the Hebrew and the Aramaic scripts had an impact on the writing of peoples which possessed a lesser measure of cultural independence.

5. *The Scripts of Israel's Neighbours*

In addition to the three peoples which developed national writing traditions — the Phoenicians, the Hebrews and the Aramaeans — there were

55. See for example, H. Torczyner (Tur-Sinai), *Lachish*, I: *The Lachish Letters*, London 1938, p. 46 (the reverse of Letter III) as well as Y. Aharoni (above, n. 24), p. 86, No. 54.
56. Peckham (above, n. 4), p. 188.
57. W. B. Hennig, The Monuments and Inscriptions of Tang-i Sarvak, *Asia Major* 2 (1951/2), pp. 151-178; A. D. H. Bivar and S. Shaked, The Inscription at Shimbar, *BSOAS* 27 (1964), pp. 265-290.

other ethnic groups living in the area: the Philistines in the south-west and the Ammonites, Moabites and Edomites in the south-east, that is, in Transjordan. As we mentioned in our survey of the Hebrew script, the earliest example of the independent Hebrew script appears in the stele of king Mesha of Moab. The language of this mid-ninth-century B.C. inscription is Moabite, but the script is Hebrew. In this period the Moabites were under Israel's political and cultural influence. They used the script current in Israel, their suzerain, and did not develop their own writing tradition. Later, Israel's political influence in Moab came to an end. In the last third of the eighth century B.C., the Assyrians — who at that time adopted the Aramaic script and language and promulgated them as an international means of communication — appeared on the King's Highway south of Damascus. The script of some seventh-century seals, in which the names are compounded with the Moabite theophoric element Kemoš (=biblical Chemosh, the name of the chief Moabite deity), manifests some affinities with the Hebrew script, together with some non-Hebrew elements. The *mem* has a large head, sometimes almost half the height of the letter, and the two vertical bars do not cut across the horizontal line. This kind of *mem* occurs in the seals of *kmšṣdq, kmšyḥy, kmšʿm kmšʾl hspr* (Kemošʿam [son of] Kemošʾel the scribe) and *kmšntn* (Fig. 88; Pl. 12:A).

Fig. 88. Three Moabite seals

However, a very similar script is also found on seals bearing names which are not compounded with the element Kemoš; the *mem* has the same large head as the *mem* in the above-mentioned seals. Thus we would classify as Moabite the seals of "Amoz the scribe" and "Manasse, son of the king" (Fig. 89). Examining the two seals bearing the name Meša, which are dated to the sixth century B.C., we see that in addition to the large-headed *mem* there is an open ʿ*ayin* and that the *shin* consists of three fingers meeting at one point (Fig. 90; Pl. 12:B). Thus it can be said that the forms of the ʿ*ayin* and the *shin* clearly manifest an intrusion of Aramaic elements into the script of the Moabites.[58]

The script used by the Edomites (the southern neighbours of the Moabites) underwent the same process. Although no ninth-century Edomite inscription has been found so far, the epigraphic material found at Tell Kheleifeh, in the vicinity of Elath, and at Umm el-Biyara and Buseirah, near Petra, provide some data on the script of the Edomites. The seal from Kheleifeh inscribed *lytm* should be read "(belonging) to Yatom" (a fairly common West Semitic name meaning "orphan"), and not "(belonging) to Yotam", i.e. Jotham the son of Uzziah king of Judah.[59] The seal *lytm* is Edomite and not Hebrew (Fig. 91). This correction is based both on orthographic criteria and on the large-headed *mem*, familiar from Moabite seals. This *mem* is also found on the jar stamps *lqwsʿnl* ʿ*bd hmlk* "(belonging) to Qausʿanali servant of the king" (Fig. 92), and on an ostracon which includes theophorous Edomite names (compounded with the element Qaus, the Edomite deity) from Tell Kheleifeh, No. 6043 (Fig. 93; Pl. 12:D), as well as on a bulla inscribed *lqwsg[br] mlk* ʾ*[dm]*, "(belonging) to Qausga[bri] king of E[dom]" (Pl. 12:C) and on an ostracon from Umm el-Biyara. Qausgabri king of Edom is mentioned in the inscriptions of the Assyrian kings Esarhaddon (680-669 B.C.) and Ashurbanipal (669-633 B.C.). However, in most of these inscriptions from Tell Kheleifeh and Umm el-Biyara, we find also the typical Aramaic open ʿ*ayin* and a *waw* shaped like an inverted h. On the Tell Kheleifeh ostracon most of the letter forms are Aramaic and only a few letters resemble their Hebrew equivalents. Most of these inscriptions

58. J. Naveh, The Scripts of Two Ostraca from Elath, *BASOR* 183 (1966), pp. 28-30 and the bibliography there; idem (above, n. 53), pp. 280-283. L. G. Herr's thesis on the Moabite, Edomite and Ammonite scripts (The Formal Scripts of Iron Age Transjordan, *BASOR* 238 [1980], pp. 21-34) is in my opinion incorrect.

59. N. Avigad, The Jotham Seal from Elath, *BASOR* 163 (1961), pp. 18-22; idem, Hebrew Epigraphic Sources, *The World History of the Jewish People, The Age of the Monarchies: Political History*, Massada Press, Jerusalem 1979, p. 43.

Fig. 89. The seals of "Amos the scribe" and "Manasse, son of the king"

Fig. 90. The seal of Mesha, (son of) 'Ada'el

 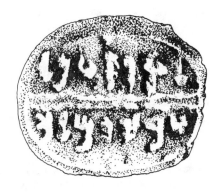

Fig. 91. The seal of Yatom from
Tell el-Kheleifeh

Fig. 92. The stamp of Quas'anali from
Tell el-Kheleifeh

belong to the seventh century B.C., but the *lytm* seal can be dated to the late eighth century, and the Tell Kheleifeh ostracon, with its predominant Aramaic elements, to the sixth century B.C.[60]

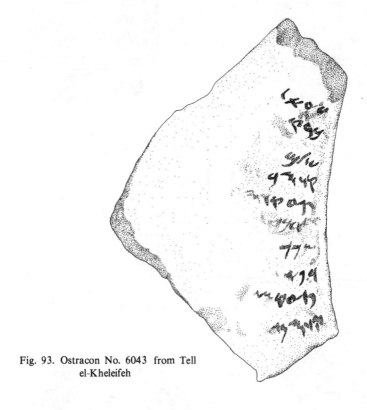

Fig. 93. Ostracon No. 6043 from Tell el-Kheleifeh

Under the political influence of Israel and Judah, respectively, the Moabites and the Edomites, adopted the script used in those kingdoms, presumably along with other cultural features. However, from the late

60. See the discussion and the bibliographical data in the articles mentioned in n. 58. See also E. Peuch, Documents épigraphiques de Buseirah, *Levant* 9 (1977), pp. 11-20; F. Israel, Miscellanea Idumea, *Rivista Biblica* 27 (1979), pp. 171-203 and the bibliography there.

eighth century, when the Assyrians appeared on the scene, the script of these peoples began to absorb Aramaic elements; by the sixth century, it was closer to Aramaic than to Hebrew. This development prompts the assumption that, in the Persian period, the Edomites and Moabites wrote texts in their native tongues (Canaanite dialects) using the Aramaic script.

The fact that these two neighbouring peoples adopted the same script may be indicative of a common political fate. Both the Moabites and the Edomites may have been open to the influence of foreign writing traditions because their own cultural identity was not sufficiently well-established to foster native scripts. The only independently-produced feature in their common script was the large-headed *mem*.

In the Persian and Hellenistic periods, Moab had already ceased to exist as a political entity, while Edom (Idumea) was expanding into southern Judah and the northern Negev.[61] A short and fragmentary text written in the early fifth century B.C. in lapidary Aramaic script, was found on a small altar at Lachish. It has been claimed that the inscription may contain an Edomite text: in addition to the word *bn* ("son") one can also read what may be the person's title beginning with the Canaanite article *h-*.[62]

The Ammonites lived along the King's Highway to the north of Moab. The corpus of Ammonite inscriptions is still scanty, but it has grown considerably in the last thirty years, especially in the last decade. The inscriptions date from the ninth to the fifth century B.C. In Amman three fragmentary inscriptions have been found: one on the statue of

61. J. Naveh, The Aramaic Ostraca from Tel Beer-Sheba (Seasons 1971-1976), *Tel Aviv* 6 (1979), pp. 182-198.
62. F. M. Cross, Two Notes on Palestinian Inscriptions of the Persian period, *BASOR* 193 (1969), pp. 21-24. Contrary to what was stated in my paper "Hebrew Texts in Aramaic Script in the Persian Period?" (*BASOR* 203 [1971], pp. 27-32 both the Lachish altar and the stamp *šlmy h'd* ("Šalmay the notary") may be of Jewish origin. In a bilingual society a person's name, including his title, does not determine the language of the text (see below, n. 90). As for the third-century B.C. ostracon from el-Kom (L. T. Geraty, The Khirbet el-Kom Bilingual Ostracon, *BASOR* 220 [1975], pp. 55-61), where an Edomite person Qosyada' *bar* (sic!) Hanna is mentioned, the Semitic text is no doubt Aramaic.

Fig. 94. The isncription of Yeraḥ'azar

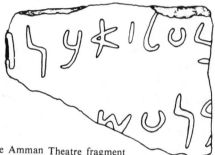

Fig. 95. The Amman Theatre fragment

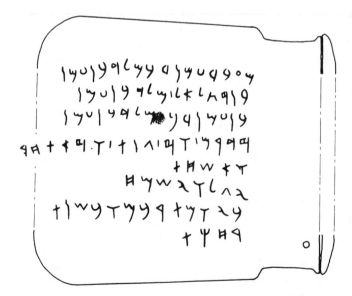

Fig. 96. Inscription on juglet from Tell Siran

Yeraḥ'azar (Fig. 94),[63] one known as the Citadel Inscription (Pl. 13:A),[64] and another called Theatre Inscription (Fig. 95).[65] In Tell Siran a juglet was discovered on which was incised a complete Ammonite text describing briefly "the works of Amminadab, king of the Ammonites, the son of Hiṣṣil'el king of the Ammonites, the son of Amminadab king of the Ammonites" (Fig. 96).[66] In the excavations at Heshbon, five Ammonite ostraca were found: Nos. I, II, IV (Fig. 97), V and XI;[67] all except No. XI contain personal names. In this context the plaster inscriptions from Tell Deir 'Alla should also be mentioned, although their language is still a matter of dispute.[68] The main source for Ammonite personal names is the group of some scores of Ammonite seals (Fig. 98; Pl. 12:E-G).[69] Some of them were found at Amman, but most are of unknown provenance and have only recently been classified as Ammonite seals. Today we know that the Ammonites spoke a Canaanite dialect,[70] but that they wrote in the script adopted from their northern neighbour, Aram-Damascus.[71] On

63. R. D. Barnett, Four Sculptures from Amman, *ADAJ* 1 (1951), p. 35, Pl. XXXI.

64. S. H. Horn, The Amman Citadel Inscription, *BASOR* 193 (1969), pp. 2-13; F. M. Cross, Epigraphic Notes on the Amman Citadel Inscription, *BASOR* 193 (1969), pp. 13-19.

65. R. W. Dajani, The Amman Theater Fragment *ADAJ* 12-13 (1967-68), pp. 65-67, Pl. XXXIX.

66. H. O. Thompson and F. Zayadine, The Tell Siran Inscription, *BASOR* 212 (1973), pp. 5-11; F. M. Cross, Notes on the Ammonite Inscription from Tell Siran, *BASOR* 212 (1973), pp. 12-15.

67. F. M. Cross, An Ostracon from Heshbon, *AUSS* 7 (1969), pp. 223-229, Pl. XXV; idem, Heshbon Ostracon II, *AUSS* 11 (1973), pp. 126-131 Pl. XVIA; idem, Heshbon Ostraca IV-VII, *AUSS* 13 (1975), pp. 1-19 Pl. I; idem, Heshbon Ostracon XI, *AUSS* 14 (1976), pp. 145-148 Pl. XVA.

68. J. Hoftijzer and G. van der Kooij, *Aramaic Texts from Deir 'Alla*, Leiden 1976. For my review on this book see *IEJ* 29 (1979), pp. 133-136.

69. Cf. L. G. Herr, *The Scripts of Ancient Northwest Semitic Seals* (Harvard Semitic Monographs, No. 18), Missoula Montana 1979, pp. 55-78.

70. G. Garbini believes that the Ammonite language should be related to Arabic; see G. Garbini, La lingua degli Ammoniti, *AION* 20 (1970), pp. 249-258.

71. Naveh (above, n. 53), p. 280.

Fig. 97. Heshbon ostracon IV

Fig. 98. Three Ammonite seals

the basis of these data, one can also identify as Ammonite the ostracon from Nimrud (biblical Calah in Assyria), which bears a list of names — most of which are also present in the above-mentioned Ammonite inscriptions — written in cursive Aramaic of the late eighth century B.C. (Pl. 13:B).[72]

The question arises whether the Ammonites used the current Aramaic script, or whether they developed a script of their own. According to Cross, the Ammonites wrote in a script which branched off from the Aramaic in the middle of the eighth century B.C., and the development of this Ammonite "national" script progressed more slowly than the contemporaneous Aramaic script.[73] Thus, if the Nimrud ostracon was written in this "national" Ammonite script, it cannot be dated to the late eighth century B.C., but to a period at least half a century later. The script of the Nimrud ostracon is much more developed than that of the Deir ʿAlla plaster inscriptions. If the script of the latter is indeed Aramaic, it may be dated to the mid-eighth century, or even one or two decades earlier.[74] Cross, suggesting that the Deir ʿAlla script does not belong to the Aramaic series, but to the "national" Ammonite script, dates it to the early seventh century B.C.[75]

In my opinion, the script of the Ammonite inscriptions cannot be considered as a national (Ammonite) script. The term national script can be applied only to those scribal traditions which developed independently without any significant foreign influence. In the first half of the first millennium B.C., only three national alphabetic scripts existed: Phoenician, Hebrew and Aramaic. Moreover, it seems unlikely that, at a time when the scripts of the Moabites and Edomites were absorbing elements of the Aramaic script current in the Assyrian empire, the script of the

72. P. Bordreuil, Les noms propres transjordaniens de l'Ostracon de Nimroud, *Revue d'Histoire et de Philosophie Religieuses* 3-4 (1979), pp. 313-317; J. Naveh, The Ostracon from Nimrud — An Ammonite Name-List, *Maarav* 2/2 (1980), pp. 163-171.
73. Cross (above, n. 66), pp. 13-14; idem (above, n. 67): *AUSS* 13, pp. 10-11.
74. J. Naveh, The Date of the Deir ʿAlla Inscription in Aramaic Script, *IEJ* 17 (1967), pp. 256-258.
75. Cross (above, n. 66), p. 14.

Ammonites (which had been Aramaic) should deviate from the Aramaic scribal tradition, evolving a distinctive, archaic style. All the letter forms in the Ammonite inscriptions can be explained within the framework of the development of the Aramaic script. There are, it is true, some local peculiarities in the script of the Ammonite inscriptions. For example, the square ʿ*ayin* in the Ammonite seals can be regarded as particular to the seal engravers of Ammon. The flag-shaped *he* in the Tell Siran inscription is perhaps a characteristic Ammonite letter form, but as it occurs only in this inscription, it may be an idiosyncrasy of the writer. According to Cross "it may be that some of the Ammonite changes took place under secondary Aramaic influence. No doubt Aramaic was known and its script read in Amman in these centuries".[76]

Cross assumes that the Ammonite national script ceased to exist in the late sixth century B.C., when there took place a "general replacement of the old national scripts, Edomite, Ammonite and Hebrew, by the Aramaic script universally used in the Persian chancelleries".[77] However, I prefer to see here three different phenomena: the script of the Edomites was continuously influenced by the Aramaic script and there was a gradual transition from Hebrew to Aramaic letter forms (see pp.102 ff.); the national Hebrew script existed side by side with the international Aramaic for many generations (see below, pp. 114 ff.); the Ammonites always wrote in the Aramaic script and did not develop a tradition of their own.

As we have seen above, this controversy affects the dating of the Ammonite inscriptions. We have already discussed the date of the Deir ʿAlla plaster inscription and that of the Nimrud ostracon. The exact dating of the Tell Siran inscription is of considerable historical significance. Cross dates its script to *c.* 600 B.C. and suggests that there were three Ammonite kings named Amminadab.[78] The inscription mentions "Amminadab the son of Hiṣṣilʾel, the son of Amminadab". In his opinion none of them can be identified with Amminadab, who was mentioned in 667 B.C. in the Assyrian lists of the twelve vassals who paid tribute to Ashur-

---

76. Cross (above, n. 67): *AUSS* 13, p. 14.
77. *Ibid.*
78. Cross (above, n. 66), pp. 13-15.

banipal. However, if the script of the Tell Siran text is regarded as belonging to the Aramaic series, it is reasonable to assume that the Tell Siran juglet belonged to Amminadab II the grandson of Amminadab I of 667 B.C.

There is also no epigraphic material that might acquaint us with the script of the Philistines. Presumably, in the twelfth century B.C. the Philistines used a Cypro-Mycenaean type of writing, but later they discarded this tradition and lost the script together with other cultural attributes they had brought with them from their homeland in Crete or elsewhere. It is reasonable to assume that in the eighth and seventh centuries, when the Philistine kings bore Semitic names like Ḥanun, Ṣidqa and Mitinti, they spoke a Semitic language and wrote in a script similar to those current in this region. The material discovered to date is very scanty. On a seal of unknown provenance we read *l'bd'l'b bn šb't 'bd mtt bn ṣdq*; its owner was a certain ʿAbdeliab, who was the servant of Mititti the son of Ṣidqa (Fig. 99).[79] Mititti (=Mitinti), king of Ashkelon, paid tribute (like Qausgabri king of Edom and Amminadab king of Ammon) to Ashurbanipal in 667 B.C. Mitinti's father Ṣidqa is mentioned as king of Ashkelon in the description of Sennacherib's campaign to Palestine in 701 B.C. Interestingly enough, this seal does not only have characters that are similar to Hebrew letters (mainly *taw*), but also Phoenician-Aramaic features (the vertical downstrokes of *mem, nun* and mainly of the *ṣade*). The sherd inscribed *]pḥr* from Ashdod does not exhibit any local characteristics,[80] but another (unpublished) sherd, also from

Fig. 99. Seal of a Philistine official

79. A. Bergman (Biran), Two Hebrew Seals of the *ʿEbed* Class, *JBL* 55 (1936), pp. 224-226.

80. M. Dothan and D. N. Freedman, Ashdod, I. *ʿAtiqot*, English Series 7 (1967), pp. 84-85 Pl. 15:8.

Ashdod,[81] has some interesting forms which may perhaps provide us with more details on the script used by the Philistines in the first half of the first millennium B.C. However, the paucity of the epigraphic material precludes further comment on the script practised by the Philistines, and we shall have to wait until archaeological excavations of Philistine sites unearth more, and perhaps longer, inscriptions.

6. *The Change from Hebrew to Jewish Script*

We have seen that in Israel and Judah there evolved a specific Hebrew national script. Towards the end of the First Temple period, the use of the Hebrew script was not restricted to scribes and individual educated persons, but there was presumably a certain stratum of the population which knew how to read and write in the national script. Nevertheless, in the Second Temple period this script had only a limited use and another, new script — the Jewish script, which is an offshoot of Aramaic — came to the fore. As early as the late third century, Hebrew biblical texts were written in the Jewish script (Fig. 100). The Hebrew script was used infrequently by Jews until the Second War against the Romans, and thereafter it was preserved only by the Samaritans.

We are faced with an extraordinary phenomenon: the Jews, a conservative nation which adhered strictly to its traditional values, abandoned their own script in favour of a foreign one. When a literate people adopts a new script, it is generally because the new script has certain advantages. It was only natural that the Assyrians should introduce the Aramaic alphabet as an official form of writing, and yet they did not abandon their own complicated cuneiform script as a medium for their native language. The modern Turks exchanged their traditional script for the Latin alphabet, a move designed to underscore their cultural affinity with Europe rather than Asia, and at the same time, to affirm the secular character of the new Turkish republic. But the foremost consideration was practicality: the Latin alphabet is without doubt an easier system

81. My thanks are due to Prof. Moshe Dothan for showing me this inscribed sherd.

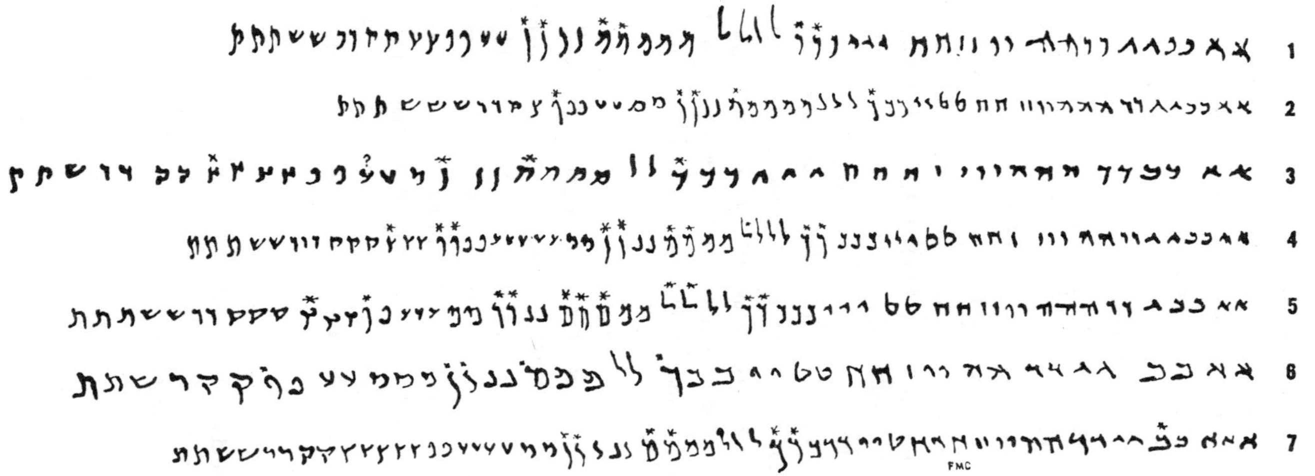

1

2

3

4

5

6

7

Fig. 100. Aramaic and early Jewish scripts: 1. Papyrus Luparensis, Aramaic cursive of c. 375-350 B.C.; 2. Papyrus from Edfu, Aramaic vulgar cursive of the early 3rd cent. B.C.; 3. An Exodus manuscript from Qumran (4QEx.f), an archaic Jewish hand of the mid-3rd cent. B.C.; 4. A ms. of Samuel (4QSam,b), Jewish formal script of the late 3rd cent. B.C.; 5. A ms. of Jeremiah (4QJer,a), formal script of c. 200-175 B.C.; 6. A ms. of Qohelet (4QQoh,a), semi-formal script of c. 175-125 B.C.; 7. 4Q Prières liturgiques A, another semi-formal hand of c. 175-125 B.C.

113

than Arabic. However, neither expediency nor ideology — at least in the Persian period — explains the Jews' preference for the Aramaic script, since the Aramaic and the Hebrew scripts had the same twenty-two letters.

As a rule, there existed in ancient times a strong bond between a language and its script. Exceptions were rare and specific in nature. Incantation texts, for instance, were universal and they passed from people to people without linguistic modification: two amulets found at Arslan Tash bear magic texts in a Canaanite dialect that were written in Aramaic characters of the seventh century B.C.[82] The demotic script was used for an Aramaic religious text written on papyrus in Egypt, probably from the Persian period.[83] A tablet from Uruk is inscribed with an Aramaic incantation text in cuneiform characters.[84] In general, however, a language and its script were closely linked. One illustration of this rule is a sixth-century B.C. seal of unknown provenance, which reads as follows: "(belonging) to Yehoyišma‘, the daughter of Šawaššaruṣur" (Pl. 14:A). The engraver, presumably a Babylonian Jew, endeavoured to use Hebrew characters for the Hebrew name Yehoyišma‘, and Aramaic ones for the Babylonian name of her father.[85]

In the Persian period, too, Jews used both languages and both scripts. Aramaic was mainly the language of administration and trade, and thus most of the inscriptions from this period found in Judah were written in the Aramaic language and script. But only one coin with the legend *yhd* (Yehud, the official Aramaic name of the province) in Aramaic letters is known. In Judah, towards the end of the Persian rule, coins were struck with Hebrew letters: in addition to the coins which mention only "Yehud", coins bearing the legend *yhzqyh hphh* ("Yeḥizkiyah the governor") have been found. On these, the language (the initial *he* as article)

82. *KAI*, No. 27; A. Caquot and R. du Mesnil du Buisson, La seconde tablette ou "petite amulette" d'Arslan-Tash, *Syria* 48 (1971), pp. 391-406.
83. R. Bowman, An Aramaic Incantation in Demotic Script, *JNES* 3 (1941), pp. 219-231.
84. J. J. Koopmans, *Aramäische Chrestomathie*, Leiden 1962, No. 56 and the bibliography there.
85. N. Avigad, Seals of Exiles, *IEJ* 15 (1965), pp. 228-230, Pl. 40E.

Fig. 101. Yehud coins:

(1) *yhd* in Aramaic letters   (2) [*y*]*ḥzq*[*yh*] *hpḥh*   (3) *yhd* in Hebrew letters

and the script are clearly Hebrew (Fig. 101: Pl. 14:B).[86] On the other hand, some decades earlier, jar handles were impressed with seals indicating the name of the Province Yehud, and sometimes the names of the government officials who were responsible for the capacity of the jars, e.g. *yhwᶜzr pḥwʾ*: the form *pḥwʾ* (with the final *alef* indicating the determinative state) is clearly Aramaic, and in this case the script used is also Aramaic (Fig. 102).[87] This usage was likewise current in Samaria. A cave in Wadi Daliyeh, east of Samaria, yielded fragments of fourth-century deeds which had been written in Samaria on papyrus in the Aramaic language and script (see above, p. 87, Fig. 80). But together with them was found a bulla bearing the text [*lyšᶜ*]*yhw bn* [*snʾ*]*blṭ pḥt šmrn*, i.e. "[belonging to Isa]iah, the son of [San]ballat, the governor of Samaria" (Fig. 103). Here the script is Hebrew and so is the language: *ben* and not the Aramaic *bar*; *Šomron* instead of the Aramaic *Šamrayin*.[88]

86. Y. Meshorer, *Jewish Coins of the Second Temple Period*, Tel-Aviv 1967, Pl. I; L. Y. Rahmani, Silver Coins of the Fourth Century B.C. from Tel Gamma, *IEJ* 21 (1971), pp. 158-160, Pl. 31; *IR*, Nos. 144-147.

87. N. Avigad, Bullae and Seals from a Post-Exilic Judaean Archive, *Qedem* 4 (1976), Fig. 17, No. 7. Avigad translates *pḥwʾ* "governor", whereas I prefer — "official", see J. Naveh, Writing and Scripts in the Persian Period, *World History of the Jewish People*, vol. V (to be published); J. C. Greenfield and J. Naveh, Hebrew and Aramaic in the Persian Period, *Cambridge History of Judaism* (to be published).

88. F. M. Cross, Papyri of the Fourth Century B.C. from Daliyeh, in D. N. Freedman and J. C. Greenfield (editors), *New Directions in Biblical Archaeology*, Garden City 1969, pp. 42-43, Figs. 34-35; *IR*, No. 148.

Fig. 102. Aramaic stamps on jars from the Province of Yehud

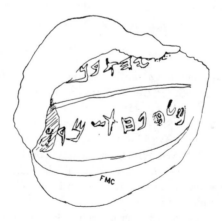

Fig. 103. Seal of the governor of Samaria impressed on a bulla

True, when dealing with such short texts consisting of personal names and titles only, the language cannot be determined. In fact, among the recently published 65 bullae of unknown provenance, but of Jewish origin, there were impressions of 12 seals, including those of Baruch, the son of Šim'i (*brwk bn šm'y*), Yiga'el, the son of Zikri (*yg'l bn zkry*) and Jeremi the scribe (*yrmy hspr*). Although these seals contain Hebrew words (*bn* and *hspr*), their script is lapidary Aramaic of the late sixth century B.C. (Fig. 104).[89] We have already seen the same phenomenon in the late ninth-century B.C. Kilamu inscription (above, p. 54) and there are many other indications that, in a bilingual society, a person's name and his title do not determine the language of the text.[90] This was surely true in the Persian period when Hebrew was still widely spoken among the Jews. Nevertheless, it seems likely that in the Persian period Hebrew texts were still being written in Hebrew characters. Further evidence for this suggestion can be found in the later coin legends: the Hasmonaean kings (135-37 B.C.), the leaders of the First Revolt (66-70 A.D.) and Bar-Kokhba (132-135 A.D.), all struck coins with Hebrew legends and

Fig. 104. Bullae of the seals of Yiga'el Baruch, Jeremi, etc.

89. Avigad (above, n. 87).
90. See e.g. the inscriptions published in N. Avigad, The Burial-Vault of a Nazirite Family on Mount Scopus, *IEJ* 21 (1971), pp. 196-198; J. Naveh, *On Stone and Mosaic, The Aramaic and Hebrew Inscriptions from Ancient Synagogues*, Jerusalem 1978, Nos. 3, 33, 80 (Hebrew).

Hebrew scripts (Fig. 105). However, when Alexander Jannaeus chose an Aramaic text — *mlk' 'lksndrws šnt kh* "the king Alexander, year 25" — it was written in the Jewish script, descendant of the Aramaic (Fig. 106).[91]

Fig. 105. Jewish coins with Hebrew legends

91. J. Naveh, Dated Coins of Alexander Janneus, *IEJ* 18 (1968), pp. 20-26.

Fig. 106. Aramaic legend on a coin of Alexander Jannaeus; *c.* 4:1

Texts written in the Hebrew script in the Second Temple period are rare. The small corpus of such texts consists of the above-mentioned coins and seal impressions, to which we can add the coins with the legend *yhdh* (Fig. 107) and the jar-handles stamped with the words *yhd* and *yršlm* (Jerusalem), from the early Hellenistic period (Fig. 108).[92] These texts are official in nature and seem to indicate that the use of the Hebrew script in this period had nationalistic connotations. However, the use of the Hebrew script in parts of the Dead Sea Scrolls of Qumran

Fig. 107. The legend *yhdh* on a coin from the early Hellenistic period

Fig. 108. *yhd* and *yršlm* stamps from the early Hellenistic period

92. P. W. Lapp, Ptolemaic Stamped Handles from Judah, *BASOR* 172 (1963), pp. 22-35; A. Kindler, Silver Coins Bearing the Name of Judea from the Early Hellenistic Period, *IEJ* 24 (1974), pp. 73-76; D. Jeselsohn, A New Coin Type with Hebrew Inscription, *ibid.*, pp. 77-78.

presumably denotes sanctity: these are Pentateuch fragments in the Hebrew script (Pl. 14:C) and some scrolls in Jewish characters, in which the Tetragrammaton (the four letters *yhwh*) and other divine names are written in Hebrew letters (Pl. 14:D).[93] A fragment of a marble slab with some Hebrew letters was found near the Temple Mount in Jerusalem.[94] A graffito on an ossuary from Jerusalem featuring the name Eleazar (Fig. 109)[95] and some single letters on ostraca and column fragments from Massada[96] seem to indicate that the Hebrew script was also used in everyday life.

Fig. 109. A graffito on an ossuary in Jewish and Hebrew characters

However, the most striking find is a seven-line epitaph found in a burial cave at Giv‘at ha-Mivtar in Jerusalem, presumably written in the Herodian period, but certainly before 70 A.D. The language is Aramaic but

93. R. S. Hanson, Paleo-Hebrew Scripts of the Hasmonaean Age, *BASOR* 175 (1964), pp. 26-42; Purvis (above, n. 54), Table III, 1-5.

94. B. Mazar, The Archaeological Excavations near the Temple Mount, in Y. Yadin (editor), *Jerusalem Revealed*, Jerusalem 1975, pp. 31-32, Fig. on p. 35.

95. M. Rosenthaler, A Paleo-Hebrew Ossuary Inscription, *IEJ* 25 (1975), pp. 138-139.

96. Y. Yadin, *Massada*, London 1966, pp. 69, 190.

the script is Hebrew (Pl. 15:A). As to its contents, the inscription is written in the first person and its translation is as follows:

"I, Abba, son of the priest Eleaz(ar), son of Aaron the high (priest), I, Abba, the oppressed and the persecuted, who was born in Jerusalem, and went into exile to Babylonia and brought (back to Jerusalem) Mattathi(ah), son of Jud(ah), and I buried him in the cave, which I acquired by the writ".

The fact that the inscription deals with a living man who performed the burial, rather than with the deceased, is extraordinary indeed. The general appearance of the inscription is also unusual, and the Hebrew characters, notwithstanding the Aramaic language, are an exceptional feature in Jewish epigraphy. Since the Hebrew script was used by the Samaritans for writing Hebrew, Aramaic and, later, even Arabic texts, an initial conclusion might be that the Abba inscription was not written by a Jew, but by a Samaritan; some letter forms even resemble those of third-century A.D. and later Samaritan inscriptions. But its contents, the unmistakably Jewish name Judah, and the fact that it was found in Jerusalem, preclude such an assumption. Thus we have to regard it as an inscription written by a Jew.[97]

The vast majority of the Pentateuch scrolls found in the Qumran caves near the Dead Sea are written in Jewish characters. There is one fragmentary text of Exodus written in a script very close to the Aramaic script of the Persian period, and for this reason Cross dated it to the mid-third century B.C. (see above, p.113, Fig. 100). This Exodus fragment is the earliest known Hebrew text written in Jewish characters rather than in Hebrew script.[98] Only in that period did the Aramaic script used by the Jews develop its characteristic Jewish features. In the Persian period, the Aramaic script was an international means of communication and the same uniform script was practised in all the provinces of the Persian em-

---

97. E. S. Rosenthal, The Givʿat ha-Mivtar Inscription, *IEJ* 23 (1973), pp. 72-81; J. Naveh, An Aramaic Tomb Inscription Written in Paleo-Hebrew Script, *ibid.*, pp. 82-91; *IR*, No. 263.

98. F. M. Cross, The Development of the Jewish Scripts, *BANE*, p. 175, Fig. 1, Line 3.

pire. The various national versions of the Aramaic script began to appear only about a century after the fall of the Persian empire, when the official language of the central government was no longer Aramaic but Greek. The Aramaic script was at that time so deeply implanted that the various nations continued to use it. But since the official language and script were no longer Aramaic, there was no unifying force to preserve the uniformity of the Aramaic script. Different nations began to develop their own versions, and thus the Jewish script evolved from the Aramaic. It seems likely that the Jews began to write Hebrew texts in the Aramaic script only when they felt that their form of the Aramaic script was distinctively Jewish. This does not constitute an entirely satisfactory explanation as to why the Jews neglected their own traditional mode of writing in favour of the new script. However, the old tradition was not entirely abandoned, and the Hebrew script did survive in some circles.

Towards the end of the Second Temple period, the Jews wrote mainly in the Jewish script while the Hebrew script was generally confined to texts of a specific nature. However, this observation holds for normative Jewish society only. We have no information regarding the attitude of the various Jewish sects to the Hebrew script. If we accept Diringer's view that the Hebrew script was in widespread use among the Sadducees, and that the Hasmonaean coin legends were struck under their influence,[99] we may presume that the Pentateuch scrolls, fragments of which were found in Qumran, were written by Sadducee scribes. Whoever was responsible, whether the Sadducees or some other Jewish sect, unmentioned in our sources, it seems likely that the Pharisees opposed the use of the Hebrew

Fig. 110. Earliest Samaritan inscription on a capital from Emmaus

99. D. Diringer, Early Hebrew Script versus Square Hebrew Script, *Essays and Studies Presented to S. A. Cook*, London 1950, pp. 46-49.

script. The negative attitude of normative Judaism to the Hebrew script receives expression in the Talmudic sources. In the Babylonian Talmud, Sanhedrin 21b, we read:

> Originally the Torah was given to Israel in the Hebrew script and in the sacred language; later, in the time of Ezra, the Torah was given in the Assyrian script [i.e. the Aramaic script, introduced by the Assyrians as an official script] and the Aramaic language. They selected for Israel the Assyrian script and the Hebrew language, leaving the Hebrew script and the Aramaic language for the ordinary people.

This *beraitha* and other passages (*ibid.*, Sanhedrin 22a; Tosefta, Sanh. V. 7: Palestinian Talmud, Megilla 71a-b) indicate that rabbinical circles were concerned with the problem and approached it in a spirit of apology. Rabbi Yehuda ha-Nasi maintained that the Torah had originally been given in the Assyrian script.

The unusual contents of the Abba inscription may perhaps support an assumption that it was written by a person with heterodox views. Abba, while emphasizing his priestly origin, says that he, 'the oppressed and the persecuted . . . was born in Jerusalem and went into exile to Babylonia'. Did he go to exile of his own free will, or was he exiled, and if so, by whom? Who was Mattathiah, son of Judah, whose bones Abba took pains to bury in Jerusalem? By whom was Abba oppressed and persecuted? All these questions remain unanswered. We may, however, hazard a guess that Abba was a separatist of some kind, who was outlawed and persecuted either by the government, because of his zealous nationalism, or by the official Jewish establishment, on account of his heterodox religious opinions.

The Samaritans, who believe that they are the true descendants of the sons of Israel, preserved the old Hebrew script. In the third century A.D. Rav Ḥisda explained that the "ordinary people" to whom the Hebrew script was conferred, were in fact the Samaritans (Babylonian Talmud, Sanhedrin 21b). The earliest Samaritan inscription is a short text written on an Ionic capital from Emmaus (Fig. 110). Since the script does not differ essentially from that of the legends on the coins of the First Revolt, the Emmaus inscription is dated to the first century A.D. Typically the Samaritan traits are discernible only in the scripts of the third-century A.D. and later Samaritan inscriptions found in Emmaus, Shechem and other sites (Fig. 111; Pl. 15:B).[100] Albright therefore suggested that the final schism between the Jews and the Samaritans should be dated to the early first century B.C., when Shechem and Samaria were conquered by the Jews.[101]

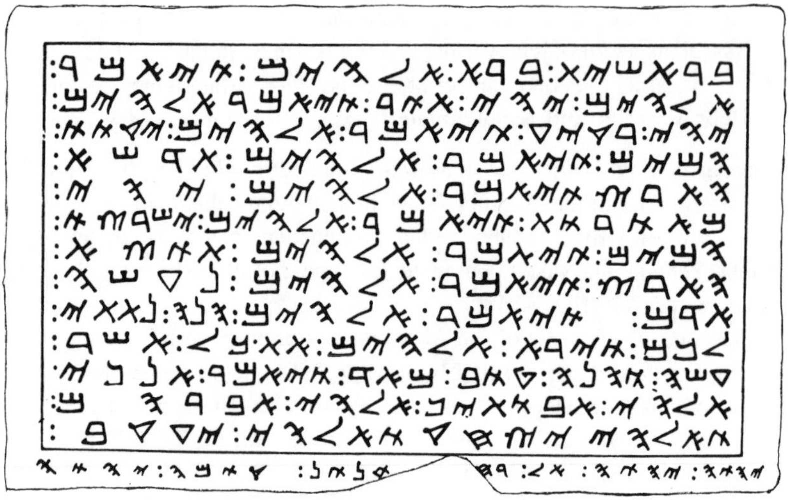

Fig. 111. A Samaritan inscription

100. For more detailed discussion on the Samaritan script see Purvis (above, n. 54) and Naveh (above, n. 97).

101. W. F. Albright, *From Stone Age to Christianity*², Garden City 1957, pp. 345-346, n. 12.

V. THE DEVELOPMENT OF THE LATER
ARAMAIC OFFSHOOTS

After the Aramaic script diverged from the Phoenician, it evolved in a single direction for about half a millennium. Aramaic was the official script of the Assyrian, Babylonian and Persian empires; as such it was uniform, and no local scripts developed even in the remotest provinces. The norms for the Aramaic language and script were established by the scribes of the royal administration. Naturally, therefore, the official Aramaic language adopted various eastern elements, such as Akkadian and Persian loan words, and was influenced by the grammar and syntax of those languages. Thus Official Aramaic can be regarded as an eastern dialect. The use of the western dialect in the Persian period was confined to private letters and other texts written or composed by Aramaeans. The Hermopolis papyri and the Proverbs of Aḥiqar belong to this category.[1] In this period the Aramaic language and script were deeply implanted in the cultures of the various peoples. With the exception of the Aramaeans, most peoples were bilingual. In places where both Aramaic and the native tongue were spoken, the Aramaic script was prevalent. For their part, the Persians did not develop a national script, and it seems that the Old Persian cuneiform syllabary writing (Fig. 112) was an artificial script employed by the Achaemenid kings for royal monuments, but not used in daily life.[2] The Jews still wrote Hebrew texts in the Hebrew script, but

---

1. J. C. Greenfield, Standard Literary Aramaic, *Actes du Premier Congrès International de Linguistique Sémitique et Chamito-Sémitique*, The Hague-Paris 1974, p. 283.
2. R. N. Frye, *The Heritage of Persia*, London 1962, pp. 74-75, 103.

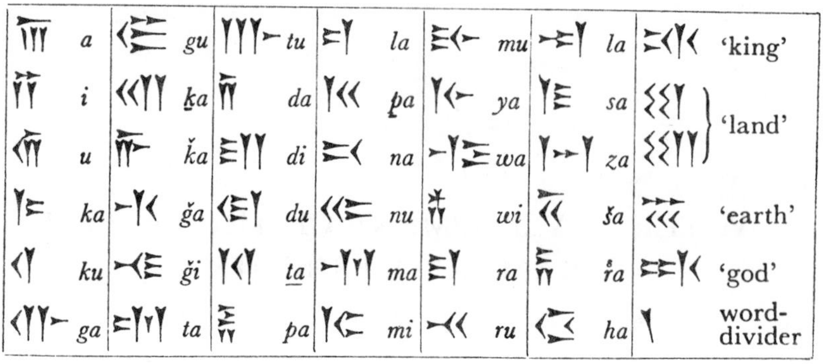

𒀀	*a*	𒄖	*gu*	𒌅	*tu*	𒆷	*la*	𒈬	*mu*	𒇲	*la*	𒈗	'king'
𒄿	*i*	𒅗	*ḵa*	𒁕	*da*	𒉺	*pa*	𒅀	*ya*	𒊓	*sa*	𒆠𒉌	} 'land'
𒌋	*u*	𒅗	*ǩa*	𒁲	*di*	𒈾	*na*	𒉿	*wa*	𒍝	*za*	𒆠𒉌	
𒅗	*ka*	𒂵	*ǧa*	𒁺	*du*	𒉡	*nu*	𒃾	*wi*	𒃻	*ša*	𒆠	'earth'
𒆪	*ku*	𒄀	*ǧi*	𒋫	*ta̱*	𒈠	*ma*	𒊏	*ra*	𒅒	*ṛa*	𒀭	'god'
𒂵	*ga*	𒋫	*ta*	𒉺	*pa*	𒈪	*mi*	𒊒	*ru*	𒄩	*ha*	𒑲	word-divider

Fig. 112. Old Persian syllabary

Aramaic was widely accepted (see above, pp. 114 ff.). Various Arab tribes, who wrote in their South Semitic scripts (Dedanite, Lihyanite and Thamudic), began to use the Aramaic script (see below, pp. 153 ff.).

After the fall of the Persian empire, vast territories came under Hellenistic rule and Greek became the language of the government. But Aramaic could not be uprooted, and various peoples continued to use the Aramaic language and script. However, since the central administration used Greek rather than Aramaic, there was no way of preserving the uniformity of the Aramaic script. Thus various nations or cultural units began to develop independent Aramaic scripts. The same period saw the start of a broad diversification among the Aramaic dialects. In the initial stage (*c.* 300 B.C.-200 A.D.), the various dialects still bear a close affinity to the official Aramaic language. Side by side with specifically local features, elements from Official Aramaic are clearly discernible in the inscriptions and manuscripts written by Jews and Nabataeans both in the west, and in Palmyra, Hatra and other centres in the east. At a later stage, a more extensive development of the various Aramaic dialects took place. East Aramaic is represented chiefly by Syriac, Babylonian Jewish Aramaic and Mandaic, and West Aramaic, by Palestinian Jewish Aramaic, Palestinian Christian Aramaic and Samaritan Aramaic.

The various Aramaic scripts can also be divided into eastern and western groups. The list of eastern Aramaic scripts includes, in addition to Syriac and Mandaic, the scripts that were practised in Palmyra, Hatra, Nisa (Turkmenistan), Armazi (Georgia), Elymais (the southern border area between modern Iraq and Iran), etc.; in the west only two scripts evolved: Jewish and Nabataean.

The classification of the scripts does not entirely parallel that of the dialects. Although a number of eastern (e.g. Syriac and Mandaic) and western dialects (Nabataean, Jewish) had their individual scripts, a western dialect could be written in an eastern Aramaic script, and vice versa. For instance, Palestinian Christian Aramaic was written in Syriac characters, while the Jewish Aramaic dialect of the Babylonian Talmud was written in the Jewish characters developed by the Jews in Palestine. Moreover, Samaritan Aramaic was not written in Aramaic but in the Samaritan script, which is a direct offshoot of the Hebrew script.

Aramaic dialects survived in some peripheral areas of the Near East. In three isolated villages of the Anti-Lebanon region, north of Damascus, a West Aramaic dialect is spoken; in Kurdistan and Azarbeijan, in the border area of Iran, Iraq, Turkey and the U.S.S.R., East Aramaic is still in use. Today, Syriac is used in the Assyrian Church, and Mandaic is still practised by the Mandaean (gnostic) sect. However, the principal modern offshoots of the Aramaic script are the Jewish and the Arabic scripts; the latter developed from the Nabataean.

1. *Aramaic Writing in the Iranian World*

Aramaic scribal traditions were developed by peoples who spoke Aramaic, or had originally spoken another Semitic language, such as Hebrew and Arabic. But there were also non-Semites, speaking Indian or Iranian languages, who wrote in Aramaic in the Persian period, and continued this practice after the fall of the Achaemenid empire. In Afghanistan and north-west India, there have come to light scores of inscriptions of King Aśoka (268-233 B.C.), containing edicts that relate to Buddhist religious precepts and moral instruction. These were written mainly in Prakrit (a Middle Indian dialect that is a direct issue of Sanskrit), but also in Greek and Aramaic (Pl. 16:A).[3] The two latter

---

3. *KAI*, Nos. 273 and 279 (2nd Edition, 1966); E. Y. Kutscher, J. Naveh and S. Shaked, The Aramaic Inscriptions of Aśoka, *Leshonenu* 34 (1970), pp. 125-136 (Hebrew, English summary, pp. 6-7).

languages had international status: Greek was introduced to this area in the wake of Alexander's conquest and Aramaic was inherited from the Persian empire. In Armenia, some Aramaic boundary inscriptions erected by Artaxias I, king of Armenia (189-160 B.C.), have been discovered (Fig. 113; Pl. 16:B). Artaxias divided the fields between the villages in the

Fig. 113. Aramaic boundary inscriptions from Armenia

course of his agrarian reform, and this act was inscribed on small stelae.[4] The wine cellars of the Parthian capital Nisa (today in Turkmenistan, U.S.S.R.), yielded over two thousand ostraca written in the Aramaic script of the first century B.C. (Pl. 17:B). These were "labels" with details

4. *KAI*, Nos. 274-275. Revised reading see in J. Naveh, The Aramaic Inscriptions on Boundary Stones in Armenia, *Die Welt des Orients* 6/1 (1971), pp. 42-46; A. Perikhanian, Les inscriptions araméennes du roi Artachès, *Revue des Études Arméniennes*, N.S. 8 (1971), pp. 169-174.

on the contents of the jars, namely, the quality of the wine or vinegar and its provenance, the year of its dispatch, and the name of the official who delivered it.[5] In Armazi, the capital of ancient Iberia, not far from modern Tbilisi, the capital of Soviet Georgia, Greek and Aramaic inscriptions from the second century A.D. were found (Fig. 114).[6] At that period the

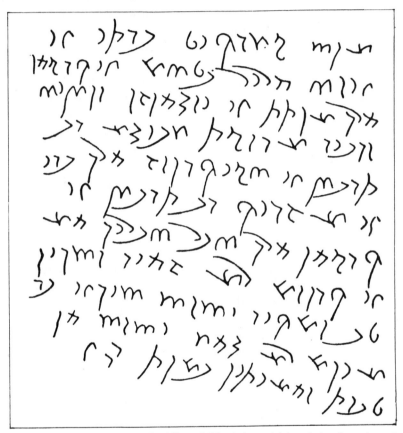

Fig. 114. The Aramaic part of a bilingual (Greek-Aramaic) inscription from Armazi

5. I. M. Diakonov and V. A. Livshitz, *Dokumenti iz Nisi*, Moscow 1960; M. Sznycer, Nouveaux ostraca de Nisa, *Semitica* 12 (1962), pp. 105-126.
6. *KAI*, No. 276; E. Y. Kutscher and J. Naveh, The Bilingual Inscription from Armazi, *Leshonenu* 34 (1970), pp. 309-313 (Hebrew, English summary).

Georgians or the Armenians did not have their own scripts. The Georgian and Armenian scripts were invented at a later date, while the Parthians, like the Persians, never developed a script of their own. The Iranian and Caucasian peoples spoke their individual languages, but for writing they used either Greek or Aramaic. Thus, since Aramaic was not a spoken language at that time, and no Aramaic dialect developed, these peoples continued to write in Official Aramaic. In the inscriptions from Armenia, Nisa and Armazi there are various deviations from standard Aramaic, in the form of non-Aramaic words and grammatical and syntactical anomalies. Most of these linguistic peculiarities are translations and loans from the language spoken by the writer.[7] Scholarly opinion is divided as to whether the Nisa and Armazi texts are a corruption of Aramaic, or an example of Parthian and Georgian ideographic writing, i.e. the use of Aramaic words to designate the equivalent Parthian words, just as the Babylonians and Assyrians wrote Sumerian words but read them in their own language.[8]

As we have mentioned, the Persians did not evolve an independent national script. Moreover, not until the Arab conquest of Persia, when the Persians began to use the Arabic script for writing their language, did they systematically adapt a script to render their own language. There is an inscription on the tomb of Darius I in Naqš-i Rustam which was written in the Aramaic script and, it seems, in the Old Persian language,[9] but generally the Persians wrote in the Aramaic script and the Aramaic language. It is doubtful whether every official in the Achaemenid kingdom knew how to read and write Aramaic. This competence was generally limited to the scribes, who could write in Aramaic a text that was dictated in Persian, and could read in Persian from the written Aramaic. Although this practice seems to us rather complicated, the Persians, Parthians and Sogdians adhered to it for a long time. Over the centuries, many Iranian words were introduced, and the Aramaic vocabulary

---

7. See Kutscher and Naveh (above, nn. 3, 4, 6).
8. W. B. Henning, Mitteliranisch, *Handbuch der Orientalistik*, 1. Abt./4. Band: Iranistik; 1. Abschnitt: Linguistik, Leiden-Köln 1958, pp. 27-28, 37-40.
9. E. Herzfeld, *Altpersische Inschriften*, Berlin 1938, p. 12, Pl. 4; Henning (above, n. 8), p. 24.

gradually declined. Later, the Aramaic language became obsolete and even the scribes were unacquainted with Aramaic grammar. Aramaic nouns and verbs had become fossilized and various Iranian suffixes were added to them. These fossilized Aramaic words are ideograms, which were written in Aramaic but read in Parthian or Persian. In the Parthian inscriptions (Pl. 17:A) the word BRY (= Aramaic "my son") was read *puhr* ("son"), whereas in Pahlavi (Middle Persian) BRH (="his son") was read *pus* ("son"). In the Sassanian period, when a Persian wished to express in writing the Pahlavi word *nišastan* (= "to sit") he wrote down the Aramaic ideogram YTYBWN (= Aramaic "they will sit") and added to it the Persian suffix -stn; *nišast* (= "he sat") was written YTYBWN-st; *butan* (= "to be") was written YHWWN-tn, comprising the Aramaic ideogram YHWWN (= Aramaic "they will be") which stands for *but* (= "he was"), and the Persian phonetic ending *tan*. The Persian word for "no" was *ne*, but it was expressed in writing by the Aramaic word L'; *šap* (= "night") — LYLY'; *dast* (= "hand") — YDH (= in fact, "his hand"); *šah* (= "king") — MLK'; *nām* (= "name") — ŠM, but *nāmak* (= "book") — ŠM-k. Certain Persian words could be written both ideographically and phonetically, e.g. "he was" could be written either YHWWNt or *bwt*.[10]

At first sight, this ideographic writing appears overly complicated. Surely, one would suppose, if the Persians had written in phonetic writing only, without the Aramaic ideograms, they could have made reading much easier. However, their conservative adherence to the ideographic system can be explained by the nature of the script which they derived from the Aramaic. Scholars who work with Middle Iranian texts know that it is considerably easier to read the Aramaic ideograms than the words written in phonetic script. As early as the first century B.C., the Nisa ostraca (written either in bad Aramaic or in ideographic Parthian), present us with difficulties in identifying various letters, on account of the cursive nature of the script, in which several letters have similar or even identical forms. The assimilation of letter forms is a progressive process. In the Pahlavi manuscripts there are only thirteen letter forms: *alef* and *ḥet* have the same form; as do *gimel, dalet* and *yod*, as well as *waw, nun,*

---

10. Henning (above, n. 8), pp. 30-37.

ʿayin and *resh*. *Ṭet* and *qof* do not exist in Pahlavi. *He*, used only as a final letter in ideograms, was written exactly like *mem*. No diacritic signs existed to differentiate between various consonants (Fig. 115).[11] It was obviously much easier for the reader to identify the fossilized Aramaic ideograms than to decipher the individual consonants of the phonetic writing.

2. The Aramaic Script in the East

In contrast to the west, where only two scripts developed from the uniform Aramaic, a large number of Aramaic scripts evolved in the east. However, since the latter have many common features which do not occur in the western scripts, we must presume either that there was once an eastern Aramaic prototype from which the various East Aramaic scripts evolved, or, alternatively, that the affinities were a consequence of close cultural relations and reciprocal influence. It is not easy to choose between these two possibilities. Only by obtaining further evidence, notably epigraphic material from the second and first centuries B.C., shall we be able to approach a solution to this problem. On the basis of their typological features, the extant eastern Aramaic scripts can be divided into three main groups, which developed in different geographical regions:

(1) The Syriac-Palmyrene branch in North Syria and on the Upper Euphrates.
(2) The North Mesopotamian branch, which evolved on the Upper Tigris and is represented mainly by the script of Hatra.
(3) The South Mesopotamian branch, to which the Mandaic script belongs.

This threefold division covers only the scripts which were used for writing Aramaic texts and does not include the Aramaic ideographic scripts which developed through the writing of Iranian dialects such as Persian, Parthian, Sogdian and Khorazmian (although these, too, should

11. H. S. Nyberg, *A Manual of Pahlavi*, I, Wiesbaden 1964, p. 129.

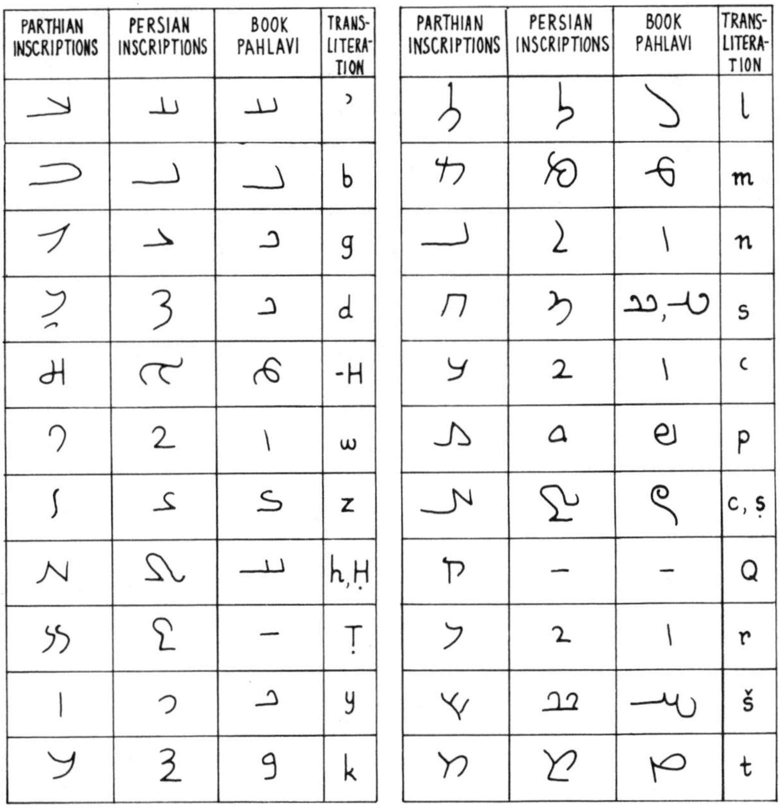

PARTHIAN INSCRIPTIONS	PERSIAN INSCRIPTIONS	BOOK PAHLAVI	TRANS-LITERA-TION	PARTHIAN INSCRIPTIONS	PERSIAN INSCRIPTIONS	BOOK PAHLAVI	TRANS-LITERA-TION
˘	⅃	⅃	ʾ	ƍ	ƍ	⟩	l
⊃	⌐	⌐	b	⌐⌐	♋	◌	m
⟋	⌐	⊃	g	⌐	⌐	\	n
⟩	3	⊃	d	⊓	⌐	⌐⌐	s
Ⅎ	⌐	⌐	-H	Ⴘ	2	\	ʿ
⟩	2	\	w	⌐⌐	◌	℮⌐	p
ʃ	⌐	S	z	⌐Ⲏ	⌐	℃	c, ṣ
Ⴈ	⌐	⌐⌐	ḥ, Ḥ	⌐⌐	—	—	Q
⌐⌐	ℂ	—	Ṭ	⌐	2	\	r
⎮	⌐	⌐	y	⌐	⌐⌐	⌐⌐	š
⌐	3	℥	k	⌐⌐	⌐⌐	⌐◌	t

Fig. 115. The Aramaic alphabet written by Iranians

be classified as eastern Aramaic scripts). We shall first describe those scripts which are remote, geographically and typologically, from the western Aramaic scripts, and then discuss the Syriac-Palmyrene branch which has certain affinities with the Jewish and Nabataean scripts.

a. *The South Mesopotamian branch*

The Mandaeans were a gnostic sect the vestige of which still exists in Khuzistan, on the Iraq-Iran border near the Persian Gulf. Their religion combined Babylonian, Persian, Jewish and Christian elements. The Mandaeans are thought to have come to this area from Palestine, and some scholars reinforce this theory with the assumption that the Mandaeans learned the Aramaic script from the Nabataeans. Their argument is based mainly on the fact that the letter *alef* has a circle-like shape in both the Nabataean and the Mandaic scripts. Lidzbarski, who supported the theory of the Mandaeans' western origin and their early settlement in Khuzistan, pointed out in 1922 that the kings of Characene (who were under Parthian suzerainty) issued coins with Mandaic legends in Khuzistan in the third century A.D.[12] Thirty years ago, Henning deciphered the rock inscriptions that accompanied the Elymaic relief monuments of Tang-i Sarvak, and the legend of a coin struck in the kingdom of Elymais in the second century A.D. (Fig. 116).[13] Then Macuch realized that this

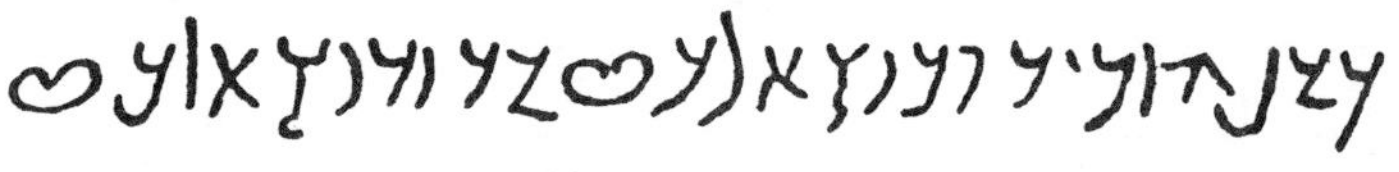

Fig. 116. Legend on an Elymaean coin

Elymaic script has much in common with the Mandaic script. He went further and stated that the Mandaeans who immigrated to Khuzistan at an earlier period brought their script with them from the west, and that the Elymaeans, the original inhabitants of this area, adopted this Mandaic script.[14]

Most Mandaean texts are manuscripts written in the Middle Ages and in the modern period, but there are also several scores of incantation texts written on bowls or on lead (Fig. 117; Pl. 17:C). The bowls are generally dated to the sixth century A.D. and some lead scrolls to *c.* 400 A.D.[15] The Mandaeans, who believed that writing was sacred, wrote their manuscripts in a skilled, formal book-hand, the incantation texts, on the

12. M. Lidzbarski, Die Münzen der Characene mit mandäischen Legenden, Mani auf Münzen seiner Zeit, *Zeitschrift für Numismatik* 33 (1922), pp. 83-96.
13. W. B. Henning, The Monuments and Inscriptions of Tang-i Sarvak, *Asia Major* 2 (1951/2), pp. 151-178.
14. R. Macuch, Anfänge der Mandäer, in F. Altheim and R. Stiehl, *Die Araber in der Alten Welt*, II, Berlin 1965, p. 146.
15. E. Yamauchi, *Mandaic Incantation Texts*, New-Haven 1967, p. 2.

Fig. 117. Mandaic incantation text on a bowl

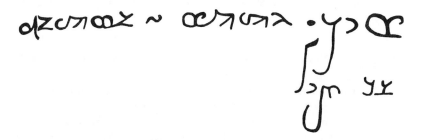

Fig. 118. Inscription from Tang-i Butan at the Shimbar Valley

other hand, were written less scrupulously. In addition to the above-mentioned Tang-i Sarvak reliefs and the coin legend, Elymaic inscriptions have been found on similar relief monuments in the Valley of Shimbar (Fig. 118), where dipinti, as yet undeciphered, were also discovered,[16] as well as on a fragmentary stele in Bard-i Nishandeh, near Mesjed-i Suleiman, and in Thaj and El-Qatif near the island of Baḥrein, about 400 km. south of the point where the Shatt el-Arab reaches the Persian Gulf.[17] The scripts used in these inscriptions belong to the same branch as that of the Characenaean coin legends and the Mandaic script; we may call this branch 'South Mesopotamian' (Fig. 119).

This script has several affinities with the other scripts of the eastern Aramaic family, whereas any similarity between Mandaic and Nabataean is simply a result of the fact that both scripts developed from a common ancestor, namely, the standard Aramaic script of the Persian period. The Elymaic script is earlier than Mandaic: this is evident not only from the letter forms, but also from the fact that the letters in the Elymaic script are generally written separately, with only a rudimentary anticipation of ligatured writing, whereas the Mandaic script is fully ligatured.[18]

Mandaic has a sign denoting the relative pronoun *ḏ* which doubtless evolved from Elymaic ligatured *zy*. It should be noted that in this branch there was no differentiation between final and medial letter forms; *kaf, nun, pe* and *ṣade* had long downstrokes in medial and final positions alike. In Mandaic these letters are nevertheless ligatured. The long *kaf, nun, pe* and *ṣade* are also used in the North Mesopotamian scripts (which did not evolve ligatures), but the Syriac-Palmyrene branch has distinctive forms for final and medial *kaf* and *nun*. This can be explained by postulating that the North and South Mesopotamian Aramaic scripts evolved from the formal style of the standard Aramaic that was used mainly for

16. A. D. H. Bivar and S. Shaked, The Inscriptions at Shimbar, *BSOAS* 27 (1964), pp. 265-290.
17. F. Altheim and R. Stiehl, *Die Araber in der Alten Welt*, V/1, Berlin 1968, pp. 77-78, 94-95, Figs. 29, 37 top; V/2, Berlin 1969, pp. 24-26, Figs. 7-8.
18. P. W. Coxon, Script Analysis and Mandaean Origins, *JSS* 15 (1970), pp. 16-30; J. Naveh, The Origin of the Mandaic Script, *BASOR* 198 (1970), pp. 32-37.

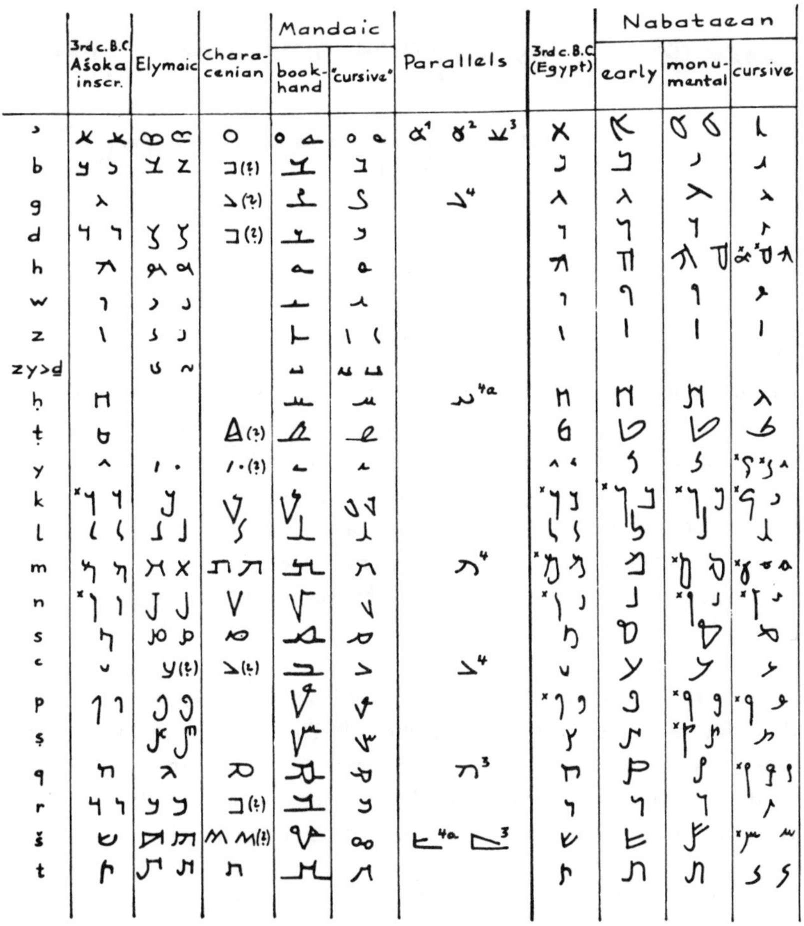

	3rd c.B.C Ašoka inscr.	Elymaic	Chara-cenian	Mandaic book-hand	Mandaic 'cursive'	Parallels	3rd c.B.C (Egypt)	Nabataean early	Nabataean monu-mental	Nabataean cursive
ʾ										
b										
g										
d										
h										
w										
z										
zy>d										
ḥ										
ṭ										
y										
k										
l										
m										
n										
s										
ʿ										
p										
ṣ										
q										
r										
š										
t										

Fig. 119. Development of the South Mesopotamian scripts (in comparison with Nabataean). Key to the parallels: (1) a bulla from Babylonia; (2) the Nash papyrus; (3) Hatra; (4) the Birecik inscription, Syriac of 6 A.D.; (4a) Syriac inscription of 165 A.D. from Samatar Harabesi (A raised x marks final forms)

engraving on stone, whereas the western Aramaic scripts and Syriac-Palmyrene followed the Aramaic book-hand, which was strongly influenced by the cursive of the Persian period.

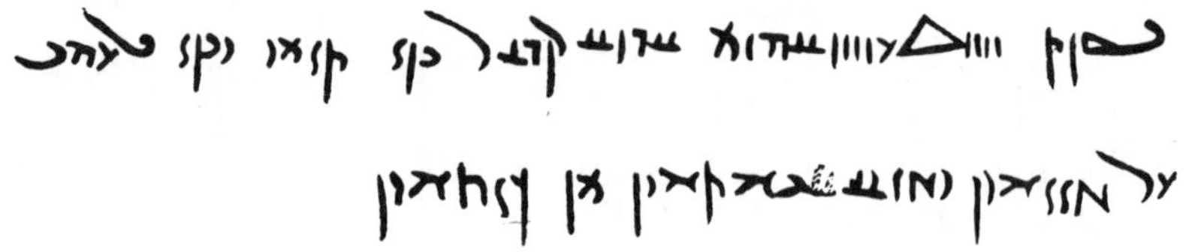

ﺳﺤﺎﻟﺐ ﺳﻖ ﺭﺍﺳﻖ ﺳﻖ ﺭﻟﻂﻑ ﻟﻟﺰﻝ ﺧﺎﻟﺤﻨﻨﻨﺮﻻﻟﻞ ﻥﺍﺣ

ﻥﺍﺭﺣﻖ ﻥﺭ ﻥﺭﺣﻦﺭﻟﺮﺣﺰﻝﻥ ﻥﺭﺭﺳﺤﻥ ﺭﻉ

Fig. 120. Hatran inscription No. 214 from 97/8 A.D.

b. *The North Mesopotamian branch*

The tolerant Parthian rulers allowed the subject nations to establish autonomous kingdoms in their empire. In addition to Elymais and Characene in South Mesopotamia, other minor states arose which preserved a cultural identity. In Hatra and Edessa there evolved independent Aramaic scripts. In Hatra, as in Edessa (and in Palmyra across the border, in the Roman empire), Arab kings had ruled since the first century B.C. The wealth of Hatra (an oasis between the Euphrates and the Tigris), like that of Palmyra, derived from the international trade which passed through the city. Archaeological excavations at Hatra revealed remains which bear witness to a rich and flourishing town. The finds include about four hundred Aramaic inscriptions.[19] These are for the most part votive inscriptions written in a script which has some affinity with the South Mesopotamian scripts, on the one hand, and with Palmyrene-Syriac, on the other, but there are other elements which are unique to this script.

About ten of the Hatran inscriptions are dated. The earliest bears the date "year 409" (= 97/8 A.D.) of the Seleucid Era, which began in October, 312 B.C. The script of this earliest dated inscription is already quite developed (Fig. 120). Unfortunately, there is no sufficient epigraphic material to indicate the earlier evolution of this script type. The latest

19. J. Naveh, The North-Mesopotamian Aramaic Script Type in the Late Parthian Period, *IOS* 2 (1972), pp. 293-294, n. 6; R. Degen, Weitere Inschriften aus Hatra (Nr. 281-335), *Neue Ephemeris für Semitische Epigraphik*, III, Wiesbaden 1978, pp. 67-111.

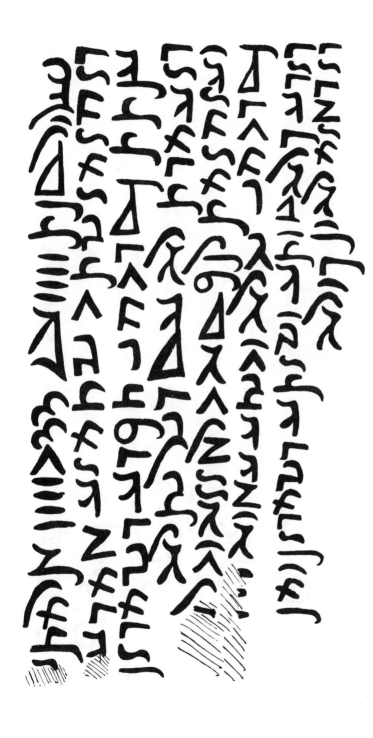

Fig. 121. Hatran inscription No. 35 from 238 A.D.

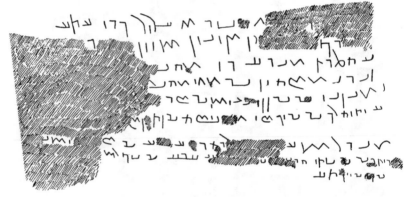

Fig. 122.
Inscription from Sari

Fig. 123. Inscription from Hassan-Kef

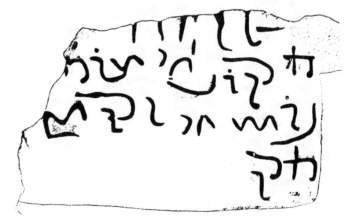

Fig. 124.
Inscription
of Garnı

140

dated inscriptions in Hatra are from 238 A.D. (Fig. 121);[20] it seems likely that soon after that date, Hatra was destroyed by the Sassanians, perhaps by Shapur I who became king in 240 A.D. Inscriptions written in this type of script were found not only in Hatra and its immediate vicinity, but also in Dura Europos on the Euphrates (Pl. 18:A) and in Assur on the Tigris. Moreover, the North Mesopotamian Aramaic script also spread to the North. Single inscriptions were discovered at two sites in Tur-ʿAbdin — Sari (Fig. 122) and Hassan-Kef (Fig. 123) — at Garni in Armenia (Fig. 124) and at Armazi in Georgia (see above, Fig. 114). All these inscriptions belong to the second half of the second century and the first half of the third century A.D.[21]

In the dated Hatran inscriptions, the evolution of the script can be followed for 140 years (98-238) during which time there were no significant changes. However, when we examine the scripts used in Tur-ʿAbdin, Armenia and Georgia, we can see substantial modifications in some letter forms (Fig. 125). These modifications were probably introduced in order to distinguish between various letters which had earlier assimilated: e.g. *he* and *ḥet*, or *gimel* and *ʿayin*. It seems likely that the Hatrans were bound to their script by tradition and therefore did not alter it; when the script was taken over by other centres, however, its users permitted themselves to introduce various changes in order to avoid confusion between similar letters. This usually meant the addition of a stroke, although sometimes the stance of a letter was shifted. In Armenia and Georgia single elements were adopted from other script types: at Garni there is a diacritic point on the *resh*, which was probably added under Syriac (or Palmyrene) influence; the Armazi script adopted *pe* and *shin* from the Parthian script.

The North Mesopotamian branch probably died out soon after the fall of the Parthian empire. None of the known inscriptions can be dated with certainty to the second half of the third century A.D. or later. Thus this script did not have time to develop a systematic ligatured form, nor did it, in common with the South Mesopotamian branch, have distinctive final

---

20. Naveh (above, n. 19), pp. 300-304, J. T. Milik, *Dédicaces faites par des dieux*, Paris 1972, pp. 353-366.
21. Naveh (above, n. 19), pp. 293-304.

Fig. 125. Development of the North Mesopotamian Aramaic script type: 1. Hatra, No. 214; 2. Hatra, No. 35; 3. Dura Europos bilingual inscription; 4. Assur; 5. 'Abrat al-Şaghīra; 6. Sari; 7. Hassan-Kef; 8. Garni; 9. Armazi

and medial letter forms. Apparently both branches developed from a common, formal prototype used for writing on stone. This assumption will be proven or refuted when the Mesopotamian soil provides us with Aramaic inscriptions from the second and first centuries B.C. Meanwhile, the scripts of the third-century B.C. Aramaic inscriptions of Aśoka (see above, p. 127) can perhaps be regarded as an early ancestor of this script type.

c. *The Palmyrene-Syriac branch*

After the Roman conquest of Syria, Palmyra, the oasis in the Syrian desert, became an important station on the trade route to the east. Forming part of the Roman empire, but located on the border of the Parthian empire, Palmyra amassed a fortune from taxes, customs and the safe conduct of trade caravans. The semi-nomadic Arabs who settled in Palmyra (and in Petra, Edessa and Hatra) adopted the Aramaic language and script, the *lingua franca* of the ancient world, and developed the script in their own way. Unlike the Nabataean, the Palmyrene and Syriac inscriptions generally have no Arab words or Arab linguistic features, and it has been suggested that the colloquial language in Palmyra and Edessa was Aramaic.

The earliest dated Palmyrene inscription is from 44 B.C. (Pl. 18:B).[22] Palmyrene inscriptions are known not only in the areas of modern Syria and north Iraq, but also in Egypt, Algeria, England, Italy, Hungary and Rumania, where isolated specimens have been discovered, indicating that persons of Palmyrene origin lived in every land in the Roman empire. Palmyra was destroyed in 272 and the latest Palmyrene inscriptions are from around that time.[23]

The Palmyrene inscriptions are mainly votive and burial inscriptions, and most of them were carved or incised on stone. A long bilingual Greek-Palmyrene inscription includes a list of customs tariffs on various goods. The script of these inscriptions is formal, and is generally termed

22. J. Starcky, Inscriptions archaïques de Palmyre, *Studi Orientalistici in onore di G. Levi della Vida*, II, Rome 1956, p. 510, Pl. I; F. M. Cross, The Development of the Jewish Script, *BANE*, p. 208, Fig. 6:2.
23. *CIS*, II Nos. 3901-4612; *Inventaire des inscriptions de Palmyre*, I-XII, Paris 1930-1975; D. Schlumberger, *La Palmyrène du Nord-Ouest*, Paris 1951.

Palmyrene monumental script (Fig. 126). However, the Palmyrenes also used cursive script, presumably for writing on papyrus and parchment. Although inscriptions on these perishable materials have not yet been found, the cursive script is known from grafitti and dipinti found at Dura Europos (Fig. 127)[24] and from a few inscriptions (Fig. 128).

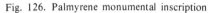

Fig. 126. Palmyrene monumental inscription

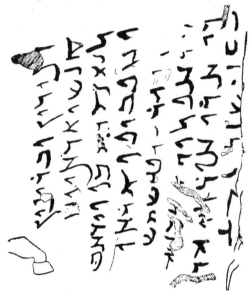

Fig. 127. Palmyrene dipinto at Dura Europos

24. R. du Mesnil du Buisson, *Inventaire des inscriptions palmyréniennes de Doura Europos*, Paris 1939. On the Palmyrene and Syriac custom of writing in ink vertically see J. Naveh, Syriac Miscellanea, 'Atiqot, English series 11 (1976), p. 103.

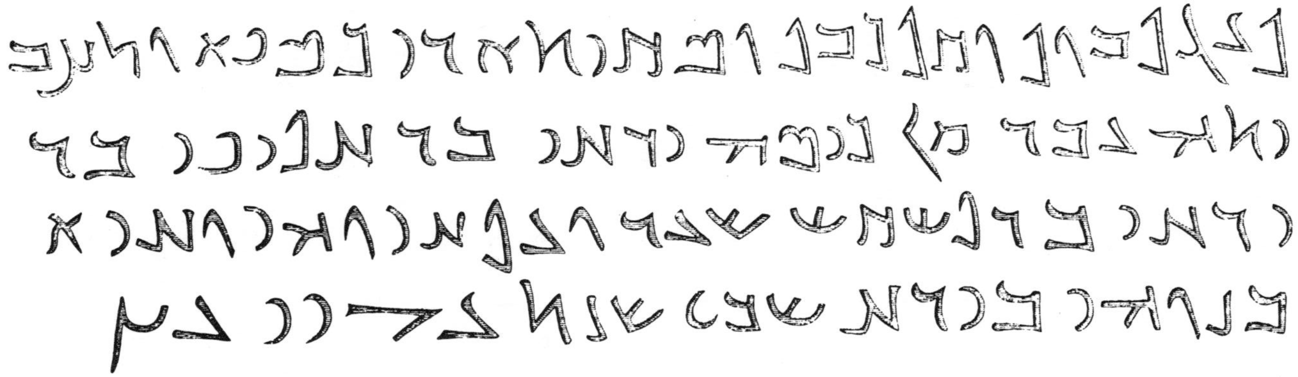

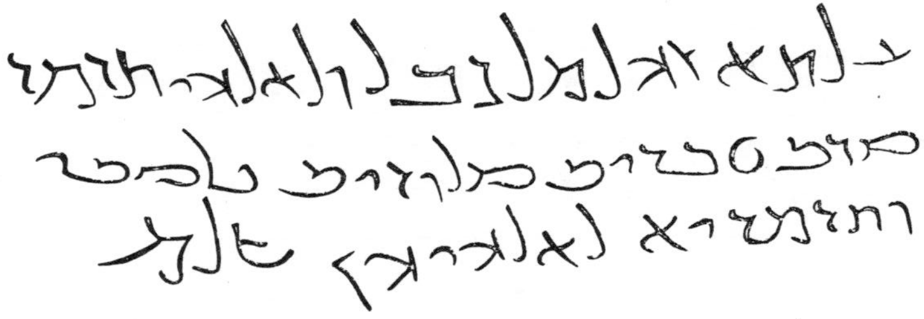

Fig. 128. Two Palmyrene cursive inscriptions
from Rome

Unattached	Joined to following letter	Joined to preceding and following letters	Joined to preceding letter	Estrangelā	Nestorian	Transliteration	Name
						'	'Ālaph
						b	Bēth
						g	Gāmal
						d	Dālath
						h	Hē
						w	Waw
						z	Zain
						ḥ	Ḥēth
						ṭ	Ṭēth
						y	Yūdh
						k	Kāph
						l	Lāmadh
						m	Mīm
						n	Nūn
						s	Semkath
						‘	‘Ē
						p	Pē
						ç	Çādhē
						q	Qōph
						r	Rēš
						š	Šīn
						t	Taw

Fig. 129. Syriac characters

Syriac is the language of the Syrian Christians whose centre was in Edessa (modern Urfa in South Turkey, near the border with Syria). Over a long period, numerous Christian manuscripts were written in this eastern Aramaic dialect and in the Syriac script. Tradition has it that the Syriac translation of the Bible, the Peshiṭta, originated in Edessa around 200 A.D. In Edessa, within the bounds of the Parthian empire, a people of Arab origin established a kingdom and later accepted Christianity, and Edessa became an important Christian centre. In the wake of schism in the Syrian Church, the Syriac script was also diversified. Best known are the following three types: *Estrangelo* (= "round script") which preserved the old, formal letters as they appear in the inscriptions; *Serto* (= "linear script"), a cursive style; and *Nestorian*, which can be described as a semi-formal script (Fig. 129).[25] The Syriac script was also employed by the Palestinian Christians, although they spoke in a western Aramaic dialect.[26] Today Syriac is the sacred language and script of what is called the "Assyrian" Church.

The earliest dated Syriac inscriptions are from 6 A.D. (from Birecik on the Euphrates, about 75 km. west of Edessa) and 73 A.D. (from Serrin, south-west of Edessa) (Figs. 130-131). From Dura Europos comes a legal

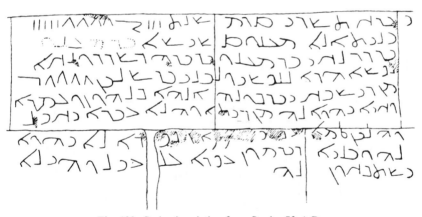

Fig. 130. Syriac inscription from Serrin, 73 A.D.

25. T. Nöldeke, *Compendious Syriac Grammar*, London 1904.
26. F. Schulthess, *Grammatik des christlich-palästinischen Aramäisch*, Tübingen 1924.

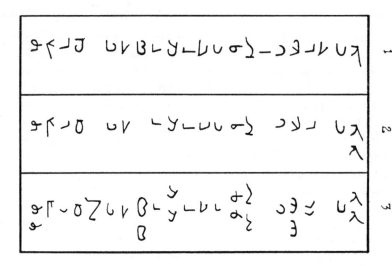

Fig. 131. Old Syriac characters.
1. Birecik, 6 A.D; 2. Serrin,
73 A.D.; 3. Sumatar, 165 A.D.

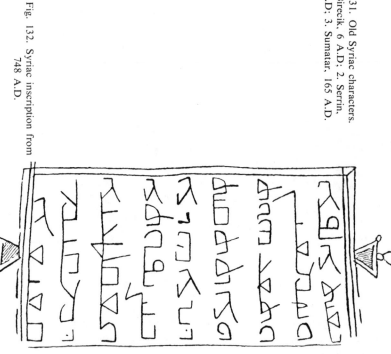

Fig. 132. Syriac inscription from
748 A.D.

document written on parchment in 243 A.D. (Pl. 19:A). A total of some seventy Old Syriac pagan texts are known to date.[27] There are also several scores of later Syriac inscriptions of Christian origin (Fig. 132; Pl. 19:B).

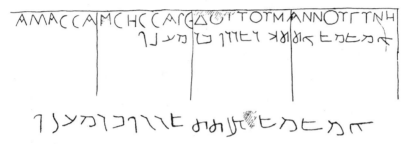

Fig. 133. Inscription of Amassamses

The close affinity between the Syriac and Palmyrene (mainly cursive Palmyrene) scripts has yet to to be properly explained. It has been convincingly argued that the inscription of Amassamses from Deir Yaʿqub near Edessa (Fig. 133), and another on the sarcophagus of "Ṣadan the queen" (probably Helene queen of Adiabene) from Jerusalem (Fig. 135) contain a mixture of Syriac and Palmyrene letter forms.[28] I would add to this category two other, rather longer, inscriptions: the so-called archaic Palmyrene inscription from Dura Europos, from 32 B.C. (Fig. 134), and the recently discovered inscription from el-Mal in South Syria from 7/6 B.C. (Fig. 136; Pl. 18:C). In these four inscriptions the script is neither Palmyrene nor Syriac, but most probably the surviving ancestral script from which both Syriac and Palmyrene evolved. This common ancestor, which can tentatively be called the 'Seleucid Aramaic' script must have existed between 250-100 B.C. as the cursive script employed by the Aramaeans in Syria and in the Seleucid state.[29] To date, no example of

27. H. J. W. Drijvers, *Old Syria (Edessean) Inscriptions*, Leiden 1972.

28. J. B. Segal, Some Syriac Inscriptions of the 2nd-3rd Century A.D., *BSOAS* 16 (1954), p. 31, n. 1; J. Pirenne, Aux origines de la graphie syriaque, *Syria* 40 (1963), pp. 101-105.

29. Cf. W. F. Albright, A Biblical Fragment from the Maccabaean Age: The Nash Papyrus, *JBL* 56 (1937), p. 171.

Fig. 134. Archaic inscription from Dura Europos

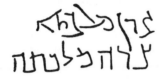

Fig. 135. Inscription of Ṣadan in "Syriac-Palmyrene" and in Jewish Aramaic

Fig. 136. Inscription from el-Mal

this early script has yet been found. However, the 'Seleucid Aramaic' script did not entirely disappear with the end of Seleucid rule. The four above-mentioned inscriptions (Dura Europos, el-Mal, Ṣadan and Amassamses) were written in this script in the first century B.C. and the first century A.D.[30]

The problem of the relationship between the Syriac and Palmyrene scripts is illustrated in another case. At Nippur and other Babylonian sites, bowls inscribed with Aramaic incantation texts from *c.* 600 A.D. have been found. They are witten in either Jewish or Mandaic characters or in a script reminiscent of Syriac but closer to the Palmyrene cursive.[31] This last-mentioned script on the magic bowls also resembles Manichaean writing, invented by Mani in the third century A.D. for writing sectarian texts in an Iranian dialect (Fig. 137). How did the cursive Palmyrene script reach Babylonia? Some scholars believe that the explanation lies in commercial links between Palmyra and Babylonia; for others, the answer is to be found in religious and cultural contacts.[32]

In an endeavour to understand the various offshoots of the East Aramaic script family, we suggest the following hypothesis. Unlike the western Aramaic scripts — Jewish and Nabataean — which followed a direct line of evolution from the (still uniform) third century B.C. Aramaic script, the eastern Aramaic scripts developed from a script which was presumably practised in the east in the third to first centuries B.C. This eastern prototype had two styles, formal and cursive. While the North Mesopotamian and the South Mesopotamian scripts followed the formal tradition, the Syrians and the Palmyrenes adopted the cursive style of the eastern script. (Monumental Palmyrene fossilized this cursive at a

30. J. Naveh, An Aramaic Inscription from El-Mal — A Survival of 'Seleucid Aramaic' Script, *IEJ* 25 (1975), pp. 117-123.
31. J. A. Montgomery, *Aramaic Incantation Texts from Nippur,* Philadelphia 1913; V. Hamilton, *Syriac Incantation Bowls,* Ann Arbor 1971.
32. Montgomery (above, n. 31), pp. 32-35; M. Lidzbarski, Die Herkunft der manichäischen Schrift, *Sitzungsberichte der Preussischen Akademie* 1916, pp. 1213-1222.

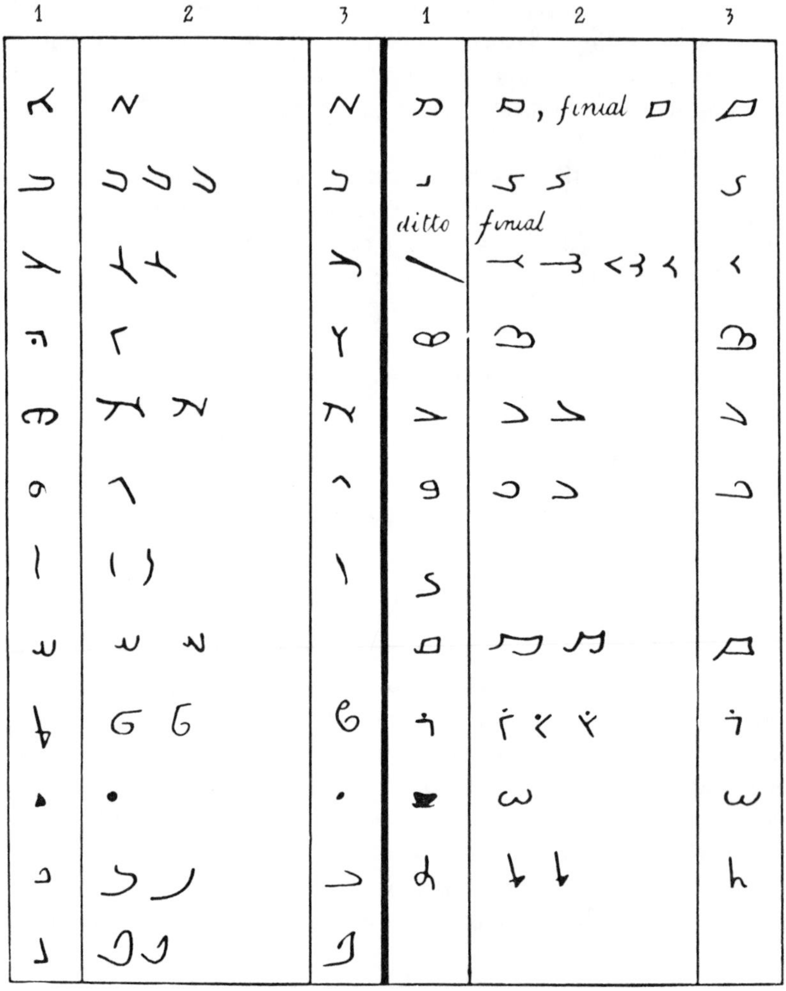
1 2 3 1 2 3
final
ditto
final

Fig. 137. Comparative table
of Estrangelo (1), script used on bowls (2), and Manichaean (3)

relatively early stage, perhaps in the first half of the first century B.C.). This eastern cursive (probably used in the Seleucid state), which was represented in the inscriptions from Dura and el-Mal and those of Sadan and Amassamses, continued to be used, presumably in some religious circles in Babylonia, and later by the Manichaean sect. The scripts on the Nippur bowls and in the Manichaean texts preserved earlier forms (closer to Palmyrene cursive), while the Syriac script, being primarily for use in secular daily life, underwent a relatively rapid development, and various alterations in letter forms took place. This reconstruction remains hypothetical until additional data become available, to support or challenge it.

3. *The Nabataean Script and the Rise of the Arabic Script*

While some Arab tribes settled in Hatra, Edessa and Palmyra, the Nabataean Arabs immigrated into the lands of biblical Edom and established their centre at Petra. However, whereas the former tribes are known only at the later stage, when their cities were already flourishing, there are some data on the early history of Arab settlement on the southern and south-eastern borders of Judah. In Nehemiah 2:19 and 6:1, a certain Geshem the Arab, or Gashmu, is mentioned among the rivals of Nehemiah. It seems likely that this person was the father of "Qainu, son of Geshem, king of Qedar", whose name is inscribed in Aramaic letters on a silver bowl dedicated to the Arab goddess Han-'Ilat, found at Tell el-Maskhuta in Wadi Tumilat (Egypt).[33] Aramaic ostraca from Arad and Beer-Sheba, from the mid-fourth century B.C. (Pl. 10:B), contain various names with the typical Arab suffix -u.[34] These Arabs also settled in Gaza and the towns to the south and east of Gaza. This explains the discovery, in the regions of northern Sinai and Raphia respectively, of a short Thamudic votive inscription from *c.* 500 B.C. (see chapter III, p. 47; Pl.

---

33. I. Rabinowitz, Aramaic Inscriptions of the Fifth Century B.C.E. from a North-Arab Shrine in Egypt, *JNES* 15 (1956), pp. 1-9; W. J. Dumbrell, The Tell el-Maskhuṭa Bowls and the 'Kingdom' of Qedar in the Persian Period, *BASOR* 203 (1971), pp. 33-44.
34. J. Naveh, The Aramaic Inscriptions from Tel Arad, *Arad Inscriptions* (ed. Y. Aharoni), Jerusalem 1981, pp. 153-176; idem, The Aramaic Ostraca from Tel Beer-Sheba (Seasons 1971-1976), *Tel-Aviv* 6 (1979), pp. 182-198; *IR*, Nos. 156-165.

2:C-D) and an Aramaic ostracon from *c.* 300 B.C., mentioning the (probably Arab) name ʿAbdmarʾan (Pl. 20:A).[35] It seems likely that on their arrival in this area, these Arabs wrote in their native (Thamudic) script, but that later, from the late fifth century onwards, they preferred to write in Aramaic. Diodorus Siculus informs us that in 312 B.C., when the Nabataeans dwelling in Petra fought against the Greeks, they sent a missive to their Greek adversaries written in Aramaic characters. All these data show that the Nabataeans and other Arab tribes adopted the uniform Aramaic script of the Persian period.

The earliest Nabataean inscription, found at Elusa in the Negev, mentions a certain "Aretas, the king of the Nabataeans" (Fig. 138). The script does not have Nabataean features; rather, it resembles the uniform Aramaic and the Jewish scripts. The inscription can be dated to the first half of the second century B.C., and the king mentioned should be identified with Aretas I who is described in 2 Macc. 5:8 as the Arab ruler with whom Jason sought refuge in Petra in 169 B.C. The votive inscription of Aṣlaḥ found in Petra bears the date "year 1 of Obodas, son of Aretas" (Fig. 139). From the script, in which only a few Nabataean elements occur, we can assume that the king mentioned is Obodas I (son of Aretas II), whose rule began in 95 B.C. Two other early Nabataean inscriptions are a dedication to El-Kutba from Wadi Tumilat, from 77 B.C., and an inscription on the statue of Rabbʾel I from Petra of 66 B.C. (Fig. 140).[36]

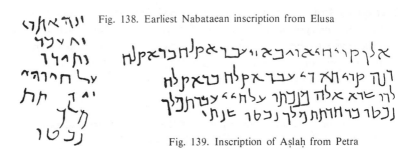

Fig. 138. Earliest Nabataean inscription from Elusa

Fig. 139. Inscription of Aṣlaḥ from Petra

35. J. Naveh, PHLṢ in a Recently Found Aramaic Ostracon, *Leshonenu* 37 (1973), pp. 270-274 (Hebrew, English summary).
36. Cross (above, n. 22), pp. 206-208, Figs. 6:1, 7:1-2.

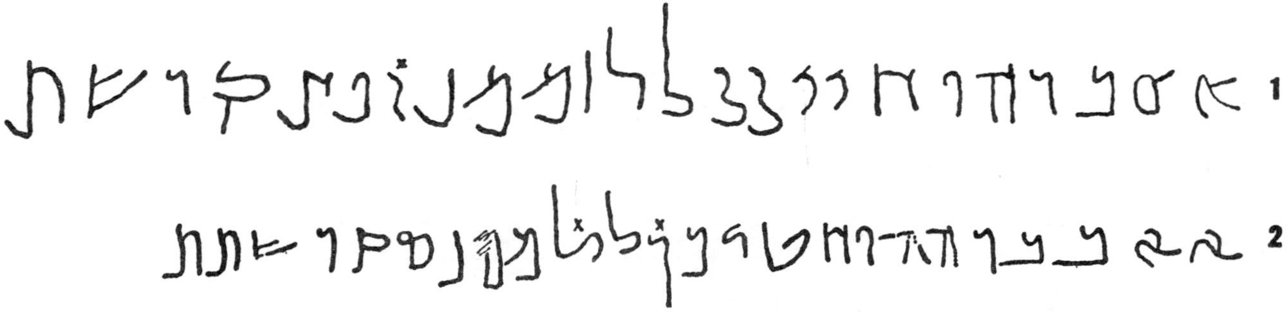

Fig. 140. Early Nabataean scripts: 1. The script of the El-Kutba inscription from Wadi Tumilat; 2. The script of the Rabb'el inscription.

Fig. 141. Nabataean monumental inscription

155

1	2	3	4	5	6	7

Fig. 142. Development of the Nabataean cursive script: 1. Elusa — *c.* 170 B.C.; 2. Aṣlaḥ — 95 B.C.; 3. Incantation text from Ḥ. Raqiq — *c.* 100 B.C.; 4. Wadi Tumilat — *c.* 77 B.C.; 5. Rabb'el — *c.* 66 B.C.; 6. Naḥal Ḥever, formal cursive — *c.* 100 A.D.; 7. Naḥal Ḥever, free cursive — *c.* 100 A.D.

An incantation text written in ink on a pebble from Ḥorvat Raqiq, northwest of Beer-Sheba represents the earliest Nabataean cursive script known so far; this should be dated around 100 B.C. (Pl. 20:B).[37] Later inscriptions show the characteristic development of this script, with a tendency to join letters and to curve the bars (Fig. 141).

Nabataean inscriptions, mainly burial and votive, have been found in Petra and in other Nabataean towns in Transjordan and the Negev, as well as at various sites in Egypt, North Arabia, Syria and even in Italy. Most of these inscriptions, and all the coins with Nabataean legends issued in Petra, antedate 106 A.D., the year in which the Romans abolished the Nabataean kingdom and annexed its territory to the Provincia Arabia. The remains of Jewish refugees who had fled from the Romans during the Second Jewish Revolt were discovered in a cave in Naḥal Ḥever, near the Dead Sea, together with Hebrew, Aramaic, Greek and Nabataean deeds written on papyrus. These documents bear exact dates: from the reign of Rabb'el II, the last Nabataean king, to the first years of Provincia Arabia (Pl. 22:A). Inscriptions later than 106 A.D. were found mainly in North Arabia.[38] The Nabataean inscriptions are written in the formal script, while the deeds from Naḥal Ḥever follow either the formal or the cursive style (Fig. 142). Nabataean cursive, which has many letter forms resembling the Arabic script, reached a well-developed stage in the late first century A.D., dispensing with certain bars and assuming a ligatured form.

A wealth of examples of the Nabataean script at the time of the Provincia Arabia can be found in the thousands of graffiti on rock faces in various wadis in Sinai. These short inscriptions, generally consisting of names and a short formula of blessing, are called Sinaitic inscriptions. Most of these texts were copied and published in line drawings about a hundred years ago (Fig. 143), but recent photographs reproduce more reliably the characteristics of the script (Pl. 21). The graffiti belong to the

---

37. J. Naveh, A Nabataean Incantation Text, *IEJ* 29 (1979), pp. 111-119.
38. G. A. Cooke, *A Text-Book of North-Semitic Inscriptions*, Oxford 1903, pp. 214-262; J. Cantineau, *Le Nabatéen*, I-II, Paris 1930-1932; Y. Yadin, Expedition D — The Cave of the Letters, *IEJ* 12 (1962), pp. 238-246; Y. Meshorer, Nabataean Coins, *Qedem* 3 (1975).

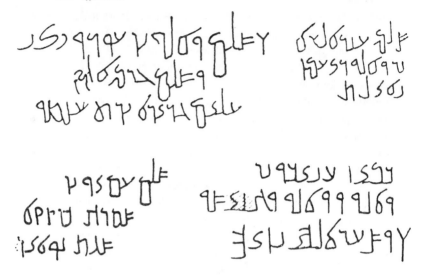

Fig. 143. Rock inscriptions from Sinai

second and third centuries A.D.; their script is generally formal, but influenced by the cursive.[39]

The language of the Nabataean inscriptions and documents is Official Aramaic, but it absorbed Arabic words and forms. Obviously, the Nabataeans spoke Arabic, and the vast majority of the persons mentioned have Arabic names. In the course of time, the Arabic elements in the language of the Nabataean inscriptions gradually increased. At Ḥejra in North Arabia there was found a burial inscription bearing the date "year 162" according to the era of Provincia Arabia, that is, 267 A.D. This is a bilingual inscription: next to the longer Nabataean text, the name of the deceased is written in Thamudic D characters (see above, p. 46; Fig. 39). The Nabataean text is written in what amounts to a mixed language, containing many Arab words and forms.[40] Another burial in-

---

39. *CIS*, II, Nos. 490-3233; A. Negev, New Dated Nabatean Graffiti from the Sinai, *IEJ* 17 (1967), pp. 250-255, Pl. 48; idem, A Nabatean Sanctuary at Jebel Moneijah, Southern Sinai, *IEJ* 27 (1977), pp. 219-231, Pls. 31-35.
40. Cantineau (above, n. 38), II, pp. 38-39.

scription dating from 328 A.D., found at Namara in the Ḥauran, mentions "Imruʾlqais, son of ʿAmru the king of all the Arabs", and is written in fairly developed Nabataean characters, although the language is Arabic (Fig. 144).[41] The latest dated inscription in this series was written in Nabataean Aramaic in Ḥejra in 356 A.D. (Fig. 145).[42]

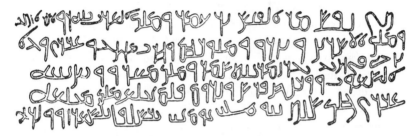

Fig. 144. The Namara inscription

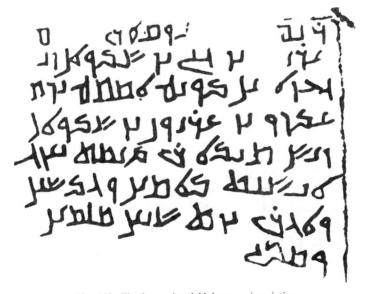

Fig. 145. The latest dated Nabataean inscription

41. Cantineau (above, n. 38), II, pp. 49-50.
42. Altheim and Stiehl (above, n. 17), V/1, pp. 305-309, Abb. 54.

No fifth-century Nabataean inscriptions are yet known, but there do exist three sixth-century Arabic inscriptions which represent an early stage of the Arabic script. Among these pre-Islamic Arabic inscriptions there is a trilingual (Greek-Syriac-Arabic) inscription from Zebed, dated to 512 A.D., a bilingual inscription (Greek-Arabic) from Ḥarran (568 A.D.) and an undated one from Umm el-Jimal which should also be dated to the sixth century A.D. (Fig. 146).[43]

There is clearly a strong link between the script of these three pre-Islamic inscriptions, on the one hand, and those of the fourth-century Nabataean inscriptions, the Sinai graffiti and, especially, the cursive scripts of the Nabataean deeds from Naḥal Ḥever, on the other. Nevertheless, Starcky suggested in 1964 that the Arabic script did not

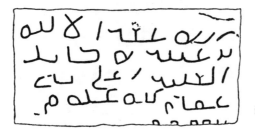

Fig. 146. Pre-Islamic Arabic inscriptions from Zebed, Ḥarran and Umm el-Jimal

43. N. Abbott, *The Rise of the North Arabic Script and its Kuranic Development*, Chicago 1931, pp. 1-16, Pl. I.

develop from Nabataean but from the Syriac cursive.[44] However, the generally accepted opinion that the Arabic script is a direct offshoot of Nabataean cannot be refuted; palaeographic evidence would corroborate this view.[45]

In the Islamic period, the Arabic script was used primarily for writing the Quran. In addition to the Kufic style (straight lines and sharp angles, employed mainly for writing on stone), there developed the Naskhi style, which was the most popular and is still in use today. After adoping the Arabic script, the Persians developed another style called Ta'liq. Whatever the individual style, the Arabic script preserved the horizontal shading, thereby adhering to a tradition which had begun in Aramaic writing as early as the eighth century B.C. Since copying the Quran was the primary function of the Arab scribes who wrote in calligraphy, the calligrapher was an artist in the truest sense, and his craft was the first which can be called a wholly Moslem art. His profession always remained one of the utmost dignity and prestige, and his work was copied onto ceramics, wood, metal objects, textiles and stone.

In the cursive Nabataean documents from Nahal Hever, there was already an assimilatory tendency between some pairs of letters: *bet* and *nun, gimel* and *het, zayin* and *resh, yod* and *taw, pe* and *qof.* This meant that a reader of early Arabic writing had to distinguish between various letters according to the context. Moreover, as the consonantal system of the Arabic language is richer than that of the Aramaic, Arab writers had to express 28 consonants using the 22 letters which existed in the Aramaic-Nabataean script. Thus, in order to make reading easier, diacritic marks were introduced to differentiate between various sounds: ـب (b), ـن (n), ـت (t), ـث (ṯ), and ـي (y) in initial or medial positions [in final position there are different forms for n (ن) and y (ي)]; ج (ǧ), ح (ḥ) and خ (ḫ); د (d) and ذ (ḏ); ر (r) and ز (z); ص (ṣ) and ض (ḍ); ط (ṭ) and ظ (ẓ); ع (') and غ (ġ); ف (f) and ق (q); س (s) and ش (š).

As a result of the cursive development, the Arabic script is ligatured. Most letters have different final forms, on the one hand, and initial and

44. J. Starcky, Petra et la Nabatène, *Dictionnaire de la Bible, Supplément* 7, Paris 1964, cols. 932-934.
45. Naveh (above, n. 18), p. 32, n. 3.

medial forms, on the other: the letter *ha* has three different forms: initial, medial and final. Some letters — *'alif, dal, dal, ra, za* and *wau* are not ligatured with the letters that follow. Early signs of the process which led to these developments are already apparent in the cursive Nabataean script of the Naḥal Ḥever documents.

The Arabic alphabetic order differs from West Semitic and does not follow the Ethiopic order (see above, p. 51). It seems likely that the Arabic letter sequence is based on similarities between the letter forms and the sounds represented by the various letters. However, the Arabs also use the twenty-two letters to denote numeric values (as in Hebrew) from 1 to 400, with the six additional consonantal signs designating numbers up to 1000: ث = 500, خ = 600, ذ = 700, ض = 800, ظ = 900 and غ = 1000.

4. *The Jewish Script*

In the Persian period the Aramaic language and script were also used widely by Jews, since Aramaic was the main language of administration and trade. But Hebrew was still spoken by a considerable proportion of the people. At that time there was a strong link between each language and its script. Hebrew texts were written in the Hebrew script, and Aramaic texts in the uniform Aramaic script. In the Hellenistic Age, however, when each of the various peoples developed the Aramaic script in their own way, the Jews created from it a specifically Jewish script, that is, a new national script of their own. At this stage the Jews also began to write Hebrew texts in this Jewish (originally Aramaic) script (for a discussion of the change of scripts among the Jews, see above, pp. 112 ff.).

Until the discovery of the Dead Sea Scrolls in 1947, the Nash papyrus was the oldest biblical manuscript representing the Jewish script in the early stage of its development (Fig. 147). This document, which was found in Egypt, is a partly damaged text of the Ten Commandments written on papyrus. In 1937 Albright suggested that it should be dated to the Hasmonaean period (165-37 B.C.), and preferably to the second half of the second century B.C.[46] The principal inscriptions known at that time

46. Albright (above, n. 29), pp. 145-176.

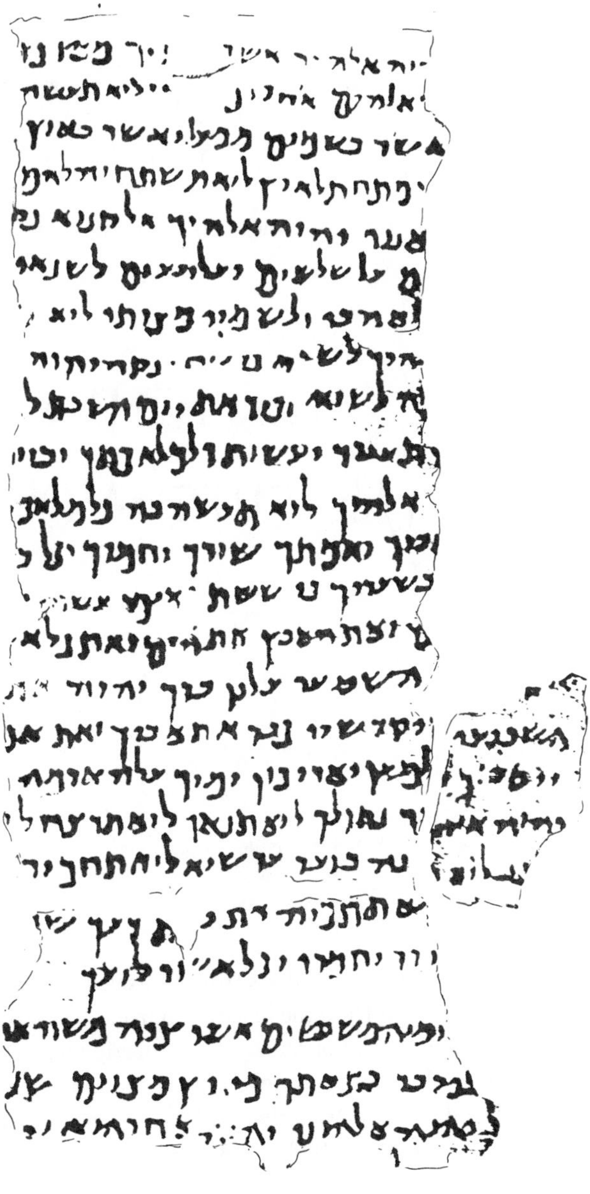

Fig. 147. The Nash Papyrus

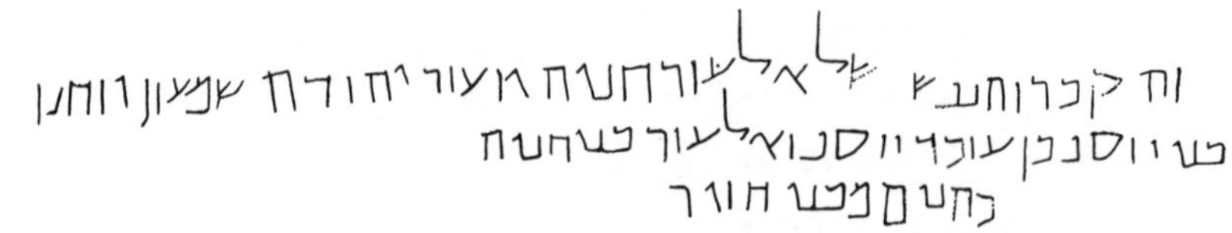

Fig. 148. The Ḥezir family tomb inscription

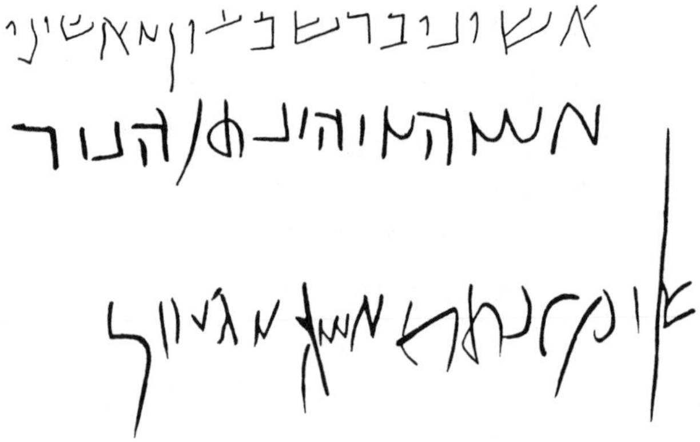

Fig. 149. Ossuary inscriptions

were some Jewish burial inscriptions from Jerusalem, such as the epitaph of king Uzziah (Pl. 23:A) and the inscription from the Ḥezir family tomb (Fig. 148), as well as scores of mostly short inscriptions or graffiti on ossuaries (Fig. 149).[47] These tomb inscriptions are thought to predate the end of Jewish settlement in Jerusalem in 70 A.D. and are generally dated to the Herodian period (37 B.C.-70 A.D.).

47. *IR*, Nos. 170, 173, 255-261.

The Dead Sea Scrolls contain biblical and other religious manuscripts written by the Dead Sea sect (Pls. 14:C-D; 23:B). They do not bear dates, but the scholars who studied them were able to conclude from palaeographic evidence that the scrolls were more or less contemporary with the above-mentioned burial inscriptions, that is, that the scrolls are to be dated to the later part of the Second Temple period. The excavations in Kh. Qumran, where the remains of a building associated with the scroll caves were found, confirmed the date. Around 70 A.D., the building was abandoned by the Dead Sea sect, or destroyed; but before they left the settlement, the sectarians endeavoured to conceal their holy scriptures in the nearby caves. However, since neither the biblical nor the sectarian manuscripts bear dates, scholars searched for historical clues in the literary works written by the sectarians, in order to fix a more exact time. As for dating the biblical texts, palaeography remains the primary criterion. Systematic palaeographic studies — mainly by Avigad and Cross — surveyed the development of the Jewish script against the background of the fifth- to third-century Aramaic scripts.[48] The early evolution of the Jewish script was divided by Cross into three phases: Archaic, or Proto-Jewish (*c.* 250-150 B.C.), Hasmonaean (*c.* 150-30 B.C.) and Herodian (*c.* 30 B.C.-70 A.D.). The various scripts were classified by Cross into four categories: (1) the formal character: essentially the successor of the late Persian Aramaic chancellery hand; (2) the semi-formal character: a subtype of the formal hand, showing the influence of the third-century B.C. Aramaic cursive on the formal character (Fig. 150); (3) the cursive hand: the successor of the early third-century B.C. Aramaic cursive; and (4) the semi-cursive: an intermediate script formed by the crossing of formal script types and the developed cursives. However, we must always bear in mind that a description of the script types, or of the writing styles, is mainly an auxiliary tool for dating the various scripts on the basis of palaeographic typology. Cross suggested dating two biblical manuscripts, found in Cave IV at Qumran, to the

48. F. M. Cross, The Oldest Manuscript from Qumran, *JBL* 74 (1955), pp. 147-172; N. Avigad, The Palaeography of the Dead Sea Scrolls and Related Documents, *Scripta Hierosolymitana* 4 (1957), pp. 56-87; Cross (above, n. 22), pp. 170-264.

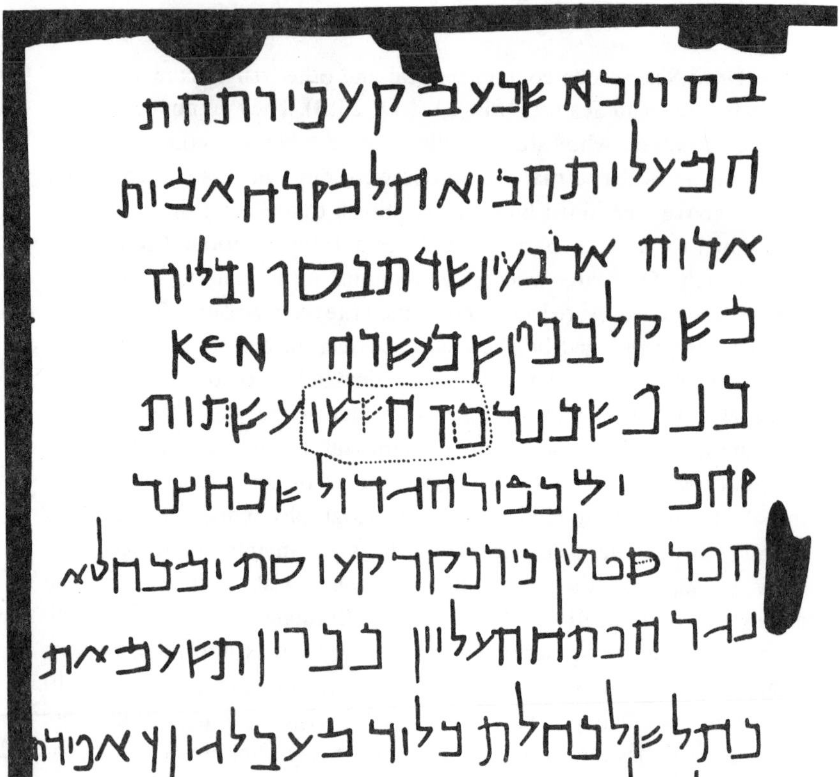

Fig. 150. Vulgar semi-formal script of the Copper Scroll

second half of the third century B.C. The script of an Exodus scroll fragment was identified as an archaic proto-Jewish hand of the mid-third century B.C., which includes letter forms evolving into the early Jewish cursive character. The script of some fragments from the Book of Samuel
was described by Cross as a proto-Jewish formal hand of the late third
century B.C. (see above, Fig. 100, lines 2-3). Even if these dates seem
very early, we are inclined to accept them because of the close affinities
between the scripts on these scroll fragments, on the one hand, and the
Aramaic formal and cursive letter forms in the fourth and third centuries
B.C., on the other. These early Jewish manuscripts indicate that towards
the end of the third century B.C. — that is, before the Hasmonaean
period — the Jews wrote Hebrew texts, or more precisely, Hebrew
biblical texts, in the Jewish script (see above, pp. 121 ff.).

After the discovery of the Dead Sea Scrolls, first Bedouin and then
archaeologists began to explore other caves in the vicinity of the Dead
Sea. Additional Jewish manuscripts came to light in two caves in Wadi
Murabbaʿat and in Naḥal Ḥever. These are mainly papyri consisting of
dispatches sent by Bar Kokhba and his officers (Pl. 22:B) and legal documents that belonged to Jewish refugees who had fled from the Romans at
the time of the Second Revolt and sought refuge in these caves (Pl. 22:C).
In the so-called "Cave of the Letters" in Naḥal Ḥever there were found
various domestic utensils and a bundle of deeds which the refugees had
brought there when they abandoned the nearby village of Ein Gedi. The
legal documents bear dates in the second century A.D., prior to the year
135 A.D., which saw the tragic end of Bar Kokhba's revolt and of the
refugees' own struggle. These manuscripts represent the various styles of
the Jewish script. Most of the messages are written in the cursive Jewish
script[49] which has some affinities with the Nabataean script. It should be
remembered that while the Nabataean monumental script absorbed cursive traits, the Jewish book-hand was hardly influenced at all by cursive
writing. The same is true in later times — indeed, it can be said that the
Jewish formal script did not undergo any significant changes in the course

49. J. T. Milik in P. Benoit et alii, *Les grottes de Murabbaʿat* (Discoveries in the
Judaean Desert, II) Oxford 1961; Y. Yadin, *Bar-Kokhba*, Jerusalem 1971;
IR, Nos. 187-194.

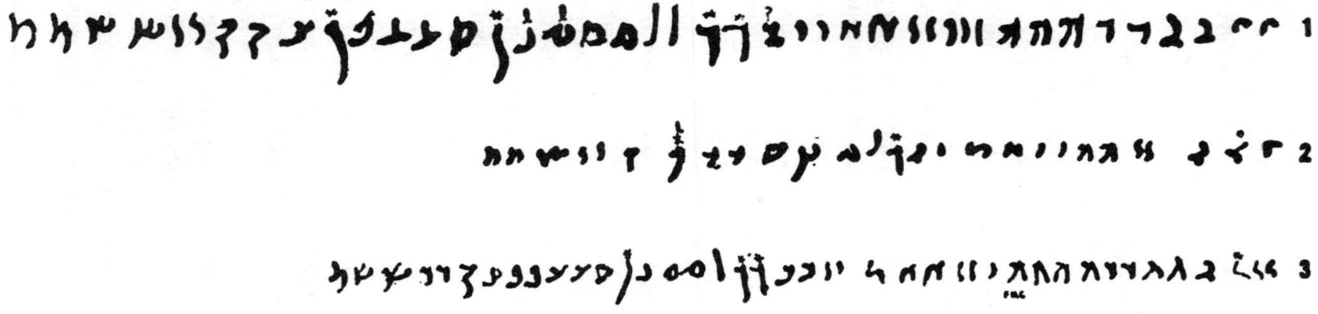

Fig. 151. Herodian and post-Herodian cursive scripts: 1. An Aramaic contract written on papyrus in 55/56 A.D. from Wadi Murabba'at; 2. An Aramaic marriage contract from 117 A.D. from Murabba'at; 3. Semi-cursive hand from an Aramaic contract of sale from 134 A.D.

of two millennia. Hence an Israeli schoolboy has no difficulty in reading the texts of the Dead Sea Scrolls. The Jewish cursive manuscripts, however, are unintelligible to all but the trained scholar. Since the Jewish book-hand was used mainly for writing the Holy Scriptures, it became a very conservative script. The cursive script, on the other hand, was always only a practical instrument, used for rapid and even hasty writing, so that it came to resemble shorthand. While the Jewish formal script survived through the ages, the cursive hand, which developed in the Second Temple period, can be traced only until the time of Bar Kokhba (Fig. 151). This cursive tradition apparently ceased to exist shortly after the defeat of the Bar Kokhba revolt. However, Jews continued to use the Jewish script for daily communication and thus developed new cursive scripts at various times and in various centres.

The extant Jewish epigraphic material produced after 135 A.D. falls into two groups: burial inscriptions, found mainly in Beth-She'arim (Fig. 152), Jaffa and Zoar (on the southern shore of the Dead Sea), and synagogue inscriptions, discovered at various sites in Palestine;[50] the latter

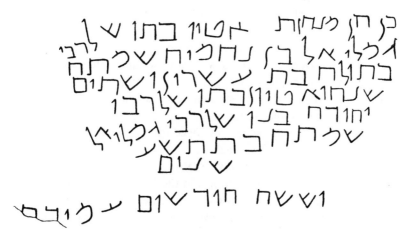

Fig. 152. Inscription on sarcophagus from Beth She'arim

50. J. B. Frey, *Corpus Inscriptionum Judaicarum*, II, Rome 1952; J. Naveh, *On Stone and Mosaic, The Aramaic and Hebrew Synagogue Inscriptions*, Jerusalem 1978 (Hebrew); *IR*, Nos. 172, 183-186.

dating mainly from the period between the fourth and the seventh centuries A.D. The main votive inscription from the synagogue of Dura Europos bears a date (245 A.D.); others can be dated by virtue of the fact that they were found under an embankment built in 256 A.D. when Dura Europos was besieged.[51] The Zoar epitaphs bear dates in the early fifth century A.D. (Fig 153).[52] At Nippur and other sites in Babylonia, Jewish incantation texts, probably from around 600 A.D., have been found.[53] Most of the above-mentioned inscriptions appear on stone, although many synagogue inscriptions were set into mosaic floors (Fig. 154; Pl. 23:C). The incantation texts were written in ink on bowls. The script used in all the above-mentioned inscriptions is formal and most of the texts do not bear dates. Dating such a conservative script by means of palaeographic criteria is difficult and sometimes impossible.

When discussing the (old) Hebrew script, we pointed out two characteristics: a conservativeness and an absence of lapidary script tradition. These traits are also found in the Jewish script. Neither in the period of the First Temple nor later was there a widespread custom of setting up monumental inscriptions. On the occasions when such inscriptions were written, the formal script was regarded as adequate. Thus the epitaph describing the burial-place of the bones of king Uzziah of Judah (Pl. 23:A), was engraved in the Herodian period in the same characters used for writing the Dead Sea Scrolls. Virtually the same letters were used in the synagogue inscriptions, whether carved in stone or set into mosaic pavements, three hundred or six hundred years later.

As we have seen, the Nabataean script evolved from a cursive tradition, whereas the Jewish script developed from the Aramaic book-hand. Both scripts have distinctive final letters. While in the Nabataean script and — especially — its derivative, the Arabic script, almost every letter has different medial and final forms, in the Jewish script there are only five differentiated final forms. Most of the latter are, in fact, the original forms. In the Persian period *kaf, mem, nun, pe* and *ṣade* were written with

51. Naveh (above, n. 50), Nos. 88-89.
52. *IR*, No. 174.
53. Montgomery (above, n. 31); C. D. Isbell, *Corpus of the Aramaic Incantation Bowls*, Missoula (Montana) 1975.

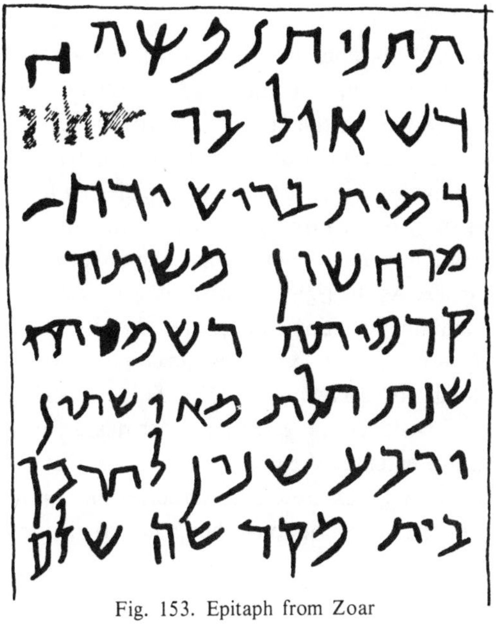

תחנעתתלקשה ה
וש אול עד אאוג
רמית בריש ירח
מרחשון משתה
קדמיתא רשמיתא
שנת תלת מאן שתין
וארבע שנען לחרבן
בית קדשה שלם

Fig. 153. Epitaph from Zoar

Fig. 154. Inscription on mosaic floor from the synagogue of Hamath Gader

long downstrokes. With time, these downstrokes began to shorten and to curve toward the next letter in the word, eventually evolving into the medial forms. However, at the end of a word, the writer slowed down, and did not curve the downstroke of the last letter, so that the long downstrokes survived in final forms. This applies to four of the Jewish final letters; the story of the fifth letter, *mem*, is only slightly different. The *mem* in the Persian period had two downstrokes, a longer right stroke and a shorter left stroke. As the right downstroke was drawn first, it was bent both in medial and final positions; but the left downstroke curved leftward only in medial position. This led to the development of the medial open *mem* and the final closed *mem* (Fig. 155). These specific features of the Nabataean and Jewish scripts, and to a lesser degree, of the Palmyrene-Syriac branch, are essentially cursive traits. Since the North and South Mesopotamian script types grew out of the formal Aramaic script employed mainly for stone inscriptions, they have no distinctive medial and final letter forms.

Fig. 155. Development of the five medial and final letters:
1. 5th-century B.C. Aramaic; 2. 1st-century B.C. Jewish; 3. Modern Hebrew

The Jewish script accompanied the Jews throughout the ages in all the communities of the Diaspora. In the Medieval Jewish script three styles can be distinguished: the formal book-hand, the semi-formal or rabbinic script, and the cursive script. The book-hand preserved its original form. Although there were differences between the Babylonian, Persian, Yemenite, Sephardic (Spanish), Italian, Ashkenazi, etc. scribal traditions, these were based on minor local characteristics, and the letter form remained essentially unchanged. The semi-formal was used mainly for writing commentaries on the Holy Scriptures and hence is called rabbinic; for instance, the Rashi script (Fig. 156) is a medieval semi-formal script

אבגדהוזחטיכךלמ
סכנספעפצדקרשת

Fig. 156. Rashi script

אבגדהוזחטיכךלמנסעפצקרשת

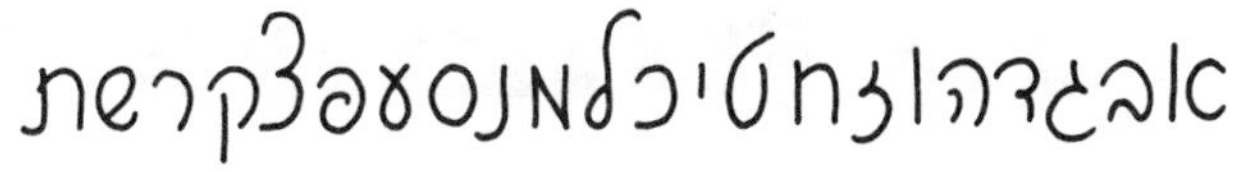

Fig. 157. Modern Hebrew cursive

developed in Italy. The cursive script was employed in daily life. A variety of Jewish cursive scripts, all stemming from the Jewish book-hand developed at various periods and in many centres. The generally accepted modern Hebrew cursive is a derivative of the Ashkenazi cursive, which began to evolve in Central and Eastern Europe in the sixteenth or seventeenth century (Fig. 157).[54]

Since the formal Jewish script was used by scribes for two millennia to write the Holy Scriptures, the ancient scribal tradition which they

54. S. A. Birnbaum, *The Hebrew Scripts*, Leiden 1971, Nos. 349-365.

followed was considered to be a religious practice. Thus they almost un-
failingly emphasized the horizontal lines, a method of shading which
follows a very ancient tradition. When the Aramaean scribes in the eighth
century B.C. wrote in ink, they held the pen in such a way that the
horizontal lines were drawn more thickly than the others. This form of
shading survived in every ink-written formal script which evolved from
the Aramaic, and is also clearly visible in the Arabic, Syriac and Mandaic
writings, as well as in Jewish, Arabic and Syriac printed lettering. Thus
the horizontal shading forms an integral part of the Jewish formal script.
(It most likely helped to preserve the square form of this script, which today is known mostly as "square Hebrew".) Although the tradition of
horizontal shading was preserved by Jews for two millennia, today we
can discern the first steps of a deviation from ancient tradition: in Israeli
newspapers many headlines are printed with letters of equally thickened
strokes, and advertisements often use square Hebrew letters with vertical
shading (Fig. 158); on most signboards in Israel, the Hebrew letters have

קורס ארצי
להכשרת מנחים
במשחקיות

Fig. 158. Vertical shading in modern Hebrew lettering

thickened downstrokes, just like the Latin letters on the English part of
the sign. (Only in the ultra-orthodox neighbourhoods of Israeli towns,
such as Mea-She'arim in Jerusalem, do people refrain from this innova-
tion.) This development is a clear reflection of the tendency in this generation to abandon ancient tradition and absorb foreign (either European or
American) cultural values. This process can be be discerned in many
spheres of life, but the recent developments in modern Hebrew script are
a striking illustration of the phenomenon.

VI. THE ANTIQUITY OF THE GREEK ALPHABET

The Greek alphabet and its principal offshoot, the Latin script, belong to classical rather than to Semitic studies. However, since the origin of the Greek alphabet and its derivation from the Semitic alphabetic script can be discussed only on the basis of a thorough knowledge of the evolution of the Semitic scripts, the problem of the antiquity of the Greek alphabet should be regarded as an intermediate field, relating to both Semitic and Greek epigraphy.

There is a consensus among scholars regarding the West Semitic origin of the Greek alphabet; however, its earliest use among the Greeks is still a subject of controversy. The consensus is based on four points:

(a) According to Greek tradition, the alphabetic characters — named *phoinikeia grammata* (Phoenician letters) or *kadmeia grammata* (the letters of Kadmos) — were introduced together with other arts by the Phoenicians who came to Greece with a person named Kadmos.
(b) The names of the letters, *alpha, beta, gamma, delta*, etc. have no meaning in Greek, but most of their Semitic equivalents, *alef, bet, gimel, dalet*, etc. are Semitic words.
(c) The letter sequence in the Greek alphabet is basically identical to the Phoenician (= Hebrew and Aramaic) alphabetical order.
(d) The earliest Greek letter forms are very similar, and some even identical, to the equivalent West Semitic letters.

"Obviously the Greek alphabet must have branched off from the Semitic at the point where the chronologically contemporary resemblances are strongest, i.e. where the two sets of alphabets most nearly agree in the forms of letters." This generally accepted statement was made by Rhys Carpenter in 1933.[1] Its application, however, is a matter of scholarly controversy. Moreover, there are certain other epigraphic traits which have to be taken into consideration. The main characteristics of the archaic Greek alphabet can be summarized as five points:

(1) The earliest Greek inscriptions known today belong to the eighth century B.C.

(2) The archaic Greek script used the twenty-two West Semitic letters, some of which designated vowels, and gradually introduced five supplementary letters: Y, then Φ, X, Ψ and finally, Ω.

(3) The archaic Greek script was not uniform — it had some local variations.

(4) It was lapidary in style.

(5) The direction of writing and the letter stances were not stable. The archaic Greeks wrote in horizontal lines, either from right to left, or from left to right, or in horizontal boustrophedon.

Some scholars maintain that the deviations from the West Semitic prototype, mainly the introduction of vowel letters and supplementary letters, and the alteration of some letter forms, must have taken place over a considerable period. It is assumed that at a former stage, prior to the eighth century B.C., the Greek alphabet was closer to the West Semitic and that the archaic Greek script in the earliest known inscriptions was itself the result of an evolution. Nowadays there is little support for such a theory of a standard Greek 'Uralphabet'. Carpenter, who dates the Greek adoption of the alphabet to the second half of the eighth century, states that "the *argumentum a silentio* [i.e. the fact that no Greek inscription pre-dating the eighth century has yet been discovered] grows every year more formidable and more conclusive."[2]

The adoption of the alphabet by the Greeks is a complex problem. In studying it, scholars also take into consideration the Homeric question and the first witnessed date of the Olympic games (776 B.C.); in addition, they seek to determine the actual place at which the Greeks could have

1. Rhys Carpenter, The Antiquity of the Greek Alphabet, *AJA* 37 (1933), p. 10.
2. *Ibid.*, p. 27.

adopted the Semitic alphabet. The results seem to corroborate the assumption that the Greeks learned the Phoenician alphabet in the eighth century B.C. At that time, following three hundred years of decay in the wake of the Dorian invasion (*c.* 1100 B.C.), Greece once again began to flourish and there is evidence of commercial contacts between Phoenicians and Greeks. However, the problem centres mainly on epigraphic indications. Although we cannot demonstrate that Greek inscriptions existed earlier that the eighth century B.C., a comparative analysis of the characteristic traits of the West Semitic script and those of archaic Greek writing, leads to the assumption that the Greek borrowing of the alphabet should be dated some three hundred years earlier than the earliest known Greek inscriptions.

True, the "argument from silence" cannot be disregarded; but how conclusive is it? The Hebrews adopted the alphabet in the twelfth or eleventh century B.C., but only one Hebrew inscription — the Gezer Calendar (which may, in fact, be Phoenician) — is known to be older than the eighth century B.C. Although it is likely that the Hebrew script was widely used in the ninth century, even by Israel's eastern neighbours (cf. the Mesha inscription), virtually no ninth-century Hebrew inscriptions are known to date. The Aramaeans began to use the alphabet slightly later than the Hebrews, but all we know of are a few early Aramaic inscriptions. However, from the eighth century onward, the number of Hebrew and Aramaic inscriptions gradually increases, testifying to the spread of writing. The progress of literacy in Greece was probably very similar to that in the East.

It is commonly held that the Greeks adopted the Semitic practice of writing from right to left and that the earliest Greek inscriptions followed this practice; according to this view, the Greeks subsequently wrote in boustrophedon, and then from left to right. But Lilian Jeffery, who argues for an initial date in the mid-eighth century, has pointed out that all three systems existed concurrently even at the early stage of archaic Greek writing. She also maintains that boustrophedon writing "simply implies a pictorial conception of letters as outlined figures which can be turned in either direction according to need".[3] This means that if the Greeks adopt-

3. L. H. Jeffery, *The Local Scripts of Archaic Greece*, Oxford 1961, p. 46.

ed the Phoenician alphabet in the eighth century, when it was already a systematic linear script (see above, pp. 53 ff.), they neglected its achievements and turned it into a more primitive, almost pictographic script. Thus we have to look for a West Semitic model in which vertical writing ceased to exist, but the left-to-right direction of writing as well as horizontal boustrophedon were still in use. This stage of evolution is represented by the Proto-Canaanite script of the late twelfth century and first half of the eleventh century B.C., i.e. just before right-to-left writing became the standard practice, around 1050 B.C.

The Greek letters are considerably less cursive than the eighth- or even ninth-century Pheonician letters. This cannot be explained merely by the fact that most of the archaic Greek inscriptions known to date are graffiti and unofficial texts that were written on stone and pottery. The Greeks must have borrowed their script from a lapidary Semitic prototype. It is hardly conceivable that they did so in the eighth century and yet ignored most of the cursive achievements of the Phoenician script. A more plausible assumption is that the Greeks adopted a lapidary style of writing because it was the only existing model.

The most ancient Greek inscriptions known today, i.e. those from the eighth century, include inscribed vases from Athens (Fig. 159) and Mount Hymettos, inscribed sherds from Corinth (Fig. 160) and rock-cut inscriptions from Thera (Fig. 161).[4] In the scripts of these early texts and in the other archaic inscriptions down to the fifth century B.C., local variations are discernable. These local scripts were in use until the fourth century B.C., when the Ionian was adopted universally and became the classical Greek script. In all the archaic local scripts, *alpha, epsilon* and *omicron* were used as signs for *a, e* and *o*, respectively, whereas *iota* before or after a consonant indicated *i*. *Upsilon* — the first supplementary letter — denoted the vowel *u*. The direction of writing and letter profiles were erratic in all the local scripts (Pl. 24:A). Only from the fourth century onwards, when the archaic local scripts were replaced by the uniform classical script, did left-to-right writing with fixed letter forms become common practice for all Greeks.

4. *Ibid.*, Pls. 1:1, 3; 18:1; 61:1.

Fig. 159. The Dipylon jug inscription from Athens

Fig. 160. Inscribed sherds from Corinth

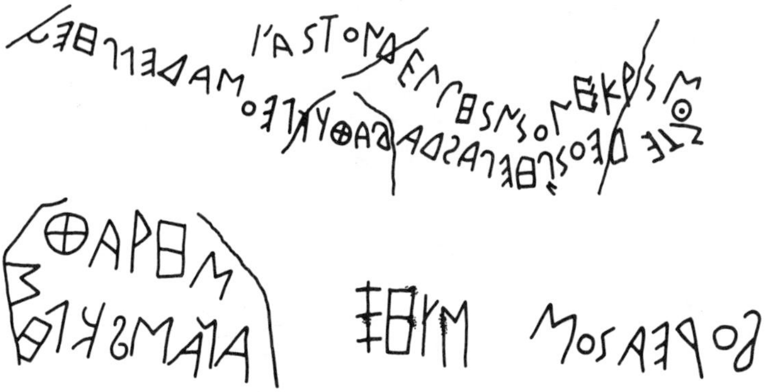

Fig. 161. Rock-cut inscriptions from Thera

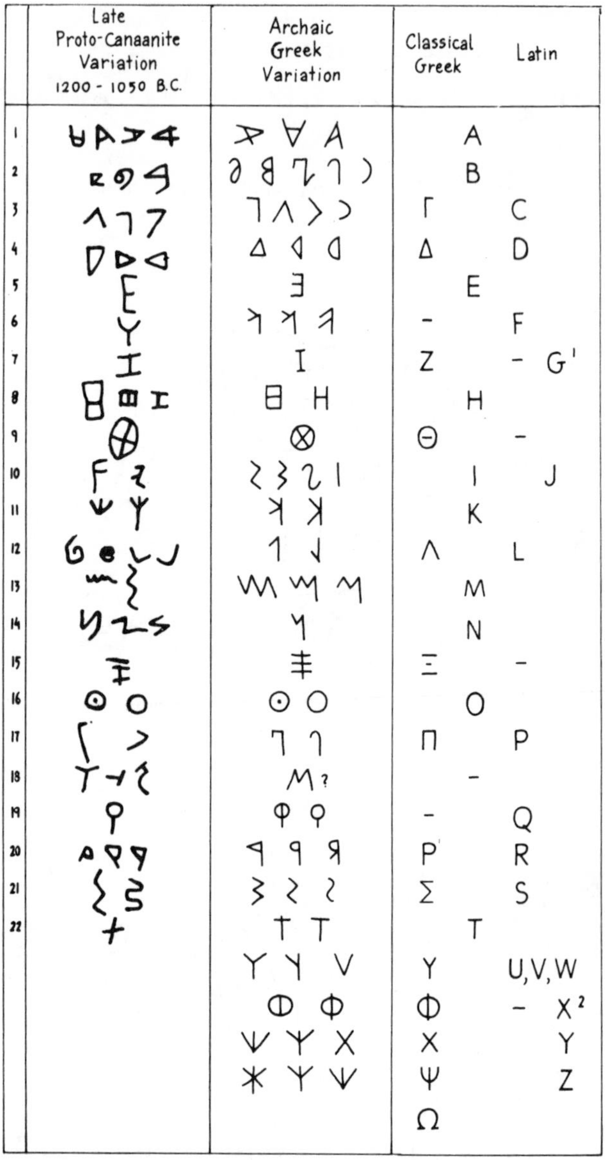

	Late Proto-Canaanite Variation 1200 - 1050 B.C.	Archaic Greek Variation	Classical Greek	Latin
1	৮ A コ ⪦	⪫ ∀ A	A	
2	⼉ ⊙ ◁	∂ 8 ˥ ˥)	B	
3	∧ ˥ ˥	˥ ∧ ⟩ ⟩	Γ	C
4	▽ ▷ ◁	Δ ◁ ◁	Δ	D
5	E	⊒	E	
6	Y	˥ ˥ ˥	–	F
7	I	I	Z	– G¹
8	⊟ ⊞ I	⊟ H	H	
9	⊕	⊗	Θ	–
10	F ⪜	⟨ ⪛ ⪜ I	I	J
11	⪜ Y	⪫ ⪫	K	
12	⏚ ● ↲	˥ ↲	∧	L
13	⌐ ⪛	M M M	M	
14	⪗ ⪜ ⪥	⪗	N	
15	⪥	⪥	Ξ	–
16	⊙ O	⊙ O	O	
17	⟨ ⟩	˥ ˥	Π	P
18	Υ ⪕	M ?	–	
19	⪭	Φ φ	–	Q
20	⪬ ⪬ ⪬	⪬ ⪬ ⪬	P	R
21	⟨ ⪛	⪛ ⪛ ⪛	Σ	S
22	✝	┳ ┳	T	
		Υ ⪤ V	Υ	U,V,W
		Φ Φ	Φ	– X²
		Ψ Υ X	X	Y
		✳ Υ ⪥	Ψ	Z
			Ω	

1 G is variation of C   2 X from Greek Ξ

Fig. 162. The Proto-Canaanite script, ancestor of archaic and classical Greek and Latin scripts

Deviation from the West Semitic letter forms and the introduction of vowel signs to improve the West Semitic consonantal system must have been a lengthy process. There were some archaic Greek letters, however, which preserved the original Proto-Canaanite prototypes (Fig. 162). The *sigma* (ξ) has the shape of the thirteenth- and twelfth-century vertical *shin*, as it is inscribed on the ewer and the bowls from Lachish and Qubur el-Walaydah. The *san* (M) does not seem to have evolved from Semitic *ṣade* (although in some abecedaries, e.g. the one from Marsiliana [Fig. 163],[5] it is placed between *pi* and *qoppa*), but is another rotation of *shin-*

Fig. 163. The abecedary from Marsiliana (Etruria) as inscribed on a school tablet

sigma. The *mu* of five equal strokes (ᴡᴡ) as it appears in the local scripts of Crete (see Pl. 24:A), Melos, Euboia and its colonies,[6] resembles the pictographic *mem* designating water. The *omicron* with the dot in its centre (Ⓞ) is thought to be a result of cutting with a compass; but it seems more likely to represent the pictographic form of the *ʿayin*, i.e. an eye with the pupil, which still occurs in the eleventh century Proto-Canaanite inscriptions. To these examples we may add the box-shaped *heta* (Ⱶ), the tall, I-shaped *zeta* (I), as well as the forms of *delta* (Δ), *epsilon* (Ɛ), *nu* (ᴎ), *ksi* (Ŧ), *pi* (Ⲅ), *qoppa* (Ϙ) and *rho* (P). All resemble their late Proto-Canaanite equivalents.

If the Greeks adopted the Proto-Canaanite alphabet when its letters were still in a process of evolution from pictographic to linear forms, this would explain the variations in the stances of certain letters. For example, the *lambda* was written with its crook at the top or at the base (Ⲅ, ⱱ): this does not mean that one of the two versions was incorrect, but simply that the pictographic conception allowed for both forms. The archaic *gamma* could be written either Γ, or Λ, or ᐸ. On the eighth-century Dipylon vase from Athens (Fig. 159), *alpha* has a ninety degrees rotation (ᐳ), and on the painted aryballos of the Museum of Fine Arts at Boston

5. *Ibid.*, Pl. 48:18.
6. *Ibid.*, p. 31, Fig. 13:4.

|o꒐ᒕ⅃ISᎸ⅂Ꮇ⅄Ǝꙅⅎ|oꙅᎷꙅoᕼ⅄⅂

Fig. 164. Inscription on the painted aryballos from Boston

(Fig. 164; Pl. 24:B), the *alpha* is "inverted" (Ɐ).[7] These are not errors, but rather realisations of the pictorial conception of the letter forms, which were inherited from the Proto-Canaanite script. Although the tenth-century Phoenician script still had two *gimel* forms — ٦ and ٨ — from the ninth century onwards only one form prevailed. *Alef* and *lamed*, however, were stabilized c. 1050 B.C.

In addition to letters which preserved the old Proto-Canaanite forms, there were some archaic Greek letters which underwent longer or shorter evolutions from their Semitic prototypes. While *beta* (Β), *vau* (Ϝ) and the straight, vertical *iota* (Ι) are the product of a relatively long evolution, *tau* (Τ) and some local forms of *rho* (Ρ) and *sigma* (Ϛ, Ϛ) show shorter Greek developments.

The fact that the archaic Greek alphabet had not one set of letters, but various local forms, also poses a problem. Cook and Woodhead presumed that there were certain local Phoenician scripts, from which Greek individuals and groups learned their local scripts at some time in the second half of the eighth century.[8] However, we know that the Phoenician script was a uniform one, without regional variations. In the second half of the eighth century, the Hebrew and the Aramaic scripts had already developed independent traditions of writing, without any local variations. It is hardly feasible that the local archaic Greek scripts could have developed from more than one West Semitic script. Certainly, one Semitic tradition was adopted, and the evolution of the local scripts must be explained as a Greek phenomenon, a process which could not have been accomplished in one generation.

It has been suggested that the eighth-century *waw* as it appears in the Samaria ostraca (see above, p. 72, Fig. 65) may have been the prototype

7. *Ibid.*, Pls. 1:1; 6:22.
8. R. M. Cook and A. G. Woodhead, The Diffusion of the Greek Alphabet, *AJA* 63 (1959), pp. 175-178.

of the archaic Greek *vau*.[9] However, as we have stated above, we cannot assume that the Greeks adopted Phoenician and Hebrew (or even Aramaic) letter forms at the same time. The *vau* must have been developed from the Proto-Canaanite *waw* of *c.* 1100 B.C., which was also the ancestor of the Hebrew *waw*. Therefore, if some forms of the *vau* resemble the eighth-century Hebrew *waw*, this should be seen only as the result of parallel developments. There is no reason to assume that there was any connection between the Hebrew and the archaic Greek scripts.

Another theory has it that the Greek alphabet evolved from Aramaic. This is based mainly on the assumption that the final -a in the names *alpha, beta, gamma, delta,* etc. was probably adopted from the Aramaeans; in Aramaic, final -a designates the determinative state of the nouns.[10] However, the letter names *iota, pi* and *rho* indicate that they were not taken from Aramaic, but from a Canaanite language: *yod* in Phoenician is "hand" (in Hebrew and Aramaic *yad*); *pe* means "mouth" (in Aramaic *pum*); *rosh* = "head" (in Aramaic *resh*). Moreover, if *alpha, beta,* etc., were Aramaic, they would appear in the names of the Syriac alphabet; that alphabet, however, has no names with final -a. Interestingly enough, the Aramaic name *resh* survives in Hebrew tradition, whereas the Canaanite form is preserved in the Greek *rho*.

The transition from the defective spelling of the Proto-Canaanite and Phoenician writing to the Greek vocalization system appears to pose a problem. In the earliest Aramaic and Hebrew inscriptions *matres lectionis* were used, a fact which scholars adduced as partial evidence for the argument that the Greeks adopted the alphabet from the Aramaeans. However, the idea of *matres lectionis* was known as early as the thirteenth century B.C. The North Canaanites in Ugarit used *yod* in certain instances to designate *i*;[11] they also introduced the supplementary letters *'u* and *'i* and turned the original *'alef* into *'a* (see above, pp. 30 f.).

There is, however, one archaic Greek letter which could not have been adopted from the eleventh-century Phoenician script. This is the *kappa,*

9. Jeffery (above, n. 3), pp. 24-25.
10. S. Segert, Altaramäische Schrift und Anfänge des griechischen Alphabets, *Klio* 41 (1963), pp. 38-57.
11. C. H. Gordon, *Ugaritic Textbook,* Rome 1965, p. 18.

which in all local scrips is written Ϝ or Κ. Until the tenth century, its West Semitic equivalent, the *kaf*, was written in the form of three fingers meeting at a common base ∨. However, an identical reproduction of this early *kaf* can be found in the local western Greek scripts as a supplementary letter denoting *khi*. Thus it may well be that the letter shaped like three fingers served for both *k* and *kh* in the Greek alphabet of the eleventh and tenth centuries. Later, in the ninth century, wishing to differentiate between these two sounds, the Greeks borrowed the contemporary Phoenician *kaf*, which in the meantime had developed a downstroke (⟩), and used it for *k*; the older form thenceforth denoted *kh* only.

Another Greek letter, *upsilon*, was adopted from the Phoenician script after the eleventh century. In the alphabetic sequence, *upsilon* (Υ) follows Τ. It was the first supplementary letter, and it served to represent the vowel *u*. When the Greeks adopted the Proto-Canaanite script, they presumably used the *waw* (= Greek *vau*) to write the consonant *w*, as did the Canaanites. Later, in the tenth and ninth centuries, the Greek *vau* underwent certain changes and its shape became Ϝ. When the Greeks invented their system of vocalization, the twenty-two letters supplied them with signs for *a* (*aleph-alpha*), *e* (*he-epsilon*), *i* (*yod-iota*) and *o* (ʿ*ayin-omicron*), but they did not find a "free" letter to use for *u* (*waw-vau* was used in archaic Greek as a consonant). Since the Greeks were always aware of the origin of their alphabet (cf. their tradition), whenever they needed an additional letter, they looked primarily for Phoenician models. So they chose the *waw* (which by then had a form different from their *vau*, though it had evolved from the same letter) as suitable for *u*. This happened possibly around the tenth century B.C., but at any rate before the invention of the *kappa*. This much is indicated by the fact that *upsilon* is the first supplementary letter, while *khi* is the third (after *phi*).

The antiquity of the Greek alphabet is not a question of epigraphy alone; it is also, and primarily, a historical issue. It is widely maintained that, after the disappearance of the Mycenaean script together with the Late Helladic civilization, Greece knew a Dark Age of illiteracy which lasted until the eighth century; this view cannot be substantiated. It is a common belief that the Greek adoption of the alphabet took place in a bilingual environment, where Greeks and Semites lived as neighbours. Recent archaeological excavations have yielded evidence of a Greek settlement at Tell Sukas in Phoenicia (today southern Lebanon) as early as the late ninth century B.C.[12] However, ninth-century Phoenician inscriptions were found long ago in Cyprus and Sardinia. Since most of the features of the archaic Greek alphabet resemble those of the West Semitic script of *c.* 1100 B.C., we have to give serious consideration to the theory of the early adoption of the alphabet by the Greeks. We suggest, therefore, that the Greeks learned the West Semitic writing at approximately the same time that the Hebrews and Aramaeans achieved literacy. These two peoples followed the practice of their Canaanite-Phoenician neighbours for some two centuries before they began to develop their own national scripts. Greeks living in more distant parts may perhaps have borrowed the Semitic alphabet after seeing it used by Canaanite merchants visiting the Aegean islands. It is also possible that in some areas, only a few Greeks might have used the new writing over a fairly long period. Since it was in Crete and Thera that the most archaic letter forms were preserved, it may well be that the inhabitants of these islands were the first Greeks to employ the alphabetic writing. Later it spread to the Greek mainland and to other islands.

The above-mentioned evidence formed the basis of observations published in 1973.[13] Whereas classical epigraphists did not react, Semitic epigraphists, who could not ignore the evidence, tried to compromise between the conventional view and the new proposition. Millard's conclusion was: "Unsatisfactory though the position may be, no more precise date can be given for the adoption of the alphabet by the Greeks than the three centuries and a half, 1100 to 750 B.C."[14] McCarter surmised "that the Greeks, though their script did not diverge as an independent tradition before *c.* 800, had experimented with the Semitic alphabet as early as *c.* 1100 ... The memory of the earlier experimentation survived long enough ... to exert a limited influence upon the final formulation of the

12. P. J. Riis, *Sukas*, I: *The North-East Sanctuary and the First Settling of Greeks in Syria and Palestine*, Copenhagen 1970, pp. 126-127; 159-162.
13. J. Naveh, Some Semitic Epigraphical Considerations on the Antiquity of the Greek Alphabet, *AJA* 77 (1973), pp. 1-8.
14. A. R. Millard, The Canaanite Linear Alphabet and its Passage to the Greeks, *Kadmos* 15 (1976), p. 142.

Greek alphabet years later."[15] This impossible formula reflects the hesitation that McCarter shared with his teacher, Cross.[16] However, after discussing the inscriptions found recently in Qubur el-Walaydah and Izbet Sartah, and, especially, the inscription from Crete (see pp. 36 ff., Figs. 30, 31, 36), Cross concludes as follows: "These new data must be said to give added support to the thesis of Joseph Naveh for the high antiquity of the earliest use by the Greeks of the alphabet, and remove obstacles to dating their borrowing to the time of transition from Old Canaanite to Linear Phoenician toward 1100 B.C.E."[17]

The local archaic Greek scripts were also used by peoples who did not speak Greek, such as the Phrygians, Lydians, Lycians, Carians, etc. in Asia Minor, and by peoples who lived in Italy — Etruscans, Umbrians, Oscans, etc. The Roman, or Latin, alphabet — which probably evolved from Etruscan — eventually became the script of Western civilization.

15. P. K. McCarter, The Early Diffusion of the Alphabet, *BA* 37 (1974), p. 68; idem, *The Antiquity of the Greek Alphabet and the Early Phoenician Scripts* (Harvard Semitic Monographs, No. 9), Missoula (Montana) 1976.
16. F. M. Cross, Early Alphabetic Scripts, *Symposia Celebrating the 75th Anniversary of the Founding of the American Schools of Oriental Research*, I: *Archaeology and Early Israelite History* (ed. F. M. Cross), Cambridge (Mass.) 1979, pp. 105-111.
17. F. M. Cross, Newly Found Inscriptions in Old Canaanite and Early Phoenician Script, *BASOR* 238 (1980), p. 17.

ABBREVIATIONS

AASOR	Annual of the American Schools of Oriental Research
ADAJ	Annual of the Department of Antiquities of Jordan
AION	Annali dell'Istituto Orientale Universitario di Napoli
AJA	American Journal of Archaeology
AUSS	Andrews University Seminary Studies
BA	The Biblical Archaeologist
BANE	*The Bible and the Ancient Near East*, Essays in honor of W. F. Albright, edited by G. E. Wright, Garden City (N.Y.) 1965 (Paperback edition)
BASOR	Bulletin of the American Schools of Oriental Research
BIFAO	Bulletin de l'Institut Français d'Archéologie Orientale
BJPES	Bulletin of the Jewish Palestine Exploration Society
BMB	Bulletin du Musée de Beyrouth
BSOAS	Bulletin of the School of Oriental and African Studies
CBQ	The Catholic Biblical Quarterly
CIS	Corpus Inscriptionum Semiticarum
EI	Eretz-Israel
Enṣ. Miqr.	Enṣiqlopediya Miqra'it (Encyclopaedia Biblica).
Gibson	J. C. L. Gibson, *Textbook of Syrian Semitic Inscriptions*, I-II, Oxford 1971, 1975
HTR	Harvard Theological Review
IEJ	Israel Exploration Journal
IOS	Israel Oriental Studies
IR	*Inscriptions Revealed*, Israel Museum Catalogue No. 100, Jerusalem 1973
JBL	Journal of Biblical Literature
JEA	Journal of Egyptian Archaeology
JNES	Journal of Near Eastern Studies
JPOS	Journal of the Palestinian Oriental Society
JRAS	Journal of the Royal Asiatic Society
JSS	Journal of Semitic Studies
KAI	*Kanaanäische und aramäische Inschriften*, I-III, by H. Donner and W. Röllig, Wiesbaden 1962-1964
Lidz., *Hb.*	M. Lidzbarski, *Handbuch der nordsemitischen Epigraphik*, I-II, Weimar 1898

ILLUSTRATIONS

Figures

		Page
1.	Family tree of the early alphabetic scripts	10
2.	Sumerian pictographic inscription (From *Enṣ. Miqr.*, I, col. 375)	12
3.	Babylonian cuneiform text (From *Enṣ. Miqr.*, I, col. 376)	12
4.	Pictographic origin of ten cuneiform signs (From I. J. Gelb, *A Study of Writing*, Chicago 1963, p. 70, Fig. 31)	12
5.	The uniconsonantal signs in the Egyptian hieroglyphic script (From A. Gardiner, *Egyptian Grammar*, Oxford 1927, p. 27)	15
6.	Egyptian hieroglyphs engraved on a stele (From *Enṣ. Miqr.*, I, col. 373)	16
7.	Hieratic and demotic scripts with hieroglyphic transcription in a modern Egyptological hand (From A. Gardiner, *Egyptian Grammar*, Oxford 1927, Pl. II, opp. p. 10)	17
8.	Hittite pictographic script (From *Enṣ. Miqr.*, I, cols. 373-374)	18
9.	The opening phrase of the Karatepe bilingual (Hittite and Phoenician) inscription; the text in square Hebrew letters is a word-by-word translation of the Hittite into Phoenician (From *Enṣ. Miqr.*, I, cols. 375-376)	18
10.	Cretan pictographic script (From A. J. Evans, *Scripta Minoa*, Oxford 1909, Pl. XII.)	19
11.	Cypriote syllabary (From I. J. Gelb, *A Study of Writing*, Chicago 1963, p. 155, Fig. 81)	20
12.	Linear B script	20
13.	Enigmatic inscription from Byblos (From M. Dunand, *Byblia Grammata*, Beirut 1945, p. 77)	21
14.	Enigmatic inscription on a stele from Baluʻah (From G. Horsfield and L. H. Vincent, *RB* 41 [1932], p. 425)	22
15.	A tablet from Deir ʻAlla	22
16.	The word *(l)bʻlt* in the Proto-Sinaitic inscriptions	24

17. Albright's chart of letters in the Proto-Sinaitic inscriptions
    (From W. F. Albright, *The Proto-Sinaitic Inscriptions and their Decipherment*, Cambridge [Mass.] 1966, Fig. 1 opp. p. 12) 25

18. Early Proto-Canaanite inscription from Shechem
    (From S. Yeivin, *The History of the Jewish Script*, Jerusalem 1939, p. 94, Fig. 18) 26

19. Early Proto-Canaanite letters (*klb*) on a potsherd from Gezer
    (From *Enṣ. Miqr.*, I, col. 383) 26

20. Early Proto-Canaanite letters on a dagger from Lachish
    (From *Enṣ. Miqr.*, I, col. 384) 26

21. Cuneiform alphabetic script from Ugarit 28

22. Cuneiform alphabetic script from Beth-Shemesh
    (From S. Yeivin, *The History of the Jewish Script*, Jerusalem 1939, p. 72, Fig. 16) 28

23. Cuneiform alphabetic text from Taʻanach
    (From D. R. Hillers, *BASOR* 173 [194], p. 48, Fig. 3) 29

24. Cuneiform alphabetic text from Naḥal Tavor 29

25. An abecedary from Ugarit
    (From *Enṣ. Miqr.*, I, Pl. IV, opp. col. 81) 30

26. Phonemic systems in West and South Semitic 32

27. Two inscriptions from Serabit el-Khadem
    (From W. F. Albright, *The Proto-Sinaitic Inscriptions and their Decipherment*, Cambridge [Mass.] 1966, Fig. 4) 34

28. A 13th-century B.C. Proto-Canaanite text on the Lachish Ewer
    (From *Enṣ. Miqr.*, I, col. 385) 35

29. Proto-Canaanite text on an ostracon from Beth Shemesh
    (From F. M. Cross, *EI* 8 [1967], p. 18*, Fig. 3) 35

30. A fragmentary Proto-Canaanite inscription on a bowl from Qubur el-Walaydah 36

31. The ostracon from Izbet Sartah
    (From F. M. Cross, *BASOR* 238 [1980], p. 8, Fig. 9) 37

32. The inscribed arrow-heads from el-Khader
    (From F. M. Cross, *BASOR* 238 [1980], pp. 4-6, Figs. 3,5,8) 38

33. Inscribed arrow-heads from the first half of the 11th century B.C.
    (From F. M. Cross, *EI* 8 [1967], p. 21*, Fig. 4) 39

34. Inscribed arrow-head from Biqaʻ 40

35. The Nora fragment
    (From F. M. Cross, *CBQ* 36 [1974], p. 490, Fig. 1) 40

36. Inscribed bronze bowl from Crete
    (From F. M. Cross, *BASOR* 238 [1980], p. 15, Fig. 12) 41

37. A South Arabic inscription from Ur
    (From W. F. Albright, *BASOR* 128 [1952], p. 40, Fig. 1) 44
38. South Arabic characters on a jar from Tell el-Kheleifeh 45
39. The bilingual (Nabataean-Thamudic) inscription from Ḥejra
    (From J. Cantineau, *Le Nabatéen*, II, Paris 1932, p. 38) 46
40. A Lihyanic text mentioning Gashm
    (From F. V. Winnett, *A Study of Lihyanite and Thamudic
    Inscriptions*, Toronto 1937, Pl. VIII) 47
41. An archaic South Arabian inscription in vertical columns
    (From A. Jamme, *BASOR* 137 [1955], p. 33) 48
42. Characters of the Ethiopic Alphabet
    (From A. Dillmann, *Ethiopic Grammar*, London 1907, Table I) 50
43. The inscription of Yeḥimilk from Byblos 52
44. The inscription of Eliba'al from Byblos 52
45. The stele of Kilamu king of Yadi
    (From F. von Luschan, *Ausgrabungen in Sendschirli*, IV, Berlin
    1911, p. 375, Fig. 273) 55
46. Part of the Phoenician inscription in Karatepe 56
47. The 9th-century B.C. Nora inscription
    (From W. F. Albright, *BASOR* 83 [1941], p. 18, Fig. 2) 58
48. Archaic Phoenician inscription from Cyprus
    (From W. F. Albright, *BASOR* 83 [1941], p. 15, Fig. 1) 58
49. 5th-century B.C. burial inscription of Tabnit king of Sidon
    (From Lidz., *Hb.*, Pl. IV:1) 58
50. The jar-inscription *lb'lṣlḥ* from Bat-Yam 59
51. A Neo-punic votive inscription with cursive letter forms
    (From Lidz., *Hb.*, Pl. XVIII:4) 60
52. 5th-century B.C. Phoenician graffiti at Abydos in Egypt
    (From M. Lidzbarski, *Ephemeris für semitische Epigraphik*, III,
    Giessen 1915, Pl. X., Nos. 47-48) 61
53. A Punic inscription from Carthage
    (From Lidz., *Hb.*, Pl. XIV:1) 61
54. The Gezer Calendar 63
55. The Mesha stele
    (From Lidz., *Hb.*, Pl. I) 64
56. The fragmentary inscription mentioning Mesha's father, Kmošyat .. 65
57. A short Hebrew votive inscription on a stone vessel from
    Kuntilet 'Ajrud 66
58. Relatively early Hebrew letters on an ostracon from Arad
    (From Y. Aharoni, *Arad Inscriptions*, Jerusalem 1981, p. 99, No. 76). 67

59. The Royal Steward inscription
 (From N. Avigad, *IEJ* 3 [1953], Pl. 9:B) 68
60. The Siloam inscription 68
61. Two Hebrew seals from the late 7th century B.C. 69
62. The *bt lmlk* inscription on the shoulder of a jar from Lachish 70
63. Jar-handles with *lmlk* stamps 71
64. Two Hebrew seals from the 8th century B.C. 71
65. Two ostraca from Samaria
 (From G. A. Reisner et alii, *Harvard Excavations at Samaria*, I,
 Cambridge [Mass.] 1924, pp. 239 f., Nos. 12 and 18) 72
66. An early 6th-century B.C. ostracon from Arad
 (From Y. Aharoni, *Arad Inscriptions*, Jerusalem 1981, p. 47,
 No. 24) 72
67. Late 7th-century petition from Meṣad Ḥashavyahu 73
68. An early 6th-century letter from Lachish
 (From H. Torczyner, *Lachish*, I: *The Lachish Letters*, London
 1938, p. 77, No. 4) 74
69. Some inscribed jar-handles from Gibeon
 (From J. B. Pritchard, *Hebrew Inscriptions and Stamps from
 Gibeon*, Philadelphia 1959, Fig. 2) 75
70. Development of the Hebrew script 77
71. Inscription of Bar-Rakib king of Sam'al
 (From Lidz., *Hb.*, Pl. XXIV:1) 79
72. Inscription of Bar-Hadad, king of Damascus
 (From F. M. Cross, *BASOR* 205 [1972], p. 38, Fig. 1) 80
73. Inscription of Zakur, king of Hamath
 (From H. Pognon, *Inscriptions sémitiques de la Syrie, de la
 Mésopotamie et de la région de Mossoul*, Paris 1907, Pl. XXV,
 No. 86) 81
74. An inscribed brick from Hamath 81
75. Letter of Adon found at Saqqarah in Egypt 82
76. Stele from Nerab
 (From Lidz., *Hb.*, Pl. XXV:1) 83
77. A lapidary inscription from Gözne in Asia-Minor
 (From R. S. Hanson, *BASOR* 192 [1968], p. 10, Fig 6) 84
78. Petition to the Governor of Judah from Elephantine,
 408 B.C. 85
79. An ostracon from Elephantine
 (From M. Lidzbarski, *Ephemeris für semitische Epigraphik*, III,
 Giessen 1915, p. 122) 86

80. Script samples of two papyri from Wadi Daliyah
(From F. M. Cross, *AASOR* 41 [1974], Pl. 59) 87
81. Development of the *alef* 90
82. Development of the *bet* 91
83. Development of the *he* 93
84. Development of the *waw* 94
85. Development of the *zayin* 95
86. Development of the *ḥet* 96
87. Comparative chart of scripts at the beginning of the 6th
century B.C.
(From J. Naveh, *The Development of the Aramaic Script*,
Jerusalem 1970, Fig. 12, opp. p. 49) 98
88. Three Moabite seals 101
89. The seals of "Amoz the scribe" and "Manasse, son of the king" ... 103
90. The seal of Mesha, (son of) 'Ada'el
(From N. Avigad, *EI* 1 [1951], p. 34, Fig. 4) 103
91. The seal of Yatom from Tell el-Kheleifeh
(From *Enṣ. Miqr.*, III, col. 622) 103
92. The stamp of Qaus'anali from Tell el-Kheleifeh 103
93. Ostracon No. 6043 from Tell el-Kheleifeh 104
94. The inscription of Yeraḥ'azar
(From Y. Aharoni, *IEJ* 1 [1951], p. 220, Fig. 1) 106
95. The Amman Theatre fragment
(From W. J. Fulco, *JNES* 38 [1979], p. 37, Fig. 1) 106
96. Inscription on juglet from Tell Siran
(From H. O. Thompson and F. Zayadine, *BASOR* 212 [1973],
p. 7, Fig.1) 106
97. Heshbon ostracon IV
(From F. M. Cross, *AUSS* 13 [1975], p. 3, Fig. 1) 108
98. Three Ammonite seals 108
99. Seal of a Philistine official 111
100. Aramaic and early Jewish scripts
(From F. M. Cross, *BANE*, p. 175, Fig. 1) 113
101. Yehud coins: (1) *yhd* in Aramaic letters; (2) [*y*]*ḥzq*[*yh*] *ḥpḥh*
and (3) *yhd* in Hebrew letters
(From N. Avigad, *Qedem* 4 [1976], Fig. 17, Nos. 16-18) 115
102. Aramaic stamps on jars from the Province of Yehud
(From N. Avigad, *Qedem* 4 [1976], Fig. 17, Nos. 1-11) 116
103. Seal of the governor of Samaria impressed on a bulla
(From F. M. Cross, *AASOR* 41 [1974], Pl. 61) 116

104. Bullae of the seals of Yiga'el, Baruch, Jeremi, etc.
(From N. Avigad, *Qedem* 4 [1976], pp. 7-9, Figs. 6-10) 117
105. Jewish coins with Hebrew legends
(From Lidz., *Hb.*, Pl. XXI:2-6) 118
106. Aramaic legend on a coin of Alexander Jannaeus; *c.* 4:1
(From J. Naveh, *IEJ* 18 [1968], p. 22, Fig. 1) 119
107. The legend *yhdh* on a coin from the early Hellenistic period
(From N. Avigad, *Qedem* 4 [1976], Fig. 17, No. 19) 119
108. *yhd* and *yršlm* stamps from the early Hellenistic period 119
109. A graffito on an ossuary in Jewish and Hebrew characters
(From M. Rosenthaler, *IEJ* 25 [1975], p. 138, Fig.1) 120
110. Earliest Samaritan inscription on a capital from Emmaus
(From Lidz., *Hb.*, Pl. XXI:7) 122
111. A Samaritan inscription
(From Lidz., *Hb.*, Pl. XXI:8) 124
112. Old Persian syllabary
(From G. R. Driver, *Semitic Writing from Pictograph to
Alphabet*[3], London 1976, p. 132, Fig. 79) 126
113. Aramaic boundary inscriptions from Armenia 128
114. The Aramaic part of a bilingual (Greek-Aramaic) inscription
from Armazi
(From G. Tsereteli, *A Bilingual Inscription from Armazi near
Mcheta in Georgia*, Tbilissi 1942, p. 15) 129
115. The Aramaic alphabet written by Iranians 133
116. Legend on an Elymaean coin
(From W. B. Henning, *Asia Major* 2 [1951/2], p. 164) 134
117. Mandaic incantation text on a bowl
(From H. Pognon, *Inscriptions mandaïtes des coupes de
Khouabir*, Paris 1898/9, No. 2) 135
118. Inscription from Tang-i Butan at the Shimbar Valley
(From A. D. H. Bivar and S. Shaked, *BSOAS* 27 [1964],
p. 273, Fig. 2) 135
119. Development of the South Mesopotamian scripts
(From J. Naveh, *BASOR* 198 [1970], p. 35) 137
120. Hatran inscription No. 214 from 97/8 A.D.
(From F. Safar, *Sumer* 21 [1965], p. 31) 138
121. Hatran inscription No. 35 from 238 A.D.
(From F. Safar, *Sumer* 9 [1953], following p. 20) 139
122. Inscription from Sari
(From J. Naveh, *IOS* 2 [1972], p. 295, Fig. 1b) 140

123. Inscription from Hassan-Kef
   (From H. Pognon, *Inscriptions sémitiques de la Syrie* ...,
   Paris 1907, Pl. XXVII, No. 61) 140

124. Inscription of Garni
   (From A. G. Perikhanian, *Istoriko-filologičeskiy Žurnal,*
   Akademiya Nauk Armyanskoy SSR, 1964, No. 3 [26], p. 124) 140

125. Development of the North Mesopotamian Aramaic script type
   (From J. Naveh, *IOS* 2 [1972], p. 299, Fig. 4) 142

126. Palmyrene monumental inscription
   (From Lidz., *Hb.*, Pl. XXXVIII:4) 144

127. Palmyrene dipinto at Dura Europos
   (From R. du Mesnil du Buisson, *Inventaire des inscriptions*
   palmyréniennes de Doura Europos, Paris 1939, p. 15, No. 25) 144

128. Two Palmyrene cursive inscriptions from Rome
   (From Lidz., *Hb.*, Pl. XLII: 9-10) 145

129. Syriac characters
   (From T. H. Robinson, *Paradigms and Exercises in Syriac*
   Grammar[4], Oxford 1962, p. 4) 146

130. Syriac inscription from Serrin, 73 A.D.
   (From H. Pognon, *Inscriptions sémitiques de la Syrie* ...,
   Paris 1907, Pl. XIV, No. 2) 147

131. Old Syriac characters
   (From A. Maricq, *Syria* 39 [1962], p. 94) 148

132. Syriac inscription from 748 A.D.
   (From H. Pognon, *Inscriptions sémitiques de la Syrie* ...,
   Paris 1907, Pl. XXVI, No. 56) 148

133. Inscription of Amassamses
   (From H. Pognon, *Inscriptions sémitiques de la Syrie* ...,
   Paris 1907, Pl. XXVI, Nos. 57-58) 149

134. Archaic inscription from Dura Europos
   (From R. du Mesnil du Buisson, *Inventaire des inscriptions*
   palmyréniennes de Doura Europos, Paris 1939, No. 1) 150

135. Inscription of Ṣadan in "Syriac-Palmyrene" and in Jewish
   Aramaic (From Lidz., *Hb.*, Pl. XLIII:7) 150

136. Inscription from el-Mal
   (From J. Naveh, *IEJ* 25 [1975], p. 117, No. 1) 150

137. Comparative table of Estrangelo (1), script used on bowls (2),
   and Manichaean (3)
   (From J. A. Montgomery, *Aramaic Incantation Texts from*
   Nippur, Philadelphia 1913, Pl. XL) 152

138. Earliest Nabataean inscription from Elusa
     (From J. Cantineau, *Le Nabatéen*, II, Paris 1932, p. 43) 154
139. Inscription of Aṣlaḥ from Petra
     (From J. Cantineau, *Le Nabatéen*, II, Paris 1932, p. 2) 154
140. Early Nabataean scripts
     (From F. M. Cross, *BANE*, p. 211, Fig. 7) 155
141. Nabataean monumental inscription
     (From Lidz., *Hb.*, Pl. XXX:2) 155
142. Development of the Nabataean cursive script
     (From J. Naveh, *IEJ* 29 [1979], p. 115, Fig. 1) 156
143. Rock inscriptions from Sinai
     (From Lidz., *Hb.*, Pl. XXXVI:1-4) 158
144. The Namara inscription
     (From R. Dussaud, *Revue Archéologique* 41 [1902], p. 410) 159
145. The latest dated Nabataean inscription
     (From S. Noja, *Biblia e Oriente* 21 [1979], p. 292, No. 3) 159
146. Pre-Islamic Arabic inscriptions from Zebed, Ḥarran and Umm el-Jimal
     (From N. Abbot, *The Rise of the North Arabic Script* ...,
     Chicago 1931, Pl. I) 160
147. The Nash Papyrus 163
148. The Ḥezir family tomb inscription
     (From N. Avigad, *Ancient Monuments in the Kidron Valley*,
     Jerusalem 1954, p. 60 [Hebrew]) 164
149. Ossuary inscriptions
     (From N. Avigad, *IEJ* 21 [1971], pp. 197, 199, Figs. 8-9) 164
150. Vulgar semi-formal script of the Copper Scroll
     (From M. Baillet et alii, *Les 'petites grottes' de Qumran*,
     [Discoveries in the Judaean Desert, III], Oxford 1962, Pl. 48) 166
151. Herodian and post-Herodian cursive scripts
     (From F. M. Cross, *BANE*, p. 209, Fig. 5) 168
152. Inscription on sarcophagus from Beth She‘arim
     (From N. Avigad, *IEJ* 7 [1957], p. 240, Fig. 5) 169
153. Epitaph from Zoar
     (From E. L. Sukenik, *Qedem* 2 [1945], p. 84, Fig. 1) 171
154. Inscription on mosaic floor from the synagogue of Hamath Gader
     (From E. L. Sukenik, *JPOS* 15 [1935], p. 130, Fig. 13) 171
155. Development of the five medial and final letters 172
156. Rashi script 173

157. Modern Hebrew cursive 173
158. Vertical shading in modern Hebrew lettering 174
159. The Dipylon jug inscription from Athens 179
160. Inscribed sherds from Corinth 179
161. Rock-cut inscriptions from Thera 179
162. The Proto-Canaanite script, ancestor of archaic and classical Greek and Latin scripts 180
163. The abecedary from Marsiliana (Etruria) as inscribed on a school tablet 181
164. Inscription on the painted aryballos from Boston 182

Plates

PLATE 1
A. Proto-Sinaitic inscription. The pictographs at the bottom compose the word *lb'lt*
(Courtesy of Dr. G. Gerster, Zürich)
B. Early Proto-Canaanite inscription from Gezer
(Courtesy of the Israel Department of Antiquities; Photo Israel Museum)
C. Late Proto-Canaanite inscription from Qubur el-Walaydah
(Courtesy of the Israel Department of Antiquities)

PLATE 2
A. Sabaean inscription from Beit el-'Ashwal, Yemen
(Courtesy of M. Chr. Robin and *Bible et Terre Sainte*)
B. Thamudic D inscription from the Negev
(From J. Naveh, *EI* 12 [1975], Pl. 27:1; Courtesy of the Israel Department of Antiquities)
C-D. Thamudic B inscription on a bowl carried by a winged figure
(From J. Naveh and E. Stern, *IEJ* 24 [1974], Pls. 12-13)

PLATE 3
A. Phoenician text on an ivory box from Ur
(From R. D. Barnett, *A Catalogue of the Nimrud Ivories in the British Museum*, London 1957, Pl. CXXXII, U11; Courtesy of the Trustees of the British Museum)

B.   A Phoenician ink inscription on a marble slab from Kition, Cyprus
      (*CIS* I, 86B; Courtesy of the Trustees of the British Museum)
C.   A Phoenician ostracon from Egypt
      (Courtesy of the Egyptian Museum, Cairo)

PLATE 4
      Phoenician papyrus from Saqqarah
      (Courtesy of the Egyptian Museum, Cairo)

PLATE 5
A.   Phoenician inscriptions on jars from Elephantine
      (Courtesy of the Egyptian Museum, Cairo)
B.   Phoenician ostracon from Tell Kheleifeh
      (Courtesy of the American Schools of Oriental Research)
C.   Phoenician papyrus of *c.* 300 B.C. from Egypt
      (Courtesy of the Egyptian Museum, Cairo)

PLATE 6
A.   A fragmentary Hebrew inscription on ivory from Nimrud
      (Courtesy of Dr. A. R. Millard)
B.   Seal and impression of Elyashiv from Arad, early 6th-century B.C.
      Hebrew
      (From Y. Aharoni, *Arad Inscriptions,* Jerusalem 1981, No. 106; Courtesy
      of the Israel Department of Antiquities)
C.   The Hebrew palimpsest papyrus from Murabba'at
      (Courtesy of the Israel Department of Antiquities)

PLATE 7
A.   Seal of Shemaryau, presumably from Samaria, 8th-century B.C. Hebrew
      (Courtesy of the Israel Department of Antiquities)
B.   An incised ostracon from Samaria, 8th-century B.C. Hebrew
      (Courtesy of the Israel Department of Antiquities)
C.   An ostracon from Arad, early 6th-century B.C. Hebrew
      (From Y. Aharoni, *Arad Inscriptions,* Jerusalem 1981, No. 1)

PLATE 8
A.   An Aramaic docket inscribed on a clay tablet, 570 B.C.
      (From J. Starcky, *Syria* 37 [1960], p. 101)
B.   One of the Hermopolis papyri *c.* 500 B.C. Aramaic
      (From E. Bresciani and M. Kamil, *Memorie di Scienze morali, storiche e
      filologiche, Accademia Nazionale dei Lincei*, VII, Serie 8 [1966], pp. 361-
      428, Pl. III; Courtesy of Accademia Nazionale dei Lincei)

PLATE 9

Aramaic letter of Arsham written on parchment

(Courtesy of Oxford University Press)

PLATE 10

A. An Aramaic ostracon from Elephantine, 5th century B.C.

(Courtesy of the Egyptian Museum, Cairo)

B. A 4th-century B.C. Aramaic ostracon from Tel Beer-Sheba

(From J. Naveh, *Tel-Aviv* 6 [1979], pp. 182-198, No. 33)

C. An early 3rd-century B.C. Aramaic ostracon from Edfu in Egypt

(From E. Sachau, *Aramäische Papyrus und Ostraka*, Leipzig 1911, Pl. 68:2)

PLATE 11

A. A Lydian-Aramaic bilingual inscription from Sardis. The Aramaic text is written in the 4th-century B.C. Aramaic lapidary script

(From H. Buckler, *Sardis*, VI/II, Leiden 1924, Pl. 1)

B. A 3rd-century B.C. Aramaic papyrus from Egypt

(From E. Bresciani, *Rendiconti di Scienze morali, storiche e filologiche, Accademia Nazionale dei Lincei* XVII [1962], Serie VIII, pp. 258-264, Pl. 1; Courtesy of Accademia Nazionale dei Lincei)

PLATE 12

A-B. Two Moabite seals from the 8th and 6th centuries, respectively

(From A. Reifenberg, *BJPES* 12 [1945-46], Pl. 2:3-4)

C. Both sides of a bulla found at Umm el-Biyara; on the obverse can be read "Belonging to Qausga[bri], king of E[dom]"

(Courtesy of the *Revue Biblique*)

D. The Edomite ostracon from Tell Kheleifeh

(Courtesy of the American Schools of Oriental Research)

E-G. Three Ammonite seals

(E — From A. Reifenberg, *Ancient Hebrew Seals*, London 1950, No. 36; F — *IR*, No. 135; G — H. Gressmann, *Altorientalische Bilder zum Alten Testament*, Berlin 1927, Pl. CCXXV, No. 579)

PLATE 13

A. The Ammonite Citadel Inscription from Amman

(From S. H. Horn, *BASOR* 193 [1969], p. 3; Courtesy of the American Schools of Oriental Research)

B. The Ammonite ostracon from Nimrud

(From J. B. Segal, *Iraq* 19 [1957], Pl. XXXIV; Courtesy of Prof. J. B. Segal and the editor of *Iraq*)

PLATE 14

A. The seal of Yehoyišmaʿ daughter of Šawaš-šar-uṣur
    (Courtesy of Prof. N. Avigad)
B. Coin with the legend *yhd* in Hebrew letters
    (Courtesy of the Israel Museum)
C. Fragment of Leviticus Scroll in Palaeo-Hebrew
    (Courtesy of the Shrine of the Book)
D. Fragment of the Psalms Scroll written in Jewish characters, but *yhwh* —
    in Palaeo-Hebrew
    (Courtesy of the Shrine of the Book)

PLATE 15

A. Aramaic burial inscription written in Palaeo-Hebrew letters
    (Courtesy of the Israel Department of Antiquities)
B. A Samaritan inscription
    (Courtesy of the Israel Museum)

PLATE 16

A. An Aramaic inscription of Aśoka from Kandahar, Afghanistan
    (From G. Pugliese Carratelli and G. Levi Della Vida, *Un editto bilingue
    greco-aramaico di Aśoka* [*Serie orientale Roma*, XXI], Rome 1958;
    Courtesy of Istituto Italiano per il Medio ed Estremo Oriente)
B. An Aramaic inscription on a boundary stone from Armenia
    (From A. Pèrikhanian, *Revue des Études Arméniennes* N.S. 8 [1971], pp.
    169-174)

PLATE 17

A. Parthian document written on parchment in 53 A.D. from Avroman,
    Kurdistan
    (From A. Cowley, *JRAS* 1919, Pl. opposite p. 147)
B. An ostracon from Nisa
    (From I. M. Diakonov and V. A. Livshitz, *Dokumenti iz Nisi*, Moscow
    1960, No. 113)
C. Lead roll inscribed with Mandaic incantation
    (From J. Naveh, *IOS* 5 [1975], pp. 47-53)

PLATE 18

A. Hatran Aramaic and Greek bilingual inscription from Dura Europos
    (From R. du Mesnil du Buisson, *Syria* 19 [1938], p. 148)
B. Earliest Palmyrene inscription

(From J. Teixidor, *Inventaire des Inscriptions de Palmyre*, XI, Beyrouth 1965, Pl. XIII, No. 100)
C. Aramaic inscription from el-Mal, southern Syria
(From J. Naveh, *IEJ* 25 [1975], Pl. 13:A)

PLATE 19
A. Old Syriac deed of sale on parchment from Dura-Europos
(Courtesy of the Yale University Art Gallery, Dura Europos Collection)
B. Syriac inscription on the mosaic pavement of the Nestorian monastery in Jericho
(Courtesy of the Israel Department of Antiquities)

PLATE 20
A. Aramaic ostracon from Raphia area, *c.* 300 B.C.
(From J. Naveh, *Leshonenu* 37 [1973], p. 270)
B. Nabataean incantation text
(From J. Naveh, *IEJ* 29 [1979], Pl. 14; Courtesy of the Israel Department of Antiquities)

PLATE 21
Nabataean graffiti on a rock in Sinai
(to be published by the author)

PLATE 22
A. Nabataean and Jewish Aramaic endorsements on a Greek deed from Naḥal Ḥever
(From J. H. Polotsky, *EI* 8, [1967], Pl. 10; Courtesy of the Shrine of the Book)
B. Aramaic message of Shimeon (Bar Kosiba) on papyrus from Naḥal Ḥever
(Courtesy of Prof. Y. Yadin)
C. The beginning of a Hebrew deed written in Ein Gedi
(Courtesy of Prof. Y. Yadin)

PLATE 23
A. Tombstone of King Uzziah
(Courtesy of the Israel Museum)
B. Some lines from the War Scroll from Qumran
(Courtesy of the Shrine of the Book)
C. Mosaic inscription found on the floor of the ancient synagogue in Na'aran near Jericho
(Courtesy of the Israel Department of Antiquities)

PLATE 24

A. Archaic Greek inscription from Crete written in the 5th century B.C., in boustrophedon
    (From M. Guarducci, *Epigrafica Greca*, I, Rome 1967, p. 186, Fig. 58; Courtesy of Istituto Poligrafico Dello Stato, Rome)

B. Aryballos with a 7th century archaic Greek inscription
    (Courtesy of the Museum of Fine Arts, Boston)

INDEX

Abbot, N. 160
abecedary 11 30 37 181
Abiba'al 54
Abydos (in Egypt) 3 61-62
Achaemenid 125 127 130
acrophonic 23 27 42
Adon 82
Aegean islands 185
Afghanistan 83 127
Africa 51 57 59
Aharoni, Y. 66 70 86 100
Aḥiqar, Proverbs of 87 125
Aḥiram 53
Aimé-Giron, N. 59 60
'Ajjul, Tell el- 42
Akhenaton 27
Akkadian 1 9 13-14 27-28 85 89 125
Akko, Tel 60
Aksum 50-51
Albright, W. F. 24 27 33-34 36 43 124
    149 162
Alexander the Great 128
Alexander Jannaeus 118-119
Alexander, P. S. 5
Algeria 143
alphabetic cuneiform script 2-3 28-30
Altheim, F. 134 136 159
Amarna, Tell el- 27
Amenhotep 27
Amman 105-107 111
Amminadab 107 110-111
Ammon 111
Ammonite(s) 9 88 101-102 105-110
Amorite 28

'Anat 39
Anatolian 54
Anti-Lebanon 127
Aphek, Tel 36
Arab(s) 43-51 126 130 138 143 147
    158 161-162
Arabia 9 43 45-47 83 85 157-158
Arabic 9 31-33 36 88 107 114 121
    127 130 153-154 157-162 170 174
Arad, Tel 66-67 72 76-77 86 153
Aram 107
Aramaean(s) 54-56 62 78 82 88
    99-100 125 149 174 177 183 185
Aramaic 3 5 9-11 14 31-33 53-57 62
    67 76-175 177 182-183
Aretas 154
Armazi 126 129-130 141-142
Armenia 128-130 141
Armenian 130
Arsham 86-87
Arslan Tash 114
Artaxias 128
Ashdod 111-112
Ashkelon 111
Ashurbanipal 102 110
Asia 112
Asia Minor 83-85 186
Aśoka 127 143
Assuan 86
Assur 88 141-142
Assyria 69 88 109
Assyrian(s) 1 9 13-14 23 82 84 88
    101-102 105 109-110 112 123 125
    130

Assyrian Church 127 147
Assyrian (= square Hebrew) script 11 123
Athens 178-181
Ausan 43
Avigad, N. 102 114-117 165
Azarbeijan 127
Azitawadda 18 54

Babylonia 44 78 88 120 123 137 151-153 170
Babylonian(s) 1 9 12-14 78 82 84 88 97 114 123-125 130 133 151 173
Babylonian Jewish Aramaic 125-127
Baḥrein 136
Baluʻah 22
Bard-i Nishandeh 136
Bar-Hadad 80
Bar-Kokhba 78 96 117 167-169
Ba-Rakib 79-80
Barnett, R. D. 107
Bat-Yam 59
Beer-Sheba 86 105 153 157
Beeston, A. F. L. 43
Behistun 87
Benoit, P. 167
Bergman (Biran), A. 111
Bethlehem 37
Beth Sheʻarim 169
Beth Shemesh 28-29 35 37
Biqaʻ 40
Birecik 137 147-148
Birnbaum, S. A. 173
Bivar, A. D. H. 100 136
Bordreuil, P. 109
boustrophedon 40-42 49 176-178
Bowman, R. 114
Bresciani, E. 85
Buddhist 127
bulla 4 70 102 115-117 137

burial inscription 3 5 58-59 85 120 143 157-158 164-165 169-171
Buseirah 102-104
Byblos 21-22 52 54 57 65

Calah see Nimrud
calligraphy 161
Canaan 65
Canaanite(s) 9 23-24 27-32 42 54 65-66 105-107 114 183-186
Cantineau, J. 157-159
Caquot, A. 84 114
Carians 186
Carpenter, R. 176
Carthage 3 57 61
Caucasian 130
Chaldaean 44
Characene 134-138
Chemosh see Kemoš
Cilicia 18 54 59 85
coin 4 85 91-93 96 114-119 122-123 134-136 157
Conti Rossini, K. 43
Cook, R. M. 182
Cooke, G. A. 5 157
Corinth 178-179
Cowley, A. E. 86
Coxon, P. W. 136
Crete 19 40-41, 59 111 181 185-186
Cross, F. M. 11 27 30 33-37 40-42 59 62 75 78 105-110 115 121 143 154 165-167 186
cuneiform 1 12-14 18 22 28-31 88 112-114 125
cursive 7-8 16 44 60-62 66-69 75-76 80-82 84-94 96-100 109 131 137 144-145 147-153 156-162 165-173 178
Cyprian 57
Cypriote syllabary 19-20

Cypro-Minoan 22-23
Cypro-Mycenaean 111
Cyprus 57-60 90 185
Cyrillic 11

Dahood, M. 28
Dajani, R. W. 107
Daliyah, Wadi 86-87 115
Damascus 80 101 107 127
Darius 130
Dead Sea 70 119 121 157 162 165-170
Dedan 44-45
Dedanite 126
dedicatory *see* votive inscription
Degen, R. 138
Deir 'Alla, Tell 22, 107-110
Deir Ya'qub 149
demotic 16-17 114
De Vaux, R. 76
diacritic mark 132, 141, 161
Diakonov, I. M. 129
Dillmann, A. 51
Diodorus Siculus 23 154
dipinto 4 136 144
Diringer, D. 22 122
Dorian invasion 20 177
Dothan, M. 60 111-112
Drijvers, H. J. W. 149
Driver, G. R. 22 86
Du Mesnil du Buisson, R. 114 144
Dupont-Sommer, A. 84
Dura Europos 141-142 144 147-152 170

Ebla 28
Edessa 138 143 147-149 153
Edom 111, 153
Edomite(s) 78 101-105 109-110

Egypt 1 3 5 14 27 59-60 82-83 85-87 114 143 153 157 162
Egyptian(s) 13-18 23-25 28 42 62 82
Ein Gedi 167
Elamites 14
El-'Arish 47
Elath 44 60 102
Elephantine 59 85-88
Eliba'al 52 54
El-Khader 37-39
El-Kom 105
El-Mal 149-152
El-Qatif 136
El-'Ula 44
Elusa 154 156
Elymaeans 134
Elymaic 100 134-136
Elymais 126 134 138
Emmaus 122-123
England 143
Ephraim 76
epigraphy 2 5-6 59 70 72 75-76 86 88 100 102 111-112 121 132 138 169 175-177 184-185
epistolography 5
epitaph *see* burial inscription
Esarhaddon 102
Eshmun 60
Estrangelo 147 152
Ethiopian 9 49-51 162
Etruria 181
Etruscans 186
Euboia 181
Euphrates 132 138 141 147
Europe 59 112
Ezra 123

Fakhariyah, Tell 89
Fertile Crescent 2
Fitzmyer, J. A. 5

France 59
Freedman, D. N. 62 78 111 115
Frey, J. B. 169
Friedrich, J. 57
Frye, R. N. 125

Gamma, Tel 115
Garbini, G. 42 107
Gardiner, A. 23
Garni 140-142
Gashmu 47 153
Gaza 42 60 153
Gelb, I. J. 9-11 22, 28
Georgia 130 141
Geraty, L. T. 105
German 18
Geshem *see* Gashmu
Gezer 26 63 65 76-77 177
Gibeon 75
Giv'at ha-Mivtar 93 120-121
Glueck, N. 43 99
Gordon, C. H. 29 183
Gözne 84
graffito 3 45-47 62 98 120 144 157-160 164 178
Greece 4 19 23 59 175 177 184
Greek(s) 1 9-11 14 18-20 23 41-43 47 84 122 126-130 143 154 157 160 175-186
Greenfield, J. C. 28 115 125
Grimme, H. 26

Hadad 80
Hadramauth 43
Hamath 80-81
Hamath Gader 171
Hamilton, V. 151
Hamitic 16
Hanson, R. S. 120
Hanun 111

Harran 160
Harris, Z. S. 57
Hasmonaean 92-93 117 120 122 162 165-167
Hassan Kef 140-142
Hathor 23-24
Hatra 126 132 137-139 141-143 153
Hauran 159
Hebrew 9-11 28 31 36 53-54 57 62-78 88-102 105 109-125 127 157 162 167 170 175 177 182-183
Hebrews 54-56 62 65 67 76 100 169 177 185
Hejra 46 158-159
Helene 149
Helladic 184
Hellenistic 84 105 119 126 162
Henning, W. B. 100 130-131
Hermopolis 85 125
Herodian 120 164-165 168 170
Herodotos 23
Herr, L. G. 102 107
Herzfeld, E. 130
Heshbon 107-108
Hever, Nahal 156-157 160-162 167
Hezir family 164
hieratic 16-17
hieroglyphic 13-17 22-23
Hillers, D. R. 30
Hisda, Rav 123
Hissil'el 107 110
Hittite 13-14 18 23 54
Hoftijzer, J. 107
Homeric question 176
Honeyman, A. M. 51
Horn, S. H. 107
Huffmon, H. B. 28
Hungary 143
Hurrians 14
Hymettos, Mount 178

Iberia 129
ideogram 13 131-132
ideographic 130-132
Idumea *see* Edom
Imru'lqais 159
incantation text 114 134-135 151 156-157 170
India(n) 127
Indo-European 18
Ionian 178
Ipsambul 98
Iran 127-133
Iranian(s) 1 127 130-133 151
Iraq 127 133 143
Isbell, C. D. 170
Islamic period 161
Israel 11 60 69-70 78 99-101 104 112 123 174 177
Israelite(s) 26 76
Israel, F. 104
Italy 59 143 157 173 186
Izbet Sartah 36-37 186

Jaffa 169
Jamme, A. 48-49
Jason 154
Jeffery, L. H. 177, 183
Jerusalem 119-121 123 149 164 174
Jeselsohn, D. 119
Jewish 88 105 115-117 121-123 133 157 164 167
Jewish script 9-11 78 88 91 112-113 118 120-122 127 133 143 151 162-174
Jews 11 53 78 112-114 117 121-122 124-127 162 167-169 173-174
Jisr, Tell 42
Jordan 22 86
Josephus Flavius 2
Jotham 102

Judaean 66 85 87 115 167
Judah 11 69-70 76-78 82 97-99 102-105 112-114 119 153
Judaism 123

Kadmos 23 175
Kamid el-Loz 42
Kamil, M. 85
Karatepe 18 54-56
Kemoš 101
Kemošyat 65 67
Kerak 65
Kheleifeh, Tell 44-45 60 102-104
Khorazmian 132
Khuzistan 133-134
Kilamu 54-57 76 80 117
Kindler, A. 119
Kition 59
Knossos 40-41
Koopmans, J. J. 114
Kornfeld, W. 3
Kraeling, E. G. 86
Kufic 161
Kuntilet 'Ajrud 66, 69
Kurdistan 127
Kutscher, E. Y. 127, 129-130

Lachish 26 33 36-37 70 74-75 98 100 105 181
lapidary 7-8 44 59-60 66-69 84-85 90-93 95 97 105 117 170 176 178
Lapp, P. W. 119
Latin 7 9-11 18 112, 174-175 180 186
Lebanon 185
Lemaire, A. 75
Lidzbarski, M. 3 59 88 134 151
Lihyanic 45-47 126
Linear B 19-20
lingua franca 27 82 89 99 143
Livshitz, V. A. 129

Lycians 186
Lydians 4, 186

Maccabaean 149
Macuch, R. 134
Ma'in 43-45
Malta 59
Mandaean(s) 127 133-136
Mandaic 126-127 132-137 151 174
Mani 134 151
Manichaean 151-153
Mari 28
Marsiliana 181
Maskhuta, Tell el- 153
Mason, O. 59
Massada 120
mater lectionis 9 62 76 89 183
Mazar, B. 120
McCarter, P. K. 185-186
Mea She'arim 174
Mediterranean 57-59
Melos 181
Melqart 80
Meṣad Ḥashavyahu 72-73
Mesha 64-67 77 94 101 103 177
Meshel, Z. 66
Meshorer, Y. 115 157
Mesjed-i Suleiman 136
Mesopotamia 1 5 13 59 138
Mesopotamian 100 132-133 138 141-
    143 151 172
Milik, J. T. 37 141 167
Millard, A. R. 69 185
Minaean *see* Ma'in
Minoan *see* Cypro-Minoan
Mitinti 111
Moab 22 101 105
Moabite(s) 9 65-66 76-78 101-105
    109
Moneijah, Jebel 158

Montgomery, J. A. 151 170
Moran, W. L. 28
Moscati, S. 33, 70-71
Moslem 161
Murabba'at, Wadi 70 75 167-168
Mycenaean 20, 184

Nabataean(s) 3 9-11 46 126-127 133-
    137 143 151-162 167 170-172
Namara 159
Naqš-i Rustam 130
Nash Papyrus 137 149 162-163
Naskhi 161
Negev 45 105 154 157
Negev, A. 158
Nehemiah 47 153
Neo-Assyrian 82
Neo-Punic 57-62, 89-90 92 95 100
Nerab 83-84
Nestorian 147
Nimrud 69 88 109-110
Nippur 44 151 170
Nisa 126 128-131
Nöldeke, T. 147
Nora 40 57-59
numismatics 4
Nyberg, H. S. 132

Obodas 154
Old Persian syllabary 125-126
Olympic games 176
Oscans 186
ossuary 120 164
ostracon 3 5 37 59 66-67 72 75-77 79
    85-86 88 92 98 102-110 128-129
    131 153-154 182

Pahlavi 131-132
palaeography 2 5-6 57 76 161 165
    170

Palaeo-Hebrew 78 120-121
Palestine 8 13 21 27 29-30 45 59-60
  70 99 111 127 133 169 185
Palestinian 105 147
Palestinian Christian Aramaic 126-
  127
Palestinian Jewish Aramaic 126
palimpsest 70
Palmyra 126 138 142 151-153
Palmyrene(s) 11 132-133 136-138
  141-145 149-153 172
Panamu 80
papyrus 5 59-60 70 75 82 85-88 92-93
  98 114-115 125 144 157 162 167-
  168
papyrology 5
Parthian(s) 128-132 134 138 141-143
  147
Peckham, J. B. 57-59 100
Pentateuch 91 93 96 99 120-122
Perikhanian, A. 128
Persia 125 130
Persian(s) 43 47 78 82 84 86-87 105
  110 114-117 121-122 125-133 136-
  137 154 161-165 170-173
Persian Gulf 133 136
Peshitta 147
Petra 102 143 153-154 157 161
Petrie, W. M. F. 23
Pettinato, G. 28
Peuch, E. 104
Pharisees 122
Philistine(s) 22 82 101 111-112
Phoenicia 60 185
Phoenician(s) 3 9-11 23-27 31 39 42
  53-62 65-66 76-82 88-100 109 111
  125 175 177-178 182-186
Phrygians 186
pictographic script 1 12-16 19 23 53
  178 181-182

Pirenne, J. 43-44 149
Plato 23
Pliny 23
Pritchard, J. B. 30
Proto-Canaanite 9-11 26-27 30-37 42
  48-49 53 97 178 180-184
Proto-Semitic 31-32 54
Proto-Sinaitic 23-27 30-34
Provincia Arabia 157-158
Ptolemaic 119
Punic 57-59 62 90
Purvis, J. D. 99 120 124

Qataban 43 51
Qaus 102
Qausgabri 102 111
Qubur el-Walaydah 36-37 181 186
Qumran 11 78 93 96 119-122 165
Quran 161

Rabb'el 154-157
rabbinic script 173
Rahmani, L. Y. 115
Raphia 153
Raqiq, Horvat 156-157
Rashi script 173
Reed, W. L. 47 65
Riis, P. J. 185
Röllig, W. 57
Roman(s) 112 138 143 157 167 186
Rome 145
Rosenthal, E. S. 121
Rosenthaler, M. 120
Rumania 143
Ruweisah 40

Saba 43
Sachau, E. 86
Ṣadan the queen 149-152
Sadducee(s) 122

Safaitic 45
Sam'al 54-55 76 79-80
Samaria 69 72 76 86 115-116 124 182
Samaritan(s) 11 77-78 89 91-94 96 99
    112 121-124 127
Samaritan Aramaic 126-127
Sanbalat 115
Sanders, J. H. 99
Sanskrit 127
Saqqarah 59 82 88 98
Sardinia 40-41 57-59 185
Sari 140-142
Sassanian(s) 131 141
Sayce, A. H. 86
Schlumberger, D. 143
Schulthess, F. 147
Scopus, Mount 117
scroll 121-122, 162 165-170
seal 4 69-71 75 77 85 101-103 107-
    108 110-111 114-119
Segal, J. B. 88 149
Segert, S. 57 183
Seleucid 47 138 149-152
Senacherib 111
Serabit el-Khadem 23 27 34 36
Serrin 147-148
Serto 147
Shaked, S. 100 127 136
Shapur 141
Shatt el-Arab 136
Shechem 26 123-124
Shiftiba'al 54
Shimbar 100 135-136
Shiqmona 59
Sicily 59
Sidon 58 60
Sidqa 111
Siloam inscription 68-69, 77
Sinai 3 23-26 45 47 66 153 157-158
    160

Sinaitic 157
Siran, Tell 106-107 110-111
Slavic 18
Sogdian(s) 130 132
South Arabian 9 24 27 31 42-51
Spain 59
stamp 71 75 103 105 116 119
Starcky, J. 143 160-161
stele 4 55 59 64-69 83-85 94 101 128
    136
Stern, E. 47
Stiehl, R. 134 136 159
Sukas, Tell 185
Sumatar Harabesi 137 148
Sumerian(s) 1 9 12-14 18 21 130
Synagogue inscription 169-171
Syria 8 13 21 29 45 53-54 89 143
    147-149 151 157 185
Syriac 126-127 132-133 136-138 141-
    144 146-153 160-161 172 174 183
Sznycer, M. 41 59 129

Ta'anach 29
Tabnit 58
Tacitus 23
Ta'liq 161
Tang-i Butan 135
Tang-i Sarvak 100 134-136
Tavor, Nahal 29
Tbilisi 129
Teixidor, J. 30
Tetragrammaton 120
Thaj 136
Thamudic 45-47 126 153-154 158
Thera 178-179 185
Thompson, H. O. 107
Tigris 132 138 141
Timna' 51
Torczyner (Tur-Sinai), H. 100
Transjordan 45 99 100-102

Tumilat, Wadi 153 155-156
Tur 'Abdin 141
Turkey 54 127 147
Turkish 112
Turkmenistan 128

Ugarit 2 24 28-30 34 183
Ullendorf, E. 51
Umbrians 186
Umm el-Biyara 102
Umm el-Jimal 160
Ur 44
Urfa 157
Uruk 114
U.S.S.R. 127-128
Uzziah 102 164 170

Vanel, A. 60
Van Beek, G. W. 43
Van den Branden, A. 24
Van der Kooij, G. 107
Ventris, M. 19

votive inscription 3 5 24 59-62 66 69
    85 138 143 153

weight 4
Winnett, F. V. 45-47 65
Woodhead, A. G. 182
Wright, G. E. 22

Yabneh Yam 75
Yadi *see* Sam'al
Yadin, Y. 120 157 167
Yamauchi, E. 134
Yaron, R. 5
Yehud 114-116 119
Yeḥimilk 52 54
Yehuda ha-Nasi, Rabbi 123

Zakur 80-81
Zayadine, F. 107
Zebed 160
Zenjirli 54
Zoar 169-171

PLATES

PLATE 1

B. Early Proto-Canaanite
inscription from Gezer

A. Proto-Sinaitic inscription. The pictographs at the bottom
compose the word *lb'lt*

C. Late Proto-Canaanite inscription from Qubur el-Walaydah

PLATE 2

A. Sabaean inscription from Beit el-Ashwal, Yemen

C-D. Thamudic B inscription on a bowl carried by a winged figure

B. Thamudic D inscription from the Negev

PLATE 3

PHOENICIAN

C. An ostracon from Egypt

A. Inscription on an ivory box from Ur

B. An ink inscription on a marble slab from Kition, Cyprus

PLATE 4

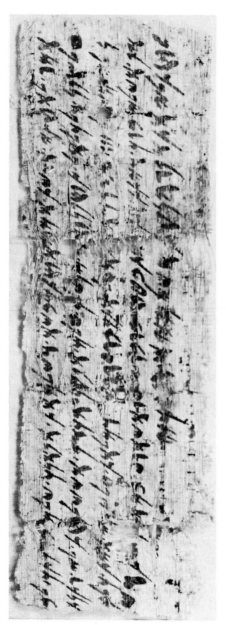

Phoenician papyrus from Saqqarah

PLATE 5

C. Papyrus of c. 300 B.C. from Egypt

B. Ostracon from Tell Kheleifeh

A. Inscriptions on jars from Elephantine

PHOENICIAN

PLATE 6   HEBREW

A. A fragmentary Hebrew inscription on ivory from Nimrud

B. Seal and impression of Elyashiv from Arad, early 6th century B.C.

C. The palimpsest papyrus from Murabba'at

A. Seal of Shemaryau,
presumably from Samaria,
8th century B.C.

B. An incised ostracon from
Samaria, 8th century B.C.

C. An ostracon from Arad, early 6th
century B.C.

PLATE 8   ARAMAIC

A. A docket inscribed on a clay tablet, 570 B.C.

B. One of the Hermopolis papyri

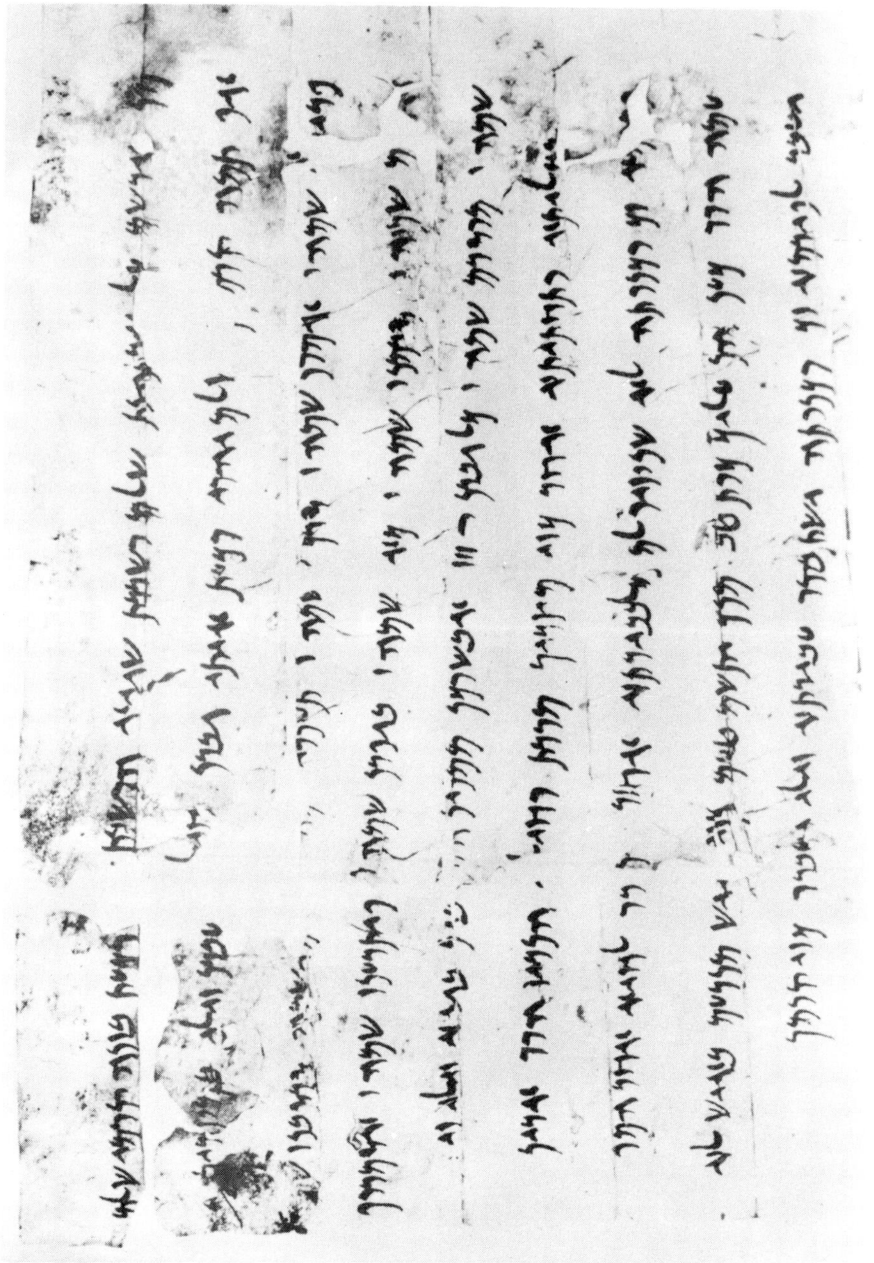

PLATE 9

An Aramaic letter of Arsham written on parchment

PLATE 10   ARAMAIC OSTRACA

B. Tel Beer-Sheba, 4th-century B.C.

A. Elephantine, 5th century B.C.

C. Edfu (Egypt) 3rd century B.C.

A. A Lydian-Aramaic bilingual inscription from Sardis. The Aramaic text is written in the 4th-century B.C. Aramaic lapidary script

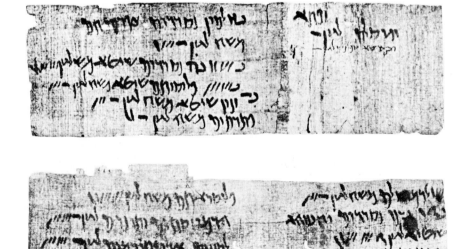

B. A 3rd-century B.C. papyrus from Egypt

PLATE 12

A-B. Two Moabite seals from the 8th and 6th centuries, respectively

C. Both sides of a bulla found at Umm el-Biyara; on the obverse can be read "Belonging to Qausga[bri], king of E[dom]"

E

D. The Edomite ostracon from Tell Kheleifeh

F

G

E-G. Three Ammonite seals

PLATE 13

B. The ostracon from Nimrud

A. The Citadel Inscription from Amman

PLATE 14

A. The seal of
Yehoyišma' daughter
of Šawaš-šar-uṣur

B. Coin with the legend *yhd*
in Hebrew letters

C. Fragment of Leviticus
Scroll in Palaeo-Hebrew

D. Fragment of the Psalms Scroll written in Jewish characters, but *yhwh* — in Palaeo-Hebrew

PLATE 15

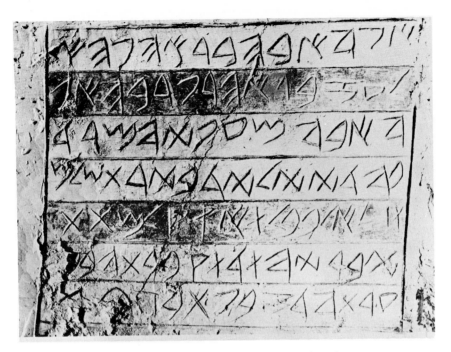

A. Aramaic burial inscription written in Palaeo-Hebrew letters

B. A Samaritan inscription

PLATE 16

A. Aramaic inscription of Aśoka from Kandahar, Afghanistan

B. Aramaic inscription on a boundary stone from Armenia

PLATE 17

A. Parthian document written on parchment in 53 A.D. from Avroman, Kurdistan

B. An ostracon from Nisa

C. Lead roll inscribed with Mandaic incantation

PLATE 18

A. Hatran Aramaic and Greek bilingual inscription from Dura Europos

B. Earliest Palmyrene inscription

C. Aramaic inscription from el-Mal, southern Syria

PLATE 19

A. Old Syriac deed of sale
on parchment
from Dura-Europos

B. Syriac inscription on the mosaic pavement of the Nestorian monastery
in Jericho

PLATE 20

A. Aramaic ostracon from Raphia area, *c.* 300 B.C.

B. Nabataean incantation text

PLATE 21

Nabataean graffiti on a rock in Sinai

PLATE 22

A. Nabataean and Jewish Aramaic endorsements on a Greek deed from Naḥal Ḥever

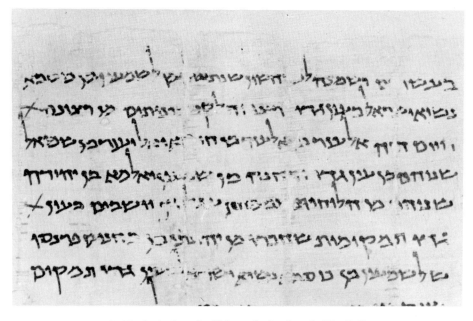

B. Aramaic message of Shimeon (Bar Kosiba) on papyrus from Naḥal Ḥever

C. The beginning of a Hebrew deed written in Ein Gedi

PLATE 23

A. Tombstone of King Uzziah

חחצוצרות תדרינה פריעות לנעד לנצח אנשי הקלע עד כלותם לזרק שלוך שבע
מעמים ואחד ותקעו להם הכוהנים בחצוצרות המשוב ובאו לוד המערכה
הריאישונה לחתיצב על מעמדם ותקעו הכוהנים בחצוצרות המקרא אישע
שלישה וגלו כרנם מך השערים ועברו בין המערבות ליוגם אנשי הרכב
מימין ומשמאל ותקעו הכוהנים בחצוצרות קול מרודד ידי סדר מלחמה
והראשות יהיו נבשטיע לסדירות אריש למעמדו ובעמדם שלשה סורים
ותקעו להם הכוהנים תריעה שנית קול עוד וסמוך ידי מגשיע עד קורבך

B. Some lines from the War Scroll
from Qumran

C. Mosaic inscription found on
the floor of the ancient synagogue
in Na'aran near Jericho

PLATE 24

A. Archaic Greek inscription from Crete written in the 5th century B.C. in boustrophedon

B. Aryballos with a 7th-century archaic Greek inscription